Praise for the Swedish edition:

First of all, I would like to express my admiration for Gunnar Karlsson's courage to tackle this difficult, complex, politically charged, and volatile subject. [...] The book contains interesting psychodynamic and phenomenological perspectives on the subject whose rich content cannot be done justice in a review. [...] I would like to thank Karlsson for a book filled with knowledge [...] The book is one of the most important entries in the psychodynamic gender debate in recent times and it should have a good chance to become a Swedish classic. [...] Gunnar Karlsson has given an extremely interesting and thought-provoking contribution to the important discussion about our gender identity.

Tomas Wånge, *Psykoterapi* [*Psychotherapy*]

Karlsson's book is a major contribution to the psychoanalytic discussions on sexes and genders and especially on the challenges of being a man. I find especially important the way Karlsson emphatically makes the distinction between sex and gender, as two ontologically different kinds of structures, the former being something one is, the latter rather as a project [...] There is much to learn from his discussion, I think, and the book should be read not only by psychoanalysts and psychotherapists, but more broadly by people interested in gender questions.

Jussi Kotkavirta, *The Scandinavian Psychoanalytic Review*

Psychoanalytic and Phenomenological Reflections on Masculinity

In this highly original volume, Gunnar Karlsson offers new answers to the question concerning the relationship between belonging to a specific sex as a male and striving for a masculine identity.

This book offers a uniquely psychoanalytic and phenomenological perspective on masculinity. Karlsson considers masculinity and traditional masculine ideals through a psychoanalytic lens before taking phenomenological concepts to chisel out the relationship between sex and gender. This perspective is developed throughout the volume to inspire readers to further their understanding of traditional gender assignment – female, male and intersex – in light of gendered characteristics such as femininity and masculinity. Chapters span topics such as the characteristics of typical, so-called "phallic masculinity", its allure and psychogenetic explanation, as well as looking at what phallic masculinity disregards. Throughout, Karlsson maintains that phallic masculinity is unattainable, as it seeks to escape the existential conditions of helplessness, vulnerability and dependence. He makes the case for the importance of considering the notion of ego-identity in the field of sex/gender studies, encouraging a liberation from gender stereotypes.

Psychoanalytic and Phenomenological Reflections on Masculinity will be of great interest to researchers, clinical psychoanalysts and psychotherapists, as well as anyone interested in masculinity, gender studies and the relationship between sex and gender.

Gunnar Karlsson is a professor in the department of Education, Stockholm University, Sweden. He is a psychoanalyst and a psychotherapist, and has published widely on psychoanalysis and phenomenology.

Psychoanalytic and Phenomenological Reflections on Masculinity

Gunnar Karlsson

Routledge
Taylor & Francis Group

LONDON AND NEW YORK

Designed cover image: francescoch / Getty Images

First published 2023
by Routledge
4 Park Square, Milton Park, Abingdon, Oxon OX14 4RN

and by Routledge
605 Third Avenue, New York, NY 10158

Routledge is an imprint of the Taylor & Francis Group, an informa business

This book was originally published under the title *Det maskulina
projektet. Psykoanalytiska och fenomenologiska reflektioner* by
Symposion Bokförlag in Sweden.

British Library Cataloguing-in-Publication Data
A catalogue record for this book is available from the British Library

ISBN: 978-1-032-40371-7 (hbk)
ISBN: 978-1-032-40277-2 (pbk)
ISBN: 978-1-003-35276-1 (ebk)

DOI: 10.4324/9781003352761

Typeset in Times New Roman
by codeMantra

Contents

Acknowledgments

While working on this book, I have been helped by the knowledge and commitment of many people. It all started quite a few years ago by Svante Tham's initiative of gathering people for a study circle concerning the psychoanalytic view of masculinity, which many collogues thought was a neglected topic in psychoanalysis. Eventually, I decided to write a book on masculinity based on my own experiences, clinical experiences as a psychoanalyst and psychotherapist and pertinent literature. I am thankful to colleagues and friends for their helpful comments on earlier versions of the Swedish edition or on this revised edition that you hold in your hand.

I hereby want to warmly thank Veronica Brunér Anjou, Emilia Degenius, John Farrow, Christina Flordh, Bozena Hautaniemi, Pirjo Lantz, Åke Lantz, Ewa Raj, Julia Romanowska, Svante Tham, Eva Tillberg, Katarzyna Maria Twaróg, Jakob Ulenius and Ulf Åkerström. I also want to express my gratitude to Bertil Wennborg's foundation for economical support in writing the book.

Introduction

In today's society, it is commonplace to view many human endeavors, behavior and choices through the prism of competition and rivalry. Matters of both a social and personal nature are treated in the same manner. Countries also compete with each other, for example, on a global scale as to whose vaccine rollout is the fastest or whose aims are the most ambitious. The achievements of educational institutes and hospital treatments are often presented in terms of targets and league tables so that each can be compared and measured against the other. The focus is on striving, competition and rivalry. But why not instead highlight the values of care, compassion, mutuality and interdependence?

In professional life, it is no longer deemed sufficient to be competent and professional, because today there is pressure to be seen as the best compared to others. Nothing is considered too important or complicated that it cannot become an item for measurement, even of a one-dimensional kind. And then there are those evenings that can be spent watching all those television shows based on some kind of contest. Due to these competitions where winners and losers are thrust into spotlight, a lack of respect and shame has gradually become the norm; those who do not make the grade are humiliated and ridiculed.

Eva-Lotta Hultén (2016) captured the spirit of the present by coining the neologism "competivism",[1] which proclaims competition as the ideology of our times. It is possible to identify a significant cluster of assorted concepts and phenomena that are embraced by the term "competition", namely rivalry, winning, winner, losing, loser, being knocked out, achieving, being best or worst, individualism, measuring up, development, comparison, hierarchy, taking control, setting records, overperforming, admiration, envy and disdain.

The role of competitiveness and rivalry has become all the more dominant in today's society and as a consequence should be taken into account when we endeavor to understand gender problems. Johanna Oksala (2016) uses both phenomenology and the later thoughts of Michel Foucault to develop a feminist philosophy related to contemporary society in the West.

DOI: 10.4324/9781003352761-1

Rather than Foucault's notion of disciplinary power, it is his thinking on biopolitics (Foucault, 2008) and his emphasis on neoliberalism's governmentality that is of primary interest in understanding the feminine subject. Oksala claims that Foucault's analysis of neoliberalism is not to be regarded as an absence of social governance; rather this governance arises from the dominant doctrine to create a society organized according to competition. Moreover, Byung-Chul Han (2015) also puts forward an argument that today's society cannot be equated with Foucault's idea of a disciplinary society, where the subject is an "obedience-subject", but instead we are today an "achieving-subject" in an achieving society. Such a society suffers from a lack of negativity and restraint. "Prohibitions, commandments, and the law are replaced by projects, initiatives and motivation" (Ibid., p. 9). What prevails is the idea of the limitless, where nothing is impossible and anything possible has to be accomplished.

I see an obvious similarity between the phallic masculine ideal and the spirit of our times: many characteristics of modern life are not in themselves new but have, however, become accentuated. Rivalry, competition, individualism, achievement, narcissism, transcending the existing and a society caught up in the idea of permanent growth and expansion are crucial components in phallic masculinity, the ideal of which has profound effects on us all, both men and women alike. Phallic masculinity is held in high repute in our culture, perhaps because it obscures the very ground on which it stands: our vulnerability and dependence. Even though it is largely an ideal that is encompassed by both men and women, it is no coincidence that it is called *masculinity* and therefore has to be aligned to a path of development primarily for boys and men.

The phallic masculine ideal corresponds also to an unsustainable global attitude. We are living in a way that threatens the whole of our planet's existence, and our response to this threat is to set our hopes first and foremost on a continuation of our technological development. It is no coincidence that men are so interested in technical matters and spend a very great deal more time than women on repairing and maintaining cars, for instance (Mellström, 1999, p. 8). My impression is that any political demand that is couched in terms of restraint provokes, especially in men, a particular strain of indignation and is often met with derision and contempt. The French psychoanalyst, Didier Anzieu, whose work has focused on the importance of establishing a containing "Skin Ego" in order to promote a feeling of security and sense of self, has underlined the necessity to set limits, not least in respect of economic expansion. Anzieu writes:

> If I had to sum up the situation of the West – and perhaps of the whole of humanity – in these closing years of the twentieth century, I would emphasise the need to set limits: on demographic expansion, on the arms race, on nuclear explosions, on the acceleration of history, on economic

growth, on insatiable consumption, on the increasing disparity between the rich nations and the Third World, on the gigantic scale of scientific projects and economic enterprise, on the invasion of the private sphere by the media of mass communication, on the compulsion endlessly to break records at the cost of over-training and drug-taking, on the ambition always to go faster and further and to spend more, with all the overcrowding, nervous tension, cardiovascular illness and general discontent that results. We need to set limits to the violence wrought on nature as well as that perpetrated on human beings. This includes the pollution of the earth, sea and atmosphere, the squandering of energy, the need to produce everything of which we are technically capable even when that means creating mechanical, architectural or biological monstrosities; it includes the jettisoning of moral laws and social rules, the absolute affirmation of individual desires, and the threat posed by technological advances to the integrity of the human body and to spiritual freedom, to the natural reproduction of human beings and to the survival of the species.

(1989, pp. 6–7)

The above description of an expansive lifestyle against which Anzieu is warning, and so illustrative of masculine striving, is endangering the development of feelings of security and of a containing ego. The theories of Anzieu on the importance of a containing Skin Ego imply a correlation between a social macro-level and an individual level, even if such a specific study, as for example this one, is limited in its focus.[2]

Sex, gender, femininity and masculinity may be studied from a variety of perspectives. This book looks at masculinity and especially the phallic masculine character and its development from the point of view of psychoanalysis and phenomenology. It is important to avoid reducing social phenomena and structures to psychological mechanisms, which has been a criticism directed at psychoanalytical gender theorists. Iris M. Young (1990), who shows considerable appreciation of Nancy J. Chodorow's contributions to the feminist understanding of gender identity, claims that Chodorow together with those feminist theorists who very much rely on psychoanalytic ideas often reduce economic and institutional repression in society to gender personalities. Gender differences are related to individuals' experiences, character and cultural categorizations. In order to fully explain male dominance, it is necessary also to take into account structural and institutional factors. In this regard, gender theories have an important role to play in showing that they are necessary but also insufficient conditions for an explanation of male dominance in society. As Young writes, "gender theory can be an enormous aid in consciousness-raising about contemporary masculinist ideologies by showing some of the sources of their misogyny" (Ibid., p. 57).

Besides the psychoanalytic perspective, phenomenology also takes a prominent position in this book. The sciences of both phenomenology and psychoanalysis have subjectivity as their focus of study, highlighting the creation of meaning in humans, although they may be said to concentrate on different levels of subjectivity.[3] This book applies primarily psychoanalysis as a developmental tool in a psychological understanding of phallic masculinity, whilst phenomenology plays a significant part in chiseling out the distinction between sex and gender as a basis for further discussions on phallic masculinity. But even with regard to relevant questions of a more existential nature, phenomenological thought offers considerable help in scrutinizing phallic masculinity.

To sum up, these are the questions that are focused on by this book: What characterizes phallic masculinity? How can it be explained from a psychogenetic angle? Why is the idea of masculinity so alluring? Why for many men is the desire to appear masculine, such a crucial aspiration? What alternatives are there to striving towards phallic masculinity? And what does phallic masculinity disregard? Let me therefore briefly present the contents of each chapter.

In Chapter 1, I discuss the conceptualizations of the terms "sex, gender and masculinity". It has certainly been quite a problem to establish a system of concepts that are consistent, stringent and generally accepted. I propose some reasons for the problems in establishing an adequate framework of concepts, whilst also trying to develop one with the use of phenomenological ideas. The phenomenological project, which aims at describing as faithfully as possible the manifestations of phenomena from a first-person perspective (i.e., from an inner perspective of *my* experience), will be here used in an attempt to constitute the meanings of such concepts as sex, gender, biology, nature and culture.

In this chapter, I will also endeavor to develop the idea of distinguishing from a first-person perspective between, on the one hand, a person's *sexual identity* and, on the other, *gender* as a possible s*triving* towards an identity or more precisely as a *project*. In other words, the two sexes – woman and man – concern identities. I simplify the discussion here and will not, for example, touch on the possibility of a nonbinary sexual identity, as it does not change my fundamental argument of the distinction between sex and gender. Sexual identity is nonacquired, and for most people it is permanent, but also requires the person to confer consent so that their identity is not experienced as wrong nor ego-dystonic. Thus, I do not consider gender as an identity, rather as a potential striving towards identity or as a project. In summary, it may be stated that identity denotes an existing being, whereas a project implies a potential that is not as yet realized. One theory I will put forward in this book is the notion that phallic masculinity as a project is unattainable since it tries to avoid the conditions of human existence of helplessness, vulnerability and dependence.

In addition to the distinction between sex and gender, I also maintain in Chapter 1 that the research area of sex/gender should encompass an ego-identity, which refers to something beyond the sex/gender dichotomy, an argument that is given greater attention later in Chapter 5. It is my hope that Chapter 1 adequately lays a firm terminological foundation in order to be able to focus on masculinity and especially phallic masculinity.

Chapter 2 is devoted to psychoanalytic theories of masculinity. After having initially affirmed the discontent in psychoanalytic circles with psychoanalytic theories about masculinity, I offer a discussion of Sigmund Freud's views on masculinity. Although his ideas on the development of masculinity can certainly be criticized in many respects, they cannot be disregarded as he managed to bring attention to crucial processes in the formation of this identity, in particular his theories concerning the processes of identification in boys as a way to understand gender development. The chapter does, however, direct criticism at Freud's neglect of the mother's significance as an object of identification for the boy as well as of his far too limited understanding of the body in the formation of the child's identity. Emphasis is placed on the boy's perception of his body in deference to the attribution of sexual identity by his environment.

Significant contributions to Freud's theoretical ideas have been developed by Robert J. Stoller and Ralph R. Greenson whose controversial theory on the importance of the boy disidentifying himself from the mother and counter-identifying himself with the father has been a catalyst for many later theoretical advancements. This chapter offers a discussion of these later ideas in the understanding of masculine gender development, which is founded on a host of complicated identification processes as well as identity-forming processes, such as the meanings ascribed to gender features and cultural norms and values by the parents and adult world. It is possible to delineate a tangible contrast between Freud's theories and modern dominant modern theories in the views of the boy's relationship to his primary caregiver/mother.[4] If both Freud and contemporary psychoanalytic gender theorists emphasize the *difference* between boy and mother, then what this difference implies is of great significance. Nowadays, this difference is considered to constitute a sorely painful experience and the basis for the boy's or man's compensatory and narcissistic phallic strivings and ideals, which is an approach quite alien to Freud's way of thinking.

Chapter 3 returns to some of the themes from Chapter 2 by refining the discussion about masculinity and especially phallic masculinity. Two other forms of masculinity are also mentioned, namely hypermasculinity and demasculinized masculinity. Hypermasculinity is characterized by its violent tendencies, sexism, xenophobia and religious terrorism, and thus may somehow be seen as an extreme form of phallic masculinity. The difference between the two will be conveyed in structural and intrapsychic terms. Somewhat paradoxically, although phallic masculinity forms a necessary backcloth to demasculinized masculinity, the latter manages to overturn and supersede the former by tearing itself away from the ideals of phallic masculinity, thus enabling a sense of relief to emerge and an experience of genuine masculinity to prevail. It is the character of phallic masculinity, which is very much realized as a rejection and disapproval of the motherly and feminine, that is the central theme of this chapter.

The description of phallic masculinity is advanced further in Chapter 4 where a more detailed perspective from the point of view of developmental psychology is presented. Whereas Chapter 3 is more devoted to the character of phallic masculinity, Chapter 4 places greater focus on a psychogenetic explanation, organized around the following three psychological challenges in the development of boys: (i) one concerning human existential conditions in terms of helplessness and dependence, (ii) the threat of castration from the preoedipal mother, and (iii) the threat of castration in relation to the father. It is primarily the first point that is discussed in detail as it has not received the attention in literature that it really deserves.

The first challenge can be seen as a kind of background feeling that the boy is carrying within himself in facing the other two challenges which deal with threats of castration in different forms. This existential challenge or dimension involves the human being's original predicament of total helplessness and dependence. With no physical care from an adult, the child would never survive, and without any emotional care, the child would end up psychologically lifeless or even, as experiences from orphanages have revealed, actually dying. The analysis undertaken in Chapter 4 shows that phallic masculinity implies both a denial of existential conditions and a rejection of the mother's containing function of these same circumstances. In other words, phallic masculinity is a reaction against humanity's frail predicament and need for nurture. What is important to emphasize in this chapter is why it is that phallic masculinity is associated with rejection of the mother's containing function, as a reaction against narcissistic hurt in the interaction with the mother and her containing/holding. In order to illustrate some of my thoughts, I have chosen a couple of episodes portrayed in the book *My Struggle. A Man in Love* by Karl Ove Knausgård (2014).

The three remaining chapters shed more light on what can be seen as having been neglected by the phallic masculine project.

Chapter 5 returns to the question raised in Chapter 1 of how to conceptualize the area of sex/gender in order to characterize the development of identity in humans. Here I argue that it is essential to introduce ego-identity into this research field. A more thorough discussion is offered of why masculinity should not be recognized as an identity but rather as a striving towards an identity or as a project (one which is also doomed to fail).

Contemporary theories about gender allow for the possibility of integrating femininity and masculinity within the same individual. By introducing ego-identity into the conceptualizations of this research area, I would like to go beyond a mere integration of femininity and masculinity in one and the same individual. My reason for this is that the formation of human identity demands a conceptualization that cannot be reduced to gender dichotomy; it concerns an ego-identity that not only in some way precedes gender but also one that transcends it, as a kind of humanization of that potential human beings have of striving towards an authentic life. With this addition of ego-identity, I would like to contend that this leads partly to a more stringent system of concepts within sex and gender research and partly to an emphasis of the dimension of authenticity in gender debate which provides a possibility to be free from the constraints of stereotyped gender ideals.

The phallic masculine project represents in a way an antithesis to the essence of care. Chapter 6 focuses on nurturing whose beginnings are to be found in an intersubjective relation that is inherently characterized by help-lessness and dependence. I look at the child's dependence on a good enough mothering in order to avoid psychological suffering resulting from painful and anxiety-arousing experiences and its fundamental role in generating enjoyment in life. Care can provide an experience of shared enjoyment for both the giver and the receiver. In certain instances, it can be difficult to differentiate between the giving and the receiving of care, as the person who feels joy in caring can also feel enveloped by it.

This discussion of motherly containing and nurturing is related to an existential and phenomenological examination of masculinity from the point of view of the dual concepts of immanence and transcendence, both of which are used in phenomenological writing but have not gained any traction in psychoanalysis. Their meaning may vary depending on their context. In the case of phenomenology's founder, Edmund Husserl, immanence is that which is present in consciousness, whilst transcendence refers to that which surmounts and goes beyond the constituting (meaning-bestowing) acts of consciousness. Here I study these concepts in relation to Simone de Beauvoir's discussion (1949/2011) about the position of men and women. Transcendence is what defines men's being, the existence of which it surmounts and goes beyond by creating and realizing already incorporated projects. On the other hand, immanence involves maintaining and preserving life in its unchanged form. Even though human existence presupposes both transcendence and immanence, according to Beauvoir, it is the male who incarnates transcendence, whilst the female's prime domain is reproduction and the family – she is relegated to the home and to immanence.

Instead of dichotomizing the concepts of immanence and transcendence, it is imperative to find a mutual and dynamic balance between them. However, as regards phallic masculinity, they are quite incompatible; only transcendence possesses any prestige, because it surpasses what is given and present by constructing something new, whilst values, associated with immanence such as preserving and accepting what already exists, are rejected. My reasoning ends up with a plea to concern ourselves with our existential conditions of helplessness, vulnerability and dependence in order to affirm and accept these conditions for our subjective lives and thereby lay a grounding for creativity, meaningfulness and enjoyment of life.

In Chapter 7, the lines of thought on exploring existential conditions are brought to a conclusion. For what can be more challenging to consider than our own finite and mortal existence? Death is hardly ever mentioned in the discussions of sex and gender. Similarly, in psychoanalytic discourse, existential death is surprisingly neglected. Existential death is death that is uncharted, foreign and yet unavoidable, uncontrollable, and can occur anytime which means the absolute end of life. So, with this starting point in the reality of existential death and its challenges for us all, not least for the masculine project, I examine its various implications for our inner life.

This concluding chapter takes a closer look at the relevance of death for phallic masculinity, although death has played a significant, but not central, role earlier in the book. In my reasoning on phallic masculinity as a project to avoid existential conditions, death can be said to constitute the final boundary on the basis of which these existential conditions may be understood. And in the discussion about the psychogenetic explanations of phallic masculinity, attention has been drawn to the boy's specific separation and loss of the mother with their painful and narcissistically humiliating consequences. If feelings of loss and separation are considered to be the most likely forerunners of an anxious relation to death, it is then not surprising that mortality presents a special dilemma for men or more precisely for phallic masculinity.

My analysis also implies that the notion of gender identity has undergone several stages of deconstruction. Briefly stated, it may be said that the deconstruction of gender identity, which shows itself to be rather a striving towards an identity or to a project – masculinity as a project – culminates in an affirmation of our finite existence: identity and mortality are antitheses. Thus, in this chapter, my intention is to demonstrate that an affirmation of death and finality offers a potential for a deeper sense of joy in life; it is not a joy of an instrumental kind that transcends or goes beyond the existent but an affirmation of what actually is given.

Renouncing a narcissistic and controlling attitude brings about a deep sense of freedom, one that can also be experienced, however difficult it is to endure, as surrender of oneself, which presents a significant challenge to us all and especially for those looking for recognition in phallic masculinity and its project. The chapter concludes with an attempt to characterize the self that is manifested in self-surrender, which the masculine project not only forfeits but also mutates into its antithesis.

Notes

1 In those cases when the quotes in the book do not exist in English, I am responsible for the translation.
2 Within the academic context, we find the so-called "psychosocial" view on masculinity developed on the basis of the psychological/psychic and social dimensions (e.g., Bornäs, 2022; Hollway, 2006; Jefferson, 2002, 2013). The argument is that both the psychic and social dimensions, both subjectivity and society, must be considered; that is to say, the psychic and social are intertwined with one another. These dimensions need to be brought together without collapsing the one into the other. Jefferson describes the psychosocial view of gender in the following way:

> The question of how (sexual) genesis and sexual difference are related can now be answered in a non-reductive, psychosocial fashion, in a way which encompasses both the messy reality of actually existing gender relations, the diversity of actual men and women's relationships to discourses of masculinity and femininity and the underlying psychological processes.
>
> (2002, p. 81)

According to the psychosocial view, academic theorizing about gender has not paid proper attention to the infant's vulnerability, dependence and anxious predicament, which plays an important part in the psychosocial view. The importance of the containing intersubjective relation between the mother (the primary caregiver) and the infant is emphasized, and accounted for by means of psychoanalytic theories. The psychoanalysts who are primarily referred to are Benjamin, Bion, Klein and Winnicott.
3 For a discussion of the relation between phenomenology and psychoanalysis, see, for example, Atwood and Stolorow (2014), Bernet (2002, 2004), Bodea and Popa (2020), Eriksson (2012), Heidegger (2001), Karlsson (2010, 2020), Lohmar and Brudzinska (2012), Merleau-Ponty (1982–83), Mishara (1990), Pontalis (1982–83), Ricoeur (1970, 2012) and Smith (2010). Works that discuss or integrate phenomenological and psychoanalytic ideas in the area of sex/gender include Beauvoir (1949/2011), Gatens (1996), Grosz (1994), Irigaray (1985, 1993), Karlsson (2014) and Owen (2012).
4 Present-day family constellations in our part of the world are quite different to those that existed a few decades ago. Nowadays, it is not unusual for a family to consist of just a single mother or single father or a same-sex couple in which neither is a biological parent of the child. Furthermore, it is more often brought to attention that there are people who do not experience themselves as either a woman or a man but rather as intersexual.

   One conceptual problem that has specifically plagued psychoanalytic theory has been the designation of the child's primary and secondary caregivers. Psychoanalytic literature often equates the primary caregiver with the mother and motherly containing or holding, even in cases where the biological mother is not necessarily involved, as the father or a male person can also function as the primary caregiver. Naturally, it is far from being straightforward to equate the primary caregiver with the mother and motherly containing, but why I have chosen to comply with this use of language demands an explanation.

   There are several reasons why I follow conventional psychoanalytic terminology and refer to the primary caregiver as the mother and motherly containing. Even if family constellations today are more complex than before, it is much more common that the primary caregiver is the biological mother or a woman than the father or a man. However, there are a couple of additional reasons that make it reasonable to equate the two: giving birth to a child is an undertaking that can only be performed by a woman, although the biological mother does not necessarily have to be the primary caregiver. Moreover, it might be supposed that a child that grows up in a family which has not complied with traditional sex-differentiated care provided by the mother as primary caregiver will anyway subsequently ascribe a traditional sex- or gender-based interpretation of nurturing because of contemporary cultural norms and customs (for more on this, see Chapter 6).

That the secondary caregiver is referred to as the father is consistent with the reasons why the primary caregiver is equated with the mother and motherly containing, but does not necessarily have to be the father or a man, though this is still the norm. The secondary caregiver or father may also be called the third in relation to the primary caregiver and child. In this way, the father or third or secondary caregiver broadens the dyad of mother and child to a triad.

The theory of phallic masculinity that I present here is furthermore bound up with the idea that earliest nurturing is intuitively related to the mother and her containing and that the father or another male makes his entry as the third, thereby dismantling the mother–child dyad.

References

Anzieu, D. (1989). *The skin ego.* Yale University Press.

Atwood, G.E. & Stolorow, R.D. (2014). *Structures of subjectivity. Explorations in psychoanalytic phenomenology and contextualism.* Routledge.

Beauvoir, S. de (1949/2011). *The second sex.* Vintage Books.

Bernet, R. (2002). Unconscious consciousness in Husserl and Freud. *Phenomenology and the Cognitive Sciences, 1*(3), 327–351. Doi:10.1023/A:1021316201873

Bernet, R. (2004). *Conscience et existence. Perspectives phénoménologiques.* Presses Universitaires de France.

Bodea, C. & Popa, D. (Eds.), (2020). *Describing the unconscious. Phenomenological perspectives on the subject of psychoanalysis.* Zeta Books.

Bornäs, H. (2022). *Subjects of violence. On gender and recognition in young men's violence against women.* Department of Child and Youth Studies, Stockholm University. Doctoral dissertation.

Eriksson, J. (2012). Freud's metapsychology – The formal a priori of psychoanalytic experience. *Scandinavian Psychoanalytic Review, 35*(1), 21–34. Doi:10.1080/01062 301.2012.10592377

Foucault, M. (2008). *The birth of biopolitics: Lectures at the Collège de France, 1978–79.* Edited by M. Senellart. Palgrave Macmillan.

Gatens, M. (1996). *Imaginary bodies: Ethics, power and corporeality.* Routledge.

Grosz, E. (1994). *Volatile bodies: Ethics, power and corporeality.* Routledge.

Han, B.-Ch. (2015). *The burnout society.* Stanford University Press.

Heidegger, M. (2001). *Zollikon seminars. Protocols – Conversations – Letters.* Edited by M. Boss. Northwestern University Press.

Hollway, W. (2006). *The capacity to care: Gender and ethical subjectivity.* Routledge.

Hultén, E.-L. (2016). *Klara färdiga gå! En bok om konkurrism.* [Ready to go! A book about competivism]. Karneval förlag.

Irigaray, L. (1985). *Speculum of the other woman.* Cornell University Press.

Irigaray, L. (1993). *An ethics of sexual difference*. Cornell University Press.

Jefferson, T. (2002). Subordinating hegemonic masculinity. *Theoretical Criminology, 6*(1), 63–88. Doi:10.1177/136248060200600103

Jefferson, T. (2013). Masculinity, sexuality and hate-motivated violence: The case of Darren. *International Journal for Crime, Justice and Social Democracy, 2*(3), 3–14. Doi:10.5204/ijcjsd.v2i3.119

Karlsson, G. (2010). *Psychoanalysis in a new light*. Cambridge University Press.

Karlsson, G. (2014). Masculinity as project. *NORMA: International Journal for Masculinity Studies, 9*(4), 249–268. Doi:10.1080/18902138.2014.908631

Karlsson, G. (2020). The function of phenomenology for psychoanalysis. In C. Bodea & D. Popa (Eds.) *Describing the unconscious. Phenomenological perspectives on the subject of psychoanalysis*. Zeta Books.

Knausgård, K.O. (2014). *My struggle. A man in love*. Book 2. Vintage Books.

Lohmar, D. & Brudzinska, J. (Eds.) (2012). *Founding psychoanalysis phenomenologically. Phenomenological theory of subjectivity and the psychoanalytic experience*. Springer.

Mellström, U. (1999). *Män och deras maskiner*. [Men and their machines]. Nya Doxa.

Merleau-Ponty, M. (1982–83). Phenomenology and psychoanalysis: Preface to Hesnard's L'oeuvre de Freud. *Review of Existential Psychology and Psychiatry, 18*(1–3), 67–72.

Mishara, A.L. (1990). Husserl and Freud: Time, memory and the unconscious. *Husserl Studies, 7*(1), 29–58. Doi:10.1007/BF00144886

Oksala, J. (2016). *Feminist experiences. Foucauldian and phenomenological investigations*. Northwestern University Press.

Owen, I.R. (2012). The phenomenological psychology of gender: How transsexuality and intersexuality express the general case of self as a cultural object. In D. Lohmar & J. Brudzinska (Eds.) *Founding psychoanalysis phenomenologically. Phenomenological theory of subjectivity and the psychoanalytic experience*. Springer.

Pontalis, J.-B. (1982–83). The problem of the unconscious in Merleau-Ponty's thought. *Review of Existential Psychology & Psychiatry, 18*(1–3), 83–96.

Ricoeur, P. (1970). *Freud and philosophy: An essay on interpretation*. Yale University Press.

Ricoeur, P. (2012). *On psychoanalysis*. Cambridge: Polity Press.

Smith, N. (2010). *Towards a phenomenology of repression – A Husserlian reply to the Freudian challenge*. Doctoral dissertation, Stockholm University.

Young, I.M. (1990). *Throwing like a girl and other essays in feminist philosophy and social theory*. Indiana University Press.

The troublesome
conceptual apparatus

Many gender theoreticians have expressed how complicated the field of sex/gender is. Sigmund Freud (1905, p. 219, footnote 1 added 1915) asserted early on that the concepts "masculine" and "feminine" "are among the most confused that occur in science". That which makes the question of gender so confused is that it moves between biology and our subjective opinions and feelings concerning the meaning of being a male and a female, respectively. To determine biologically what characterizes a male and a female is usually done without any problems, but to capture characteristic traits for masculinity and femininity is much more difficult, according to Freud "...psycho-analysis cannot elucidate the intrinsic nature of what in conventional or in biological phraseology is termed 'masculine' and 'feminine': it simply takes over the two concepts and makes them the foundation of its work" (1920, p. 171).

Despite the fact that a lot of water has flown under the sex/gender bridge since Freud's time, contemporary theorists also find reasons to point out how tangled, illogical and confused this research area is. Judith Butler (1990), in her *Gender Trouble*, remarks how entangled our relationship to sex and gender is also outside of scientific contexts. Moira Gatens points out that the sex/gender distinction "is used in both confused and confusing ways" (1991, p. 139). Furthermore, the perhaps leading figure in the field of masculinity research, R.W. Connell, claims that the terms "masculine" and "feminine" "prove remarkably elusive and difficult to define" (1995, p. 3). And if we listen to some contemporary psychoanalytic voices, we can hear that Adrienne Harris (1991) has captured this difficulty by asserting that gender is a "contradiction". Michael J. Diamond admits that "the landscape of psychoanalysis and gender abounds with conceptual, terminological, technical, and socio-political difficulties" (2013, p. 2). Finally, Emilce Dio Bleichmar writes that "(t)here is a great deal in the psychoanalytic literature about gender, spanning two decades. However, we find that, even today, neither its conceptual aspect nor its clinical application is clear" (2010, p. 177).

Hence, an urgent task within this field of research is to work out as cogent a conceptual apparatus as possible. The first step in such a clarifying

DOI: 10.4324/9781003352761-2

endeavor is to determine and specify the relationship between sex and gender. A selection of the different ways that this relationship has been defined
includes the following: sex precedes gender; gender precedes sex; gender is
simply a reflection of sex; sex is a neutral basis on which a social and constructed gender rests; sex is a construction, which means that gender in principle can be reduced to sex; sex and gender are entailed in the living body;
sex and gender are intertwined but can be distinguished analytically; sex
and gender stand in a circular relationship with each other.

The question arises as to why it is so hard to determine the relationship
between sex and gender. To formulate such a question in terms of *the relationship* between sex and gender may raise objections. A biological essentialist only acknowledges the existence of (biological) sex, and for certain
poststructuralists, only a culturally constructed gender exists, which, however, is sometimes called sex. Some theoreticians and gender researchers,
not least psychoanalysts, make the claim that both concepts are valid. However, before discussing the relationship between sex and gender, I would like
to suggest some reasons for the difficulty in determining the meaning of sex
and gender.

Why has it been so hard to determine the meaning of sex and gender?

One reason for this difficulty is that it entails a stance on the relationship
between biology and our subjective views on the meaning of sex and gender.
We have to deal with a conceptual apparatus whose implication has often
been that woman and man signify biological sex, whereas femininity and
masculinity signify gender, which supposedly consists of social and cultural
layers on the sex. Most profoundly, perhaps, the difficulty of determining the
meaning in, and the possible relationship between, sex and gender amounts
to stances taken on ontological and epistemological issues. By consulting
the phenomenological view on the intentionality of consciousness, I believe
we can avoid being trapped in various sorts of difficulties.

In order to achieve a greater clarity concerning the sex/gender issue, I
want to elucidate an important feature in the phenomenological notion of
intentionality. The concept of intentionality implies the existence of the correlation between subject and object, between the subjective pole and the
objective pole. In other words, phenomenology rejects an objectivistic idea
which presumes the existence of an object's specific property independent
of a subject. In such an objectivistic attitude, the inextricable link between
subject and object is neglected. The notion of intentionality means that our
perception or understanding of the object correlates/stands in a specific relation to the subjective horizon, which enables the object to appear in the
specific way in which it appears. However, phenomenology does not merely
reject the objectivistic position but also reject its opposite: subjectivism

in its reduction of the object to something that is exclusively imprisoned in the subject. The phenomenological notion of intentionality keeps subject and object apart, as they are simultaneously dependent on each other. Everything objective is given from a subjective horizon, and the subjective meaning bestowing or constituting is directed towards, and presupposes, the object.

More specifically, I want to claim that a failure to take into account the intentionality of consciousness, which is noticeable in the present discussion going on in the field of sex/gender research, yields two kinds of mistakes. The first mistake is to conceive of biology/nature in an objectivistic manner. The view of biologism concerning biology and nature implies precisely an objectivistic stance, and thereby biology/nature is determined not only as something noncultural but also as something that does not require a certain position/horizon from which it can be determined as biology/nature. The second kind of mistake is to reduce biology/nature to something exclusively cultural. This is the reversal of the objectivistic mistake. In this case, biology/nature becomes entirely a cultural entity, which I would claim is not a faithful description of the way in which biology/nature and cultural objects, respectively, present themselves to us in our experiences. The phenomenological project, in its attempt to describe as faithfully as possible the appearance of different phenomena, can be indispensable for determining the meaning of concepts such as sex, gender, biology, nature, culture and psychology.

Far too often, when reading literature in the field of sex/gender, I am struck by the fact that this phenomenological attitude is not considered.[1] The horizon, from which different claims concerning the character of sex/gender are given, is neglected. As said previously, the rhetoric of poststructuralism, seems to imply that if someone claims that nature is not culture, this amounts to being an objectivistic claim.[2] When it comes to poststructuralism, the only existing alternatives seem to be a kind of culturalism or objectivism in discussing biology/nature. The possibility of phenomenological reflections on ontological and epistemological issues has been overlooked. Given the phenomenological view of consciousness as intentional, it is accurate to maintain that nature is something that is given in a way that does not reduce it to culture; however, the condition for nature to appear for us is nevertheless a constituting subject. Thus, there is a third path, between the opposing views that we are either objectivists or culturalists, and if we chose it, the task will be to specify how nature and culture are given for a constituting subject. In order to be able to answer the question of the meaning of sex and gender, it will be crucial to describe how these structures are given to us from a first-person perspective.

In the literature, one can often notice that the first- and third-person perspectives are mixed up, contributing to confusion and obscurity. Let us imagine: a man with a caring occupation can be assumed to affirm a feminine trait from a third-person perspective. However, he does not need to feel that this third-person perspective corresponds with his own experience, his first-person perspective, of the meaning of gender. The failure to consider the difference between a third- and a first-person perspective often coincides with the failure to consider the difference between a purely empirical/statistical correlation between actions/feelings and sex and a specific concrete meaning bestowing of such (an abstract) empirical correlation with one self as a meaning bestowing person/subject. To concretize: a male person working in a preschool, sewing cloth bags together with a child, can easily perceive himself as being employed in a feminine occupation, from a traditional perspective, without, however, identifying himself with, or feeling as if he were, a woman or as someone who feels he is behaving like a woman. The male preschool teacher may quite simply experience that he is involved in an occupation that he finds amusing, boring, meaningful, meaningless and challenging, in line with his masculine ideals and so on, simultaneously as he understands that from a third-person perspective what he is doing can be conceived of as a typical feminine occupation. In other words, there is a difference between seeing oneself from a first-person perspective, how it feels for oneself to, for example, sew cloth bags, and seeing oneself from the outside, that is to say, to see oneself from a third-person perspective, which entails a self-objectification.

Another reason which is why the gender issue is inextricable is the fact that often, not least in the psychoanalytic literature, it is unclear whether masculinity signifies the individual's identity or libidinal object choice.[3] Ethel S. Person emphasizes that masculinity is about identity and not about object choice "(s)ince both heterosexuals and homosexuals may be masculine, masculinity is clearly not dependent on a man's sexual object choice" (2006, p. 1169). Thus, it is important not to confuse identity and object choice, even though the sexual orientation has implications for masculinity ideals in our society. In the theory of hegemonic masculinity, R.W. Connell claims that the central power relation is men's superiority over women, although even groups of men relate to one another by superiority and subordination, where the homosexual man is subjected to the most blatant form of subordinated masculinity.[4] An obvious expression of sexuality connected to masculinity is Bernie Zilbergeld's description of lasting and deeply rooted cultural ideals which masculinity is supposed to match, namely the image of a "large, powerful, untiring phallus attached to a cool controlled male, long on experience, confident, and knowledgeable enough to make women crazy with desire [...]" (from Person, 2006, p. 1174).

Thus, sex/gender and sexuality are related to one another, but my point is that sexual identity and gender, roughly speaking, can be said to precede sexual (libidinal) object choice in terms of sexual orientation. I am sceptical to the attempt to explain sexual identity on the basis of sexuality, although aspects of sexuality, naturally, can play an important role in order to understand gender/masculinity, as is obvious in the above quote from Zilbergeld. Unlike, for example, Jean Laplanche (2007), Butler (1995) and Ilka Quindeau (2013), my vantage point is not sexuality or the libidinal object choice (sexual orientation) in understanding sexual identity and gender.[5] Person (2006) stresses that the usual path of development is that the boy establishes a male sexual identity that precedes sexuality and that organizes it.

In addition, sexuality and sexual yearning possess a character that opposes the formation of identity. The creation of identity is not spurred by that which is forbidden in the way that sexuality is, but is rather pulled towards the normative. Jacqueline Schaffer writes:

> Everything that the ego finds intolerable may contribute to sexual enjoyment: breaking-in, sexual misuse of power, loss of control, abolition of limits, possession, submissiveness – in other words, "defeat" with all its polysemy.
>
> (2010, p. 139)

The shaping of identity is structuring and binding, whereas sexuality is dissolving (Karlsson, 2010, 2011). In line with Quindeau (2013, p. 187f), I understand sexuality as something, which exceeds, in a certain sense, sexual identity/gender, which orgasm is an example of. For Gilles Deleuze and Félix Guattari, sexual desire is not gendered: "Desire begins, not by desiring the sameness and stasis of the maternal body, but by seeking the radical change, flux and difference that recognizes no bounding identities or stabilities" (from Colebrook, 2004, p. 187). Sexuality breaks with the ordinary, everyday, stabilizing predictability and can be said to possess an "extraordinary" character. Extraordinary in at least two meanings, partly as an extremely strong experience and partly in the sense that the sexual experience structurally breaks with our ordinary way of being in the world (Karlsson, 2010; Stein, 1998).

Sexuality can also exert the function of coping with lacks and conflicts which primarily concern something other than (genital) sexuality. It may be about identity problems, separation problems or need for care and containment. In general, I believe that sexuality allows itself to be used for different needs and wishes, since its character is plastic and momentarily can disguise different sources of anxiety. Then there is another aspect of sexuality, namely that sexuality itself can be traumatizing and anxiety-ridden if the ego-structure is too deficient (Anzieu, 1989; Gantheret, 1983).

The sex–gender distinction

As mentioned, in the literature there are many different ways in which the relationship between sex and gender is depicted. To say something first about the biological position, biologism reduces cultural and psychological meaning (gender) to sex, in the sense that equates biology with the natural, scientific, biological body. In such a position, there is only room for a given sex and no gender.

An opposite and very influential position to the biological one, in the contemporary field of gender science, is poststructuralism where gender is exclusively a social and cultural construction. A radical version of post-structuralism is represented by the idea that even the biological sex is a con-struction (e.g., Butler, 1990); there is no given, nonconstructed sex on which a cultural and social interpretation of gender rests. The body is not some-thing biologically given which functions as a ground for the determination of gender.[6] Sex is displayed in its repeated performances; there is no natural bodily constitution, but the body is through and through the result of a cul-tural, discursive production, whose repeating character gives the impression of possessing a natural and stable core. Butler asserts "(t)hat the gendered body is performative suggests that it has no ontological status apart from the various acts which constitute its reality" (1990, p. 136). She substantiates her idea by exemplifying with drag shows, where a man, for example, por-trays femininity in an exaggerated way.

In her *Bodies That Matter*, Butler (1993) acknowledges the materiality of the body, although it concerns a materiality that is conceived of as an effect of power, as the most productive effect of power.[7] The sex is determined as the materialization of regulating norms, and these cultural norms are regulated by power discourses. Her critique concerns the domineering het-erosexual norm where two, supposedly, naturally given bodies are pulled to one another. Ironically, Butler's theory of performativity has a distinct phallocentric character in its emphasis on language, considering that the construction of sex overemphasizes form to the price of matter.[8] The body is the outcome of actions and activities, language and discourse, whilst the concrete material body is suppressed and prelinguistic, sensorial experi-ences are ruled out. The body as an exclusively social construction risks being conceived of as solely passive, a body effected by discourse without being able to effect discourse. Butler's theory has been criticized, and I will shortly mention phenomenological feminists' critique of her. But before this I will consult psychoanalysis.

According to Ethel S. Person and Lionel Ovesey, Freud was the first who substantially differentiated between sex and gender, but he did not have access to the terminological difference between sex and gender, since the German language only provides the concept "Geschlecht".

> The insight that the existence of personality differences between the sexes required an explanation was a major intellectual leap, and it is Freud who must be credited with that insight. Thus, psychoanalysis was

the first comprehensive personality theory that attempted to explain the
origins of what we now call gender.

(1983, p. 203)

It was on the basis of psychoanalytic and psychiatric treatment with, among
others, transsexuals that a terminological distinction was made between
sex and gender. An important person in this context was the psychoanalyst
Robert J. Stoller who coined the term "gender identity", which he described
as follows:

> Gender identity is the sense of knowing to which sex one belongs, that
> is, the awareness "I am a male" or "I am a female" [...] The advantage of
> the phrase "gender identity" lies in the fact that it clearly refers to one's
> self-image as regards belonging to a specific sex. Thus, of a patient who
> says: "I am not a very masculine man", it is possible to say that his gender
> identity is male although he recognizes his lack of so-called masculinity.
>
> (1964, p. 220)

Some years later, Stoller (1968, pp. 9–10) developed the terminology and
distinguished between sex, gender, gender identity and gender role. *Sex* is
restricted to a biological determination which refers to man and woman,
although there may be individuals who cannot be categorized in accordance with this binary division. *Gender* has a psychological and cultural
meaning rather than a biological one. Stoller points out that the terms "female" and "male" are used when talking about sex, whereas "feminine" and
"masculine" are the adequate terms for gender. *Gender identity* is defined
as the person's knowledge and awareness of belonging to one of the sexes
and not the other one. In the course of the individual's development, the
gender identity becomes more and more complex; the individual does not
experience himself/herself merely as, for example, a man, but as a masculine
man or a feminine man or as a man who fantasizes about being a woman.
Finally, there is the concept "gender role" which relates to the overt and
public behavior displayed together with others. That is the role one assumes
in interaction with others for the purpose of establishing a certain position
vis-à-vis others with respect to the gender dimension.

Also, in the psychoanalytic discussion, the concepts "sex and gender"
are often treated obscurely. The term "gender" is often used where it would
have been more appropriate to use the term "sex" and vice versa. In one of
Chodorow's later works, she clearly abstains from differentiating between
them, when writing: "I am calling the perspective [...] the sexual difference
perspective, though for me, it could equally be called the gender difference
perspective" (2012, p. 140). However, Michael J. Diamond takes a clear
stance for the sake of psychoanalysis by arguing for a middle road between
biology and culture. Gender becomes a kind of construction with threads
anchored in the human being's biology and anatomy.

Diamond writes:

> Rather than simply deconstructing gender dichotomies, I believe that
> sophisticated psychoanalytic theory must be able to sustain the nec-
> essary dialectical tension between traditional essentialist (either/or)
> thinking and a postmodern, constructivist (both/and) perspective.
>
> (2006, p. 1104)

However, such a middle road has been criticized for adopting a body–mind
dualism, which is a philosophical position that, I venture to say, everyone
shuns today. I will try to defend a position in which a distinction is made
between sex (female, male) and gender (femininity, masculinity), without falling into the trap of body–mind dualism. In accordance with Carol
Bigwood's (1991) thinking, I believe in the necessity, in a certain sense, to
renaturalize the body by means of Maurice Merleau-Ponty's explication of
the subjective, so-called "lived body" or better "living body" (*le corps pro-
pre, le corps vécu*). The living body is the body in its subjectivity, as opposed
to the objective body of natural science; the living body is both material and
intentional.

> The union of the soul and the body is not established through an arbi-
> trary decree that unites two mutually exclusive terms, one a subject and
> the other an object. It is accomplished at each moment in the movement
> of existence.
>
> (Merleau-Ponty 1945/2012, p. 91)[9]

Phenomenological reflections on the sex–gender distinction

Representatives of the phenomenological feminist traditions share the critique with social constructionism and poststructuralism against biologism.
However, within the phenomenological tradition, we also find criticism
against poststructuralism and Butler's theorizing with respect to different
features. Sara Heinämaa (1998) claims that Butler has not succeeded in
avoiding the sex–gender distinction, which was her intention to do.[10] Bigwood has also expressed criticism of Butler's emphasis on the discursive and
cultural production of sex which yields to a "disembodied body".

Bigwood argues for the necessity of renaturalizing the body in her reference to Merleau-Ponty's thinking, without falling into the trap of body–
mind dualism. She is critical of Butler's negligence of the noncognitive,
anonymous (nonpersonal) body, a body which is intertwined with our personal and cultural existence. For poststructuralists, nature is rendered into
something solely anthropocentric and the product of human actions; the
body loses its material, bodily character in its reduction into being an effect
of cultural, language production.

It seems to me that in her zeal to advocate a gender fluidity, Butler goes too far in her denaturalization of the body. Her Foucauldian attempt to avoid metaphysical foundationalism leaves us with a disembodied body and a free-floating gender artifice in a sea of cultural meaning production.

(Bigwood, 1991, p. 59)

According to Bigwood, Merleau-Ponty's living body possesses a certain permanence in comparison with a culturally and linguistically determined gender. However, it would be a mistake to depict the relationship between body and gender as a causal relationship; the body possesses an indeterminate constancy in its insoluble intertwinement with cultural and personal layers of meaning. The body is both natural and cultural, and these layers come into being at the same time, even though it is important to differentiate between them analytically: "The 'connatural' body is neither empirically nor logically prior to the 'cultural' body but is existentially a codeterminant of the body and thus can be at least distinguished abstractly from cultural determinants" (Ibid., p. 66).[11]

By means of phenomenology, we can understand sex/body and gender/culture within the frame of a constituting subject. The phenomenological alternative to biological objectivistic essentialism, which presupposes a nature independent of a human being, and poststructuralism, which treats the body as merely representation, is to affirm a certain bodily being in light of a constituting human being. The division between female and male as two different sexes depends on a constituting subject. Even though the body is always intertwined with historical and cultural significances, one can nevertheless discern an abstract moment in constituting the sex – an abstract moment that functions as a criterion of which category (female or male) the body in question belongs to. Likewise, gender is not a disembodied entity; the cultural gender dimension will, in the course of the individual's development, reflect the sexed body.[12]

No doubt, it is a complicated task to describe the relationship between sex and gender, but to merge them is no solution. When taking part of arguments against the sex–gender distinction, I am often struck by the fact that the relevance of sex is downplayed, as if it would only occur in a banal sense, or that the arguments, nevertheless, presuppose the existence of sex.

One may say that the categorization of the sexual difference between sex (female–male) and the gender difference (femininity–masculinity), respectively, originates from different sources.[13] The determination of a person's sex and this person's sexual identity is based on the experiences of something being given, before the acquisition of different identities, such as professional identity, significant interests that are practiced and form an experience of identity and personality traits of a more permanent kind.

The sexed body does, in a certain sense, possess an objective identity, and a person's sexual identity is not the outcome of strivings and choices. If we describe that with the sexual dimension intertwined with the gender dimension, we end up having to carry out different actions, strivings towards a certain personality and character, based, first of all, on different assimilating processes, of which identification processes with significant persons play a crucial role (more on this in the next chapter). In other words, the constitution of one's sex has to do with one's being, female or male, whereas gender involves actions, behavior, character and psychological and cultural levels of meaning.

If we, by means of phenomenological reflections, look closer at the sexual dimension (female, male), I would like to claim that a distinction can be made between a (subjective) first-person perspective and a third-person perspective. The way in which sex is "objectively" described from a third-person perspective presupposes a division of the human body in accordance with certain perceptible and/or not perceptible characteristics. Parents and the adult world have throughout history ascribed a specific sex to the newborn (usually boy or girl) on the basis of perception. This does not, of course, mean that the perception is merely a registration of objective facts: subjective aspects, such as wishes, norms and values, can affect the perception. In any case, more or less conscious and developed ideas about the historical and cultural meaning of belonging to a specific sex are always present.[14] The sexual ascription, by the surrounding world, is taken as an established fact (the first question that parents usually get asked about the newborn is what sex it is) and justified, by means of a perception of something intersubjectively (objectively) given, regardless of anyone's idiosyncratic imaginations, fantasies and wishes.

If we look at sex from a first-person perspective, we are dealing with a person's sexual *identity*. (That which I refer to as "sexual identity" corresponds to what many others call "gender identity"; more on that later.) The different sexes – female and male – are about identities. The sexual identity is a nonacquired identity and is for most people a very solid and constant one. Nevertheless, the individual must consent to it in order for it not to be experienced as fault or ego-dystonic. It has its source and origin prior to acquired identities such as, for example, a person's professional identity or one's identity as an athlete. An acquired identity requires devotion and certain actions in the development of the identity, whereas a nonacquired identity is something that is experienced as given and beyond one's will. The sexual body possesses a certain objective identity; it presents itself as something given, as something beyond one's choice. In particular, a person's sexual identity reaches thematic awareness when it fails, as is the case for the transsexual who has the experience of being born in the wrong biological body (Chiland, 2003).

It is an odd element in the sex/gender debate that the transsexual person's relationship to their sex is sometimes taken as proof of a dissolution and refutation of the validity of sexual identity, when, in fact, the transsexual person's relationship to their sex proves the opposite. If one wants to adduce an example which shows the legitimacy and urgency of belonging to a specific sex, we can refer to the transsexual, who, not rarely, affirms it by undergoing extensive sex affirmative medical procedures. For the transsexual, it is not a question of choosing an identity or trying to adopt one's behavior in line with one's given sex, but here it is a question of affirming an experienced being – that one is a specific sex.[15]

Thus, the transsexual person's experience is an example which motivates us to make a distinction between sex and gender. But there are further, subtler, examples showing the validity of such a distinction, where it can be quite difficult to draw a clear and obvious limit between sexual identity and gender which I signify as a *striving* for identity, or as a *project*. For example, in psychotherapeutic work, one can perceive men who vacillate between doubting their maleness (that is to say, the experience of their sexual belongingness) and insecurity whether they behave in a sufficiently masculine way in different contexts, such as being competent enough to satisfy their partner sexually.[16] In this case, we witness a vacillation between an insecurity concerning one's male sex and an insecurity about one's masculinity, that is to say, how successfully one lives up to the ideals connected to being a male. When the insecurity has to do with one's sexual identity, the man in question may feel confused about his sex, commenting about strange sensations in his penis and expressing doubts whether he is really built as a man. Such an experience is different from a man who does not worry about whether he is a man or not, but who feels doubtful whether he, for example, is self-assertive enough in order to appear masculine in front of others.

And if we take an everyday example where a man uncomfortably experiences his behavior as feminine, this does not need to disturb him in his sexual identity (unless possibly he is in a psychotic state of mind). On the contrary, one can claim that it is precisely due to his sexual identity as a man that he experiences his feminine behavior as uncomfortable.

Finally, it can be worth mentioning a political argument that has been used against demolishing the distinction between sex and gender; a fusion between sex and gender risks undermining the feminist project of abolishing the structural oppression of women, since this oppression is based on the denomination of the sex and not on gender traits.[17]

I will now briefly comment on an argument which is often used against the validity of a sex–gender distinction, an argument which rests on Thomas Laqueur's (1992) analysis of the biological sex as a modern construction.[18] It is not until modern time that man and woman were differentiated on the ground of biological dimorphism. The idea of the existence of two sexes on biological grounds, the so-called "two-sex model", did not come into existence until the end of 18th century, when it replaced the so-called "one-sex model". Before the Age of Enlightenment, the idea was that men and women were one and the same sex; they had the same genitals, the only difference was that the man's sex organ was outside the body, while the woman's was inside. The vagina was supposed to be an interior penis, the labia a foreskin, the uterus a scrotum and the ovaries were seen as interior testicles.

If the view underwent such a radical reformulation during the late 18th century, does this mean that sex cannot be differentiated from gender? Even with the one-sex model, there is a distinction between men and women; thus, it should not be understood as if no distinction is being made. The man is the role model due to the idea that he is regarded as being closer to the perfect cosmic order. The difference between men and women is, by all means, not motivated from the vantage point of a biological construction, but rests on metaphysical grounds; the man was assumed to stand higher in the hierarchy of perfection which different beings represented in the cosmos. Laqueur shows how hard the one-sex model was to kill before it eventually was replaced by the two-sex model, where body and sex no longer are related to a higher metaphysic order, but are thus determined on the basis of biology.

Despite the different explanatory systems, there is, nevertheless, a common vantage point in the sense that women are differentiated from men. I believe this points to a kind of indeterminate constancy that characterizes the body and which induces that something in the anatomical difference (which, by the way, also is entailed in the one-sex model) constitutes the point of departure for the categorization of women and men, before we ascribe it scientific or metaphysical ground. Laqueur writes:

> In the ordinary course of events, sexing was of course no problem. Creatures with an external penis were declared to be boys and were allowed all the privileges and obligations of that status; those with only an internal penis were assigned to the inferior category of girl.
>
> (1992, p. 135)

The fact that the anatomical difference became of such importance, not to say, played the crucial role in the differentiation between female and male, can be understood from its connection to the reproductive function. However, the different valuing of the sexes is, of course, not legitimized neither by body morphology nor by certain possible functions that the body may possess. The lesson that would be reasonable to draw is rather that no one can be both, and that we need each other.

In summary, I have maintained that sex has to do with a nonacquired identity, whereas gender can be said to be a possible *striving* for an identity or, in other words, a *project*. The focus of this book is on gender/masculinity rather than on a problematic concerning sex and sexual identity. The focus on gender/masculinity, however, does not mean that the question of sexual identity is psychologically of no importance or unproblematic. The trans-sexual person's experience of being born into the wrong body shows un-doubtedly how deeply painful a sexual identity can be experienced. From a development point of view, the identity of belonging to a specific sex also en-tails a process of disillusionment in that omnipotent wishes to be everything are to be rejected in favor of an acceptance of reality. To reconcile with the limitations of reality is a painful process but, nevertheless, worth living through and makes, after all, existence more bearable. Nevertheless, in line with my emphasis on the intertwined relationship between sex and gender dimensions, it will be obvious that the phallic masculine project involves omnipotent ideas about the meaning of belonging to the male sex.

Gender and the need to give room for ego-identity

The conceptual confusion within the field of sex/gender is not restricted to unclarities concerning the relationship between sexes (female, male, inter-sex) and gender (femininity, masculinity), but can also be seen in the dis-cussion about gender which belongs to the cultural, psychological meaning level. Today, there is a tendency to dissolve the difference between the con-cepts "feminine and masculine" in various ways. A wish is discernable to let masculinity include personality traits that traditionally are conceived of as feminine, such as, for example, that masculinity can be expressed in supportive and caring qualities or in a cooperative capacity (Person, 2006). From a semantic point of view, objections can be raised about the unnec-essary obscurity that is created if the masculine qualities and personality traits are the same as the feminine ones. What is, in such a case, the point with the masculine–feminine distinction? Sex/gender research should, of course, contain the possibility of discovering similarities between men and women, but these should not be comprehended in terms of masculinity and femininity being connoted as the same. Consequently, there is no bi-ologism smuggled in my distinction between femininity and masculinity, but this distinction is motivated, to some extent, by semantic, logical rea-sons. Whether, and to what extent, men can feel feminine and/or display feminine traits, from a third-person perspective, are empirical questions. I will argue that those factors which psychologically and culturally consti-tute masculinity involve a repudiation of the feminine, in particular of the motherly.[19]

It is often difficult to compare different theories with one another, since relevant concepts are used differently. There are some conceptual differ-ences in my work compared to what is common in the literature. First of all, I use the term "sex/sexual identity" on occasions when many other theoreti-cians would use the concept "gender identity". To the extent that the concept "sex" is used at all, it seems to be done so from a third-person perspective, whereas I elaborate on sex in the sense of sexual identity from a first-person perspective. Second, I do not talk about gender identity, but a *striving* for gender identity, or simply gender as a *project*, and in this book, it pertains to masculinity – masculinity as a project.

One way of formulating the relationship between sexual identity and gender as a project is to assert that gender represents the individual's relation to the sexually, culturally conditioned meaning. What makes the consideration of gender necessary is that all the historical, social and cultural meaning that has been identified with one's sexual identity calls for an answer, for a position on existing masculine ideals. The answer can take the form of either a striving for a gender identity or a rejection of the idea that there is such a thing as gender identity, that is, the claim that there exists a specific meaning attached to one's sex. Given that this account is valid, there are reasons to promote a concept that does not restrict the field of sex/gender to sexual identity and gender as a project.

Therefore, I will, in Chapter 5, argue that the human formation of identity requires a conceptualization which does not lock it into the gender dichotomy; we need to give room for an ego-identity that transcends femininity and masculinity. It has to do with both an ego-identity which, in a certain sense, precedes sexual identity/gender and one which develops beyond it, as a kind of humanization that is inherited in a person's possibility of striving for an authentic life. I also believe that it is essential to bring in the notion of ego-identity in order to gain greater clarity within this field of research. By introducing ego-identity into the discussion, much is gained: we will obtain a more cogent conceptual apparatus within sex/gender research; we will highlight the significance of the notion of authenticity in the sex/gender discussion which, not least, will enable us to easier liberate ourselves from stereotypical gender ideals.

Notes

1 Within the field of sex/gender research, the view of poststructuralism predominates. When it comes to masculinity studies, the phenomenological view is practically nonexistent, which is pointed out by Berggren (2014), who uses representatives of phenomenological feminism in his analysis of masculinity.
2 Seidler is critical towards the poststructuralism's

> categorical distinctions between nature and culture. When realizing the problems with these distinctions and that poststructuralist theories often claim that sexual identities are shaped only within the cultural sphere and in language, then we identify a weakness in the poststructuralist tradition which is difficult to discover for someone who has been introduced to social theory with its conceptual world.
>
> (2004, p. 19)

> Another example of a similar critique against poststructuralism is Hollway's who deplores that the distinction between sexual and gender differences "has been lost with the dominance of a social constructionist paradigm on identity

that claims that all differences are socially produced and therefore gender differences" (2006, p. 36).

3 Grosz makes an important remark concerning the risk of misunderstanding the
term "sex" in English, in that it can be mixed with "sexuality":

> In my understanding, the term 'sex' refers, not to sexual impulses, desires,
> wishes, hopes, bodies, pleasures, behaviors and practices: this I refer to the
> term 'sexuality'. 'Sex' refers to the domain of sexual difference, to the ques-
> tion of *morphologies of bodies* (italics in the original).
>
> (1995, p. 213)

4 Connell's (e.g., 1995) theory of "hegemonic masculinity" is the domineering theory within academic research and can be conceived of as a sociological theory
of masculinity. The concept "hegemony" stems from the Italian Marxist Anto-
nio Gramsci's analysis of class relations, and in Connell's theory this concept
designates the masculine ideals that become leading and ruling in the culture
and which one has to relate to. "Masculinity is shaped in relation to an overall
structure of power (the subordination of women to men), and in relation to a
general symbolism of difference (the opposition of femininity and masculinity)" (Ibid., p. 223). Important features in the theory of hegemonic masculinity
include the idea that gender structures describe power relations based on social, everyday practices. There are many masculinities, and they are changeable and should be understood from the vantage point of societal institutions
and socioeconomic processes. Gender structures, such as masculinity, can be
changed both from within itself and being the result of external factors, such
as socioeconomic changes in society. The hegemony presupposes that there is a
connection between institutional power and cultural ideals. Masculinity must
be understood as an intersectional phenomenon: "It is now common to say that
gender 'intersects' – better, interacts – with race and class. We might add that
it constantly interacts with nationality or position in the world order" (Ibid., p.
75). For example, the white man's masculinity is not the same as the black man's,
nor is the heterosexual's the same as the homosexual's. We are, thus, dealing
with multiple masculinities, and the mission is to investigate their mutual relations. However, the central power relation is not the relations between men but
men's superior position in relationship to women:

> Hegemonic masculinity can be defined as the configuration of gender prac-
> tice which embodies the currently accepted answer to the problem of the
> legitimacy of patriarchy, which guarantees (or is taken to guarantee) the
> dominant position of men and the subordination of women. (Ibid., p. 77)

Typical, but not necessarily, representatives of hegemonic masculinity are
men who hold top positions in business, military and government. And when
it comes to the positioning between men, there are, apart from the concept
hegemony, three concepts used to describe superior and inferior positioning,
namely subordination, complicity and marginalization. Connell claims that the
homosexual masculinity is the most conspicuous subordinated masculinity:
"Patriarchal culture has a simple interpretation of gay men: they lack masculinity" (Ibid., p. 143). However, there are other subordinated masculinities, since
there are heterosexual men who are associated with femininity and thereby are
excluded from belonging to a legitimate masculinity, which can be highlighted
by different derogatory epithet: wimp, milksop, nerd, sissy, mother's boy and so
on. The term "complicity" refers to the majority of men who do not reach the
level of practicing hegemonic masculinity (since they may be quite few) but who,

nevertheless, gain from hegemonic masculinity and the superior position in relationship to women. Finally, the term "marginalization" is to be understood on the basis of other structures in society that interplay with gender, such as class, race and ethnicity. Conell asserts that marginalization is relative to the authorization of hegemonic masculinity of the dominant group. Concretely, this can manifest itself in that certain men in an inferior or discriminated group (e.g., blacks, immigrants) by being stars in, for example, entertainment and sports can be role models for hegemonic masculinity, although this does not have the effect that the discriminated group (e.g., blacks, immigrants) rise up from their subordinated position to reach an equal social authority.

The theory of hegemonic masculinity has been discussed and criticized. One merit with the theory that has, for example, been emphasized is that it allows for a multiplicity of masculinities, that it entails a dimension of power and that it concerns the relation between men and women as well as between men. However, it has also been criticized for being vague and unclear when it comes to the norms that are prescribed and constitute the hegemonic masculinity. Its portraying of men is insufficient in order to understand men's positioning as sexual beings. It has been criticized for being tendentious and running the risk of reducing masculinity to a question of power relations. It neglects psychological issues and painful experiences that men may have experienced in growing up. And in line with psychoanalytic thinking, researchers have pointed out the importance of fear in men's emotional life (see, for example, Hearn, 2004; Johansson, 2008; Kimmel, 2012; Seidler, 2004; Wetherell & Edley, 1999). For a response to some of the critiques that have been launched against the theory of hegemonic masculinity, see Connell & Messerschmidt's (2005) article in which psychoanalysis is referred to as a significant source for understanding the subject's gender practice.

5 The fact that I do not postulate the libido as the starting point for the organization of sexual identity and gender does not imply a relapse to a pre-psychoanalytic idea about sexuality, as Quindeau claims. I agree that the significance of partial drives is essential in making the unconscious comprehensible. To exemplify with the first partial drive, the oral drive, it would be a mistake to consider the drive itself as sexual/gender specific. However, the manner in which the infant is breastfed can very well be sexual/gender specific, and thereby, the sexual drive plays immediately a role for determining gender ideals.

6 Even though the difference between biologism and poststructuralism is obvious on one level, there is a more significant affiliation between them, when considering some of the poststructuralists' denial of the existence of biological facts independent of social and political norms. Moi writes: "I get the impression that poststructuralists believe that if there *were* biological facts, then they would indeed give rise to social norms. In this way, they paradoxically share the fundamental belief of biological determinists" (italics in the original) (2005, p. 42).

7 Alcoff criticizes Butler's understanding of the materiality of the body:

> But if materiality is *merely* the effect of power, then it is merely an epiphenomenon, without any causal efficacy, and theorists are more likely to think they can ignore phenomenological or other accounts of materiality and address only representations and discourses (italics in the original).
>
> (2000, pp. 858–859)

8 Ever since antiquity, form and matter have been connected with different metaphors, and not least form as male/masculine and matter as female/feminine. In Aristotle, we can read that

the female always provides the material, the male that which fashions it, for this is the power we say each possess, and *this is what it is for them to be male and female* [...] While the body is from the female, it is the soul that is from the male.

(from Laqueur, 1992, p. 30) (italics in Laqueur)

Lloyd has analyzed the meaning of maleness and femaleness in the history of Western philosophy and found that the man as the representative of reason is always superior to the woman.

Associations between maleness and clear determination or definition persisted in articulations of the form-matter distinction in later Greek philosophical thought. Maleness was aligned with active, determinate form, femaleness with passive, indeterminate matter. The scene for these alignments was set by traditional Greek understanding of sexual reproduction, which saw the father as providing the formative principle, the real causal force of generation, whilst the mother provided only the matter which received form or determination, and nourished what had been produced by the father.

(Lloyd, 1984, p. 3)

9 And another clarifying quote from Merleau-Ponty:

It is impossible to superimpose upon man both a primary layer of behaviors that could be called 'natural' and a constructed cultural or spiritual world. For man, everything is constructed and everything is natural, in the sense that there is no single word or behavior that does not owe something to mere biological being – and, at the same time, there is no word or behavior that does not break free from animal life, that does not deflect vital behaviors from their direction [sens] through a sort of *escape* and a genius for ambiguity that might well serve to define man.

(italics in the original) (1945/2012, p. 195)

10 Heinämaa argues for a position in which no difference is made between sex and gender from the vantage point of Merleau-Ponty's idea of the living body. Sexual identity is understood as a stylistic unity, as a variation of a way of relating to the world, without making any essential difference between bodily properties, sexuality, cognition and so on: "The development of a sexual identity [...] is not accounted for by the concepts of inheritance and properties, but by the concepts of imitation and mimicry, repetition and modification" (Heinämaa, 2003, p. 68). And yet another quote from Heinämaa:

(w)e can understand sexual difference [...] as a difference between two styles of intentional life – that is, as a difference in ways of intending realities and idealities, and being motivated by experiences and experienceable objects. As stylistic characteristics of persons, 'manhood' and 'womanhood' are not anchored on any particular activities on objects, but are given as two different ways of relating to objectivity, acting on objects and being affected by them.

(2012, p. 236)

11 In line with Merleau-Ponty's view of the body, we have Beauvoir's conceptualization of the body as situation: "the body is not a thing, it is a situation: it is our grasp on the world and the outline of our projects" (italics in the original) (1949/2011, p. 46). Without adopting a biological essentialist position, Beauvoir recognizes that there are certain factual differences between a man's

and a woman's body, but such facts "do not carry their meaning in themselves" (Ibid., p. 47). The body as situation consists of an intertwinement between facticity and freedom, in the sense that our facticity never functions as a cause for our strivings and our freedom is never absolute.

12 Bourdieu talks about "circular causality" between biology and gender in order to explain the masculine domination.

> The social world constructs the body as a sexually defined reality and as the depository of sexually defining principles of vision and division. This embodied social programme of perception is applied to all the things of the world and firstly to the *body* itself, in its biological reality. It is this programme which constructs the difference between the biological sexes in conformity with the principles of a mythic vision of the world rooted in the arbitrary relationship of domination of men over women, itself inscribed, with the division of labour, in the reality of the social order. The *biological* difference between the *sexes*, i.e. between the male and female bodies, and, in particular, *anatomical* difference between the sex organs, can thus appear as natural justification of the socially constructed difference between the *genders*, and in particular of the social division of labour.
>
> > (italics in the original) (2001, p. 11)

Colebrook summarizes Bourdieu's position in a way that resembles Bigwood's view, when she writes: "Bourdieu's 'circularity' of the relationship between biology and gender insists that one can neither see gender differences as merely imposed, nor see them as directly caused" (2004, p. 50).

13 As pointed out in the Introduction, I simplify the discussion by not taking up the possibility of a nonbinary sexual identity, since such a possibility does not have any impact on my principal argument about the distinction between sex and gender.

14 Gatens, who is influenced by both psychoanalysis and Merleau-Ponty's living body in her conceptualization of "the imaginary body", writes:

> Masculinity and femininity as forms of sex-appropriate behaviours are manifestations of a historically based, culturally shared phantasy about male and female biologies, and as such sex and gender are not arbitrarily connected. The connection between the female body and femininity is not arbitrary in the same way that the symptom is not arbitrarily related to its etiology.
>
> > (1996, p. 13)

15 Rubin pays attention to the fact that the phenomenological approach to studies of transsexuality has been met with resistance by some feminists and poststructuralists, who claim that the choice of the transsexual to undergo operations in order to acquire a correspondence between the appearance of the look of one's body and one's sexual identity implies a legitimation of sexual normativity. The emphasis of poststructuralism on discourse analysis entails a denial of the transsexual's experience of identity. Rubin stresses the importance of investigating the transsexual person's lived experience in a phenomenological spirit:

> The critiques of transsexuals may be countered by a phenomenology that views all lived experience as worthy of description and does not deny that knowledges gleaned from such experiences are also functional to homosexual subjects [...] Most of all, phenomenology remains committed to lived experience as one legitimate source of knowledge [...] Feminist and queer studies have dismissed or coopted transsexualism before transsexuals have scarcely had a chance to speak in our own names [...] The life experiences of

transsexuals were not mined for new insights about embodiment. Instead, these experiences were held up to ideological measuring stick and eventually found to lack a proper degree of feminist political awareness. Usually, this proceeded through a critique of transsexual essentialism.

(1998, pp. 271–272)

On the basis of interviews with transsexuals (female to males = FTMs), Rubin notes that

most of the FTMs in my research [...] tend to essentialize their identities and 'fail' to frame their personal biographies in a discursive genealogy [...] As trans scholarship enters the doors of the academy via queer theory, a rift is developing between members of the trans community and this emerging scholarship.

(Ibid., p. 276)

16　Note! When I present and discuss my ideas, the term "maleness" is used exclusively in relationship to the category "sex". However, it has not been possible to systematically maintain such an order when referring to, or discussing, others' ideas. In such cases, I have chosen to comply with the language use of the author in question, but sometimes added the terminology which I find to be adequate in this specific context.

17　Benhabib writes: "A certain version of postmodernism is not only incompatible with but would undermine the very possibility of feminism as the theoretical articulation of the emancipatory aspirations of women" (1992, pp. 228–229).

18　Laqueur himself expresses such a view point when stating that "some of the so-called sex differences in biological and sociological research turn out to be gender differences after all, and the distinction between nature and culture collapses as the former folds into the latter" (1992, p. 13).

19　Moss (2012) emphasizes that *repudiation* is an important element in a masculine strategy. Repudiation can even have the double character that an original repudiation from what conventionally is conceived of as feminine is followed by a repudiation of this original repudiation with the intention, for example, of indulging into a pleasurable feminine expression. Moss talks about masculinity as masquerade.

References

Alcoff, L.M. (2000). Philosophy matters: A review of recent work in feminist philosophy. *Signs, 25*(3), 841–882.

Anzieu, D. (1989). *The skin ego.* Yale University Press.

Beauvoir, S. de (149/2011). The second sex. Vintage Books.

Benhabib, S. (1992). *Situating the self. Gender, community and postmodernism in contemporary ethics.* Polity Press.

Berggren, K. (2014). Sticky masculinity: Post-structuralism, phenomenology and subjectivity in critical studies on men. *Men and Masculinities, 17*(3), 231–252. Doi:10.1177/1097184X14539510

Bigwood, C. (1991). Renaturalizing the body (with the help of Merleau-Ponty). *Hypatia, 6*(3), 54–73. Doi:10.1111/j.1527-2001.1991.tb00255.x

Bourdieu, P. (2001). *Masculine domination.* Polity.

Butler, J. (1990). *Gender trouble: Feminism and the subversion of identity.* Routledge.

Butler, J. (1993). *Bodies that matter: On the discursive limits of "sex".* Routledge.

Butler, J. (1995). Melancholy gender – refused identification. *Psychoanalytic Dialogues, 5*(2), 165–180. Doi:10.1080/10481889509539059

Chiland, C. (2003). Sex and gender: The battle between body and soul. In A.M. Alizade (Ed.) *Masculine scenarios*. Karnac.

Chodorow, N.J. (2012). Beyond sexual difference: Same-sex/cross-generation and clinical individuality in the creation of feminine and masculine. In her *Individualizing gender and sexuality. Theory and practice*. Routledge.

Colebrook, C.L. (2004). *Gender*. Palgrave Macmillan.

Connell, R.W. (1995). *Masculinities*. Polity Press.

Connell, R.W. & Messerschmidt, J.W. (2005). Hegemonic masculinity, rethinking the concept. *Gender & Society, 19*(6), 829–859. Doi:10.1177/0891243205278639

Diamond, M.J. (2006). Masculinity unravelled: The roots of male gender identity and the shifting of male ego ideals throughout life. *Journal of the American Psychoanalytic Association, 54*(4), 1099–1130. Doi:10.1177/00030651060540040601

Diamond, M.J. (2013). Evolving perspectives on masculinities and its discontents: Reworking the internal phallic and genital positions. In E. Ester Palerm Mari & F- Thomson-Salo (Eds.) *Masculinity and femininity today*. Karnac.

Dio Bleichmar, E. (2010). The psychoanalyst's implicit theories of gender. In L. Glocer Fiorini & G. Abelin-Sas Rose (Eds.) *On Freud's "femininity"*. Karnac.

Freud, S. (1905). *Three essays on the theory of sexuality. The standard edition of the complete psychological works of Sigmund Freud, 7*.

Freud, S. (1920). The psychogenesis of a case of homosexuality in a woman. *The standard edition of the complete psychological works of Sigmund Freud, 18*.

Gantheret, F. (1983). L'impensable maternel et les fondements maternels du penser. *Nouvelle Revue de Psychoanalyse, 28*, 7–27.

Gatens, M. (1991). A critique of the gender/sex distinction. In S. Gunew (Ed.) *A reader in feminist knowledge*. Routledge.

Gatens, M. (1996). *Imaginary bodies: Ethics, power and corporeality*. Routledge.

Grosz, E. (1995). *Space, time and perversion. Essays on the politics of bodies*. Routledge.

Harris, A. (1991). Gender as contradiction. *Psychoanalytic Dialogues, 1*(2), 197–224. Doi:10.1080/10481889109538893

Hearn, J. (2004). From hegemonic masculinity to the hegemony of men. *Feminist theory, 5*(1), 49–72. Doi:10.1177/1464700104040813

Heinämaa, S. (1998). Kvinna – natur, produkt, stil? [Woman – nature, product, style?]. *Tidskrift för genusvetenskap, 19*(1), 33–48.

Heinämaa, S. (2003). *Toward a phenomenology of sexual difference. Husserl, Merleau-Ponty, Beauvoir*. Rowman & Littlefield Publishers, Inc.

Heinämaa, S. (2012). Sex, gender and embodiment. In D. Zahavi (Ed.) *The Oxford handbook of contemporary phenomenology*. Oxford University Press.

Hollway, W. (2006). *The capacity to care: Gender and ethical subjectivity*. Routledge.

Johansson, T. (2008). The full monty – masculinity undressed. *NORMA (Nordisk tidskrift för maskulinitetsstudier), 3*(1), 13–30.

Karlsson, G. (2010). *Psychoanalysis in a new light*. Cambridge University Press.

Karlsson, G. (2011). Sigmund Freud och sexualiteten. [Sigmund Freud and sexuality]. In M. Anjefelt (Ed.) *10 skäl att älska Freud*. [10 reasons to love Freud]. Natur och Kultur.

Kimmel, M. (2012). *Manhood in America. A cultural history*. Oxford University Press.

Laplanche, J. (2007). Gender, sex, and the sexual. *Studies in Gender and Sexuality, 8*(2), 201–219. Doi:10.1080/15240650701225567

Laqueur, T. (1992). *Making sex. Body and gender from the Greeks to Freud.* Harvard University Press.

Lloyd, G. (1984). *The man of reason. "Male" and "female" in Western philosophy.* Routledge.

Merleau-Ponty, M. (1945/2012). *Phenomenology of perception.* Routledge.

Moi, T. (2005). *Sex, gender, and the body. The student edition of "What is a woman?".* Oxford University Press.

Moss, D. (2012). *Thirteen ways of looking at a man. Psychoanalysis and masculinity.* Routledge.

Person, E.S. (2006). Masculinities plural. *Journal of the American Psychoanalytic Association, 54*(4), 1165–1186. Doi:10.1177/00030651060540041501

Person, E.S. & Ovesey, L. (1983). Psychoanalytic theories of gender. *Journal of the American Academy of Psychoanalysis, 11*(2), 203–226. Doi:10.1521/jaap.1.1983.11.2.203

Quindeau, I. (2013). *Seduction and desire. A psychoanalytic theory of sexuality beyond Freud.* Karnac.

Rubin, H.S. (1998). Phenomenology as method in trans studies. *GLQ: A Journal of Lesbian and Gay Studies, 4*(2), 263–281.

Schaffer, J. (2010). The riddle of the repudiation of femininity: The scandal of the feminine dimension. In L. Glocer Fiorini & G. Abelin-Sas Rose (Eds.) *On Freud's "femininity".* Karnac.

Seidler, V. (2004). Des/orienterade maskuliniteter. Kroppar, känslor och rädsla. [Dis/oriented masculinities. Bodies, emotions and fears]. *Kvinnovetenskaplig tidskrift,* no. 1–2, 11–16.

Stein, R. (1998). The poignant, the excessive and the enigmatic in sexuality. *International Journal of Psychoanalysis, 45*(2), 253–268.

Stoller, R.J. (1964). A contribution to the study of gender identity. *International Journal of Psychoanalysis, 45*(2–3), 220–226.

Stoller, R.J. (1968). *Sex and gender. The development of masculinity and femininity,* vol 1. Maresfield Reprints.

Wetherell, M. & Edley, N. (1999). Negotiating hegemonic masculinity: Imaginary positions and psycho-discursive practices. *Feminism & Psychology, 9*(3), 335–356. Doi:10.1177/0959353599009003012

2

Psychoanalytic theories about masculinity

In this chapter, I will discuss psychoanalytic theories about masculinity.[1] In Chapter 3, I will discuss three forms of masculinity with a focus on phallic masculinity.

When discussing psychoanalytic contributions to masculinity, one cannot ignore Freud. As was pointed out in Chapter 1, Person and Ovesey (1983) maintain that Freud was the first one to draw attention, in a substantial way, to the difference between biological sex and cultural, psychological gender, despite the fact that in German only one suitable term exists: "Geschlecht". His theorizing and formulation precede, in other words, the terminological distinction between sex and gender, which was introduced in the 1950s. It may be worth paying attention to Freud's contribution to the discussion in light of all the criticism which has been launched against him concerning the issue of sex/gender. In particular, the views he expressed regarding women and femininity have been criticized. His phallocentric theory (more on this later), which largely provides the foundation for the criticism that his theorization about the women has been subjected to, has been accused of having a detrimental effect also on the development of the theorizing about masculinity in psychoanalysis. Muriel Dimen and Virginia Goldner state that "Freud's idealization of phallic masculinity not only erased and debased femininity as a category and as a lived, embodied self-experience. It also delayed the theorization of masculinity in all its specificity and multiplicity" (2005, p. 99).

Other voices, within the psychoanalytic community, which have expressed a discontent with psychoanalytic knowledge include, for example, Ken Corbett (2009, p. 6) who claims that the psychoanalytic discourse about masculinity does not reach the same complexity as the one about femininity. Besides, neither has it had the same socially transforming effect as the one about femininity. Janice Lieberman (2006, p. 1059) points out that masculinity is neglected in psychoanalysis, and in the work of Quindeau (2013, p. 165), one can read that masculinity has remained a "dark continent" in psychoanalytic theory, in contrast to Freud's view that the sexual life of adult women is a "dark continent" (Freud, 1926, p. 212). Bruce Reis and

DOI: 10.4324/9781003352761-3

Robert Grossmark (2009, p. xv), on the basis of their clinical experiences, claim that there is a need to revise the ways in which masculinity has been theorized. At the same time, Dana Breen points out that the psychoanalytic understanding about masculinity has undergone a revolution since Freud's time, but it has, in her words, "gone almost unnoticed" (1993, p. 24).

On Freud's view of masculinity

According to Freud, masculinity begins as a distinguishing sexual identity during the phallic genital phase (3–5 years), in connection with the castration complex. I write "*distinguishing* sexual identity", that is to say, masculinity as opposed to femininity. Freud's idea is namely that from the beginning all individuals are small men, boys and girls. In the beginning, there is only one sex, since the vagina has not yet the status of sex, and her clitoris is assumed to be synonymous with the penis.[2] The discovery of the sexual difference takes place in the phallic genital phase, which causes the girl to suffer from penis envy and the boy to fear losing his penis; his fate is to cope with castration threat and castration anxiety. The boy's discovery that the girl/woman is castrated is accepted with much resistance, and the emotional reaction which this discovery brings about permanently determines boys' relation to women: "horror of the mutilated creature or triumphant contempt for her" (Freud, 1925, p. 252).[3]

Both the girl's and the boy's first libidinal object (love object) is, according to Freud, the mother. The girl's psychosexual development is for this reason more complicated since she has to switch both the erogenous zone (from clitoris to vagina) and the libidinal object (from mother to father), given that there will be a satisfactorily oedipal solution, in the eyes of Freud. The trajectory for the boy is simpler, since he maintains both the penis as genital organ and the mother as his libidinal object. Even though the boy's development is less complicated, he is, nevertheless, forced to fight against fairly horrible demons. The threat to the boy and man of losing their highly valued sex organ has a strong effect on their character formation, in the form of the construction of the ego-ideal and superego structure.

Freud's idealization of the male genital is never subjected to a psychoanalytic examination of ideas and fantasies, but seems to be conceived of as an objective fact. He can be criticized for neglecting to adopt a psychoanalytic view on the matter in question, which would, among other things, consist of a revelation that a possible disdain for the female genital can be considered to be a false idea or illusion. In Freud's world, it is the male genital which primarily connects to "the propagation of the species" and thereby explains this organ's highly narcissistic value: "Since the penis [...] owes its extraordinarily high narcissistic cathexis to its organic significance for the propagation of the species [...]" (Ibid., p. 257). Besides, it is difficult to avoid getting the impression that Freud thinks that it is quite in order that the man should be valued higher than the woman, when he talks about "the feminists, who are anxious to force us to regard the two sexes as completely equal in position and worth" (Ibid., p. 258). However, in fairness it should be pointed out that Freud embraced the idea of bisexual disposition, which is why the difference between men and women is not as significant as the difference between masculine and feminine characteristics. In this sense, there are no pure masculine men since masculine and feminine characteristics are mixed up with one another.

Freud's theorizing represents a traditional patriarchal thinking, in the sense that it is in the dynamic between father and son, the "higher side of man" arise. Within the "higher side of man" are included religion, morality and a social sense. "The male sex seems to have taken the lead in all these moral acquisitions; and they seem to have been transmitted to women by cross-inheritance" (1923, p. 37).

Freud's idea that from the beginning everyone is a small man – in other words, the penis is the only existing genital organ – goes by the name "phallocentrism". His phallocentric theory has been criticized ever since the 1920s, primarily because it implies a denial of the preoedipal girl's own experience of herself as a girl. Karen Horney (1924, 1926, 1932, 1933) and Ernest Jones (1927, 1933, 1935) maintained that femininity and masculinity were founded before the occurrence of the phallic phase and were caused by innate dispositions.[4]

The distinguishing sexual identity, thus, begins with the phallic genital phase in connection with the Oedipus complex. In the so-called "positive oedipal conflict", the boy wishes to marry his mother and eliminate his father. In other words, this conflict entails both incestuous wishes and aggression and murderous impulses. However, the Oedipus complex must be annihilated due to "its internal impossibility", Freud writes (1924, p. 173). The phallic phase, including the boy's narcissistic cathexis of his penis, must also recede due to the threat of castration. It is the father's task to execute the castration, although the threat most often comes from the mother.[5]

Above, I mentioned the positive oedipal conflict, but the matter is, somewhat, more complicated. Due to the existence of the bisexual constitution, the boy also wants to get rid of the mother and be an object of love for the father (the passive feminine position).[6] However, from the discovery of the woman's castration, the boy can satisfy himself neither in an active masculine way (since then he risks being punished by his rival, the father) nor passively feminine (where the wish to replace the mother and be loved by the father happens at the cost of losing his penis). Hence, in both cases, the result is castration. In the ordinary, normal development, the oedipal wishes are repressed and the boy replaces his attitude of rivalry towards his father by identifying with him, according to Freud. This reasoning presupposes two kinds of relating between children and parents: one is about the parent being a love object, someone whom the child wants to have; in the other kind of relating, the parent is an object of identification, someone whom the child wants to be. I will return to this distinction later, when discussing the phenomenon of identification, but first a few words about the polarity between active and passive.

Masculinity equals activity

A recurring theme in Freud's polarization between male/masculine and female/feminine is the depiction of active and passive. He was certainly not content with this characterization, but nevertheless he found it difficult to disregard.[7] The central thought is that the male organ, the penis, is active. The man loves by penetrating the woman. The so-called "aim" of the sexual/libidinal drive of the woman – that is, the way in which the sexual satisfaction is reached – is through passivity; she wants to be loved and vaginally penetrated. Interestingly enough, Freud emphasizes that the child's first sexual and sexually accentuated experiences with the mother is of passive nature; the baby is breastfed and is taken care of. Such an observation is interesting in light of a comment made by Freud, namely that something that is received passively generally tends to bring about an active reaction with the child. In other words, the child tries to (actively) control impressions that the environment has imposed on it (cf. Freud, 1931).

We recognize this mechanism in the compulsion to repeat in its attempt to handle traumatic experiences. What I find interesting is that Freud's reasoning makes it possible to conceive of the active masculine trait as reactive, as a kind of defense. This is a completely different way to perceive masculinity than what is customary in Freud. Later on, I will characterize masculine and feminine by means of the concepts "control" and "reception", which have a certain relation to Freud's concepts "active" and "passive".

The function of identification

Even if Freud's sex/gender theory, in many ways, is deficient, he has, nevertheless, chiseled out the field and a set of problems by means of concepts that are essential. One such concept, perhaps the most important, is identification. In general, the concept of identification is an extremely important one within psychoanalysis and has an affinity with such mechanisms as incorporation, introjection and imitation, all of which describe different aspects of assimilating processes.[8]

The mechanism of identification is relevant in different contexts; the first time Freud discusses it is in connection with hysteria, and identification is then described as an "assimilation" of others' symptoms "on the basis of a similar aetiological pretension" (1900, p. 150). Hence, identification contains both an assimilation of the other's way of being and an experience of sharing a common ground with the other. In his *Group Psychology and the Analysis of the Ego*, in which identification is discussed at length, Freud maintains

that identification is "the earliest expression of an emotional tie with another person" (1921, p. 105). *Identification* is the concept that will form the
hub of the presentation here. Roy Schafer points out that the process of
identification is unconscious with possible significant preconscious and conscious components involved. The process of identifying with an object aims
at "being like, the same as, and merged with one or more representations of
that object" (1968, p. 140). These three aims presumably cooperate with one
another in most identifications. Jean Laplanche and Jean-Bertand Pontalis,
in their psychoanalytic vocabulary, define identification as follows:

> Psychological process whereby the subject assimilates an aspect, prop-
> erty or attribute of the other and is transformed, wholly or partially,
> after the model the other provides. It is by means of a series of identifi-
> cations that the personality is constituted and specified.
>
> (1985, p. 205)

The boy's acquisition of masculinity, by means of different assimilating
processes with the father, is described as being distinctive of the masculine
character, which means that it is not a question of a passive or feminine
attitude to the father as in the case of a homosexual object choice.[9] Such an
acquired masculinity is drawn from two sources: partly it originates from
incorporation far back in a primal history and partly in the form of the boy's
oedipal identification with the father. When it comes to incorporation in a
primal history, Freud adhered to the idea that in the beginning there was a
sovereign primal father with sole access to the women. This awoke the sons'
anger, which led to the murder of the father, whereupon guilt feelings and
the need of reconciliation took place. The Totem meal, a meal of reconciliation, became an important part of the "Totem and taboo" culture, from
which Freud analyzed the acquisition of the strength of the primal father.

Masculinity as something acquired, in the form of the boy's oedipal
identification with his father, signifies an ambivalent identification. Hence,
the identification is not solely something positive, since in this phase of life
the boy wishes the father to be gone, as he is an obstacle to the realization
of the oedipal wishes towards the mother. But Freud points out that the
ambivalent identification originates from the first oral phase of the libido
organization, "in which the object that we long for and prize is assimilated
by eating and is in that way annihilated as such" (1921, p. 105). The oedipal
identification with the father has a precursor in a cannibalistic incorporation of the father, manifested in the feast of the totem meal:

> The violent primal father had doubtless been the feared and envied
> model of each one of the company of brothers: and in the act of devour-
> ing him they accomplished their identification with him, and each one
> of them acquired a portion of his strength.
>
> (1913, p. 142)

In discussing the identification of the oedipal boy, Freud states repeatedly that identification is most likely the original form of attachment. However, at the same time, he allows for an object-cathexis which may be even earlier than the identification with the father, namely an object-cathexis in relationship towards the mother in an anaclitic object choice; (the mother in her role as giving nourishment, care and protection) (1921, p. 105, 1923, p. 31).

We leave the obscurities in Freud in order to draw attention to his division of two types of attachments to other people: one type is the boy's identification with his father (apart from the later identification with his mother in the homosexual object choice), and the other attachment is a kind of object-cathexis with the mother. My point is to draw attention to the fact that the mother does not appear as an object of identification but only as a libidinal object for the boy.

An important distinction between object-cathexis (the other one as a love object) and identification object (identifying with the other) is that in the first case, one wants to *have* the other, and in the other case, one wants to *be or be like* the other. And we can see that the mother, even in the form of an anaclitic object choice, serves the function of providing what the boy wants to have, while the father is the point of reference for what the boy wants to be. Freud puts forward the idea that identification and object choice, to a large extent, are independent of one another, but that it is possible to identify oneself with someone whom one has chosen as a sexual object (cf. Freud, 1932b, p. 63). A typical case when one identifies with a love object is after the loss of it. Freud writes: "If one has lost a love-object, the most obvious reaction is to identify oneself with it, to replace it from within, as it were, by identification" (1940, p. 193).[10] As a comment to Freud's *The Dissolution of the Oedipus Complex* (1924), Bengt Warren states that "the identification is created by giving up the love relationship [...] The lost relationship creates a kind of underpressure, which has to be compensated by the identification" (2003, p. 370). It is worth paying attention to the circumstance that the process of identification is at its strongest in the absence of a beloved object.

The tradition-mediating function of identification

Identification is of great significance for mankind's mediation of traditions from one generation to the next and for cultural meaning in a broad sense (religion, moral, art). These phenomena are, first of all, understood from the father–son relation by Freud. The mother/woman is conspicuous by her absence in these contexts, fully in line with her not being an object of identification for the son. The tradition-mediating function is provided by the superego and is manifested both as a consequence of the dissolution of the Oedipus complex and in the earlier cannibalistic settlement with the primal father. Freud writes that it is the superego which is "the vehicle of tradition" and "the advocate of a striving towards perfection", which we can grasp as the "the higher side of human life" (1932b, p. 67). And, as stated, the super-ego is first a matter between the father and the son: "The super-ego arises, as we know, from an identification with the father taken as a model. Every such identification is in the nature of desexualization or even of a sublimation" (1923, p. 54).[11]

Some critical remarks

Freud's gender theory is built on sand. For example, his idea of phallus primacy (i.e., the penis as the only existing genital organ during the first years of child's life) is not compatible with the girls' experience of their vagina. And on a closer look, Freud's entire theoretical construction seems contradictory; the theory of psychosexual development does not harmonize with his phallocentric ideas. Freud describes, many times, how the preoedipal boy identifies himself with the father and has the mother as the love object long before the postulated sex differentiation takes place in the phallic–genital phase around the age of three. On one occasion, it looks like Freud gives himself away when he – after having established that the most important identification is "his identification with the father in his own personal prehistory" – makes a reservation in a footnote by writing:

> Perhaps it would be safer to say "with his parents"; for before a child has arrived at a definite knowledge of the difference between the sexes, the lack of a penis, it does not distinguish in value between its father and its mother
>
> (Ibid., p. 31, note 1).

I will limit myself to two critical remarks: (1) Freud systematically neglects the importance of the mother as an object of identification for the son and thereby the development of the son's identity; and (2) His view entails too limited an embodied centrifugal horizon from which the child's forming of identity is conceptualized.

(1) The negligence of the importance of the mother as an object of identification for the boy reflects more than anything else the boy's/the man's defense against feeling dependent on the mother and what such a dependence represents.[12] Upon reading Freud, one gets the impression that he distances himself from the thought that the woman/mother possibly could be an important object of identification, to the extent that his theorizing becomes contradictory. We can read that the process of identification is very important, most likely the original form of attachment to someone else (1932b, p. 63). In spite of this understanding of the psychology of identification, the father is the sole object of identification for the boy, except from a boy's/

man's homosexual object choice when the mother is the object of identification. The care of the mother never becomes a source of identification for the boy.

In his *Three Essays on Sexuality*, we learn that the first psychosexual phase of development is the oral or cannibalistic one and that the incorporation of the object is "the prototype of a process which, in the form of identification, is later to play such an important psychological part" (1905, p. 198). No doubt, it is interesting to note that when the oral phase and the manifestation of cannibalism achieve importance for identification, for the boy it will be about incorporating the father in the form of a phylogenetic fantasy about the totem meal as a reminder of the father murder. The real oral satisfaction that the mother's breast can provide is not given any importance.

Furthermore, Freud notes repeatedly the connection between losing the object and identifying with the object. In his discussion of the destiny of the little girl, the loss of the mother as an object of love leads to an identification with her.

> If one has lost a love-object, the most obvious reaction is to identify oneself with it, to replace it from within, as it were, by identification. This mechanism now comes to the little girl's help. Identification with her mother can take the place of attachment to her mother.
>
> (1940, p. 193)

However, when it comes to the boy's loss of the mother and her care, such as weaning or her turning away from him in order to turn, for example, to the father, the loss does not result in an identification with her.

Given that there is neither occasion nor any motive for the little boy to identify with his mother, there is no reason to be surprised that she is not supposed to provide a tradition-mediating and cultural constructing task. Possibly, she fulfills this function in a more indirect manner. Because, if she is not someone to identify with, but someone to conquer, her love is lending a great significance for the future life of the boy. "(I)f a man has been his mother's undisputed darling he retains throughout life the triumphant feeling, the confidence in success, which not seldom brings actual success along with it". In referring to Goethe's autobiography, which, I believe, has great similarities with Freud's own, Freud can write: "My strength has its roots in my relation to my mother" (1917, p. 156).

(2) The abovementioned point entailed a critique of Freud's restricted view of the constitution of the boy's development of identity based on the process of identification. Under this point, I will consider his over-restricted embodied, centrifugal horizon, from which he accounts for the child's identity formation. By the expression "embodied centrifugal horizon", I imply

partly the view that identity is restricted to be about the genital organ and partly that it takes its vantage point from the child's discovery of its genitals. The early dynamic interplay between mother and child, father and child, and mother and father and child is then, first of all, a part of a centrifugal movement; that is to say, it is the child's discovery of the sex difference in the phallic–genital phase which becomes central. There is very little of a centripetal force, influences which come from the outside, such as the surroundings' assignment of the sex and the meaning of this assignment. That which has been obvious from my presentation is that the identification, by all means, plays an important role for the child's gender development, but the basis for the identification boils down to being a question about the anatomic body, according to Freud.

In the course of the reading of this chapter, we will see that the subsequent theoretical development in psychoanalysis, in many respects, has broadened the basis for that which is considered to be essential for the child's sex/gender development.

On the view of masculinity among Freud's successors

During the past few decades, the criticism against Freud's ideas has come to cover more and more aspects of his work. Here, I will discuss some of these aspects in order to wrap up the chapter with a discussion about the enormous complexity and extended view on the formation of masculinity that has been developed from the vantage point of the child's preoedipal object relations and identifications. The point of departure for this discussion is Robert J. Stoller's and Ralph R. Greenson's much disputed theory concerning the importance of the little boy's dis-identifying from his mother. But as I said, before delving into this discussion and the rich development that has taken place within this field of research, I will mention some other aspects contributing to the groundbreaking understanding of masculinity that have occurred since Freud's days (cf. Breen, 1993).

An essential difference between Freud and today's theoreticians has to do with the view of the psychosexual development, even though the criticism against Freud's phallocentric theory goes far back. The phallic boy's/man's feeling of being better equipped than the girl/woman turned, already during the 1920s and 1930s, towards paying attention to the boy's/man's feeling of inferiority and insufficiency vis-à-vis the mother and women, as a consequence of the castration anxiety that the vagina evokes (Horney, 1932; Jones, 1933) – the big, unknown and dangerous hole which the little boy's penis is not able to offer satisfaction (Brenner, 1979; Person, 1986). Janine Chasseguet-Smirgel (1985, p. 86) is one of those psychoanalysts who have argued for a more extended castration complex, in order to give room for the pregenital child's painful feelings of not being able to satisfy the mother or to give her a baby. Other psychoanalysts also pay attention to castration anxiety in relation to the preoedipal mother, by bringing forth the separation from the mother, problems in the relation between the mother and the child, and the mother's omnipotence (Galenson & Roiphe, 1980; Person, 1986; Tyson, 1989).

The castration complex does not have the same central position as it had during Freud's time. Besides, it has been understood in a more extended fashion and in a more symbolic way by some psychoanalysts. Freud's castration anxiety was tied to the incest taboo, but also in this respect, we witness, already in the 1920s, a criticism against such a restriction. The castration anxiety can also be involved in other losses and phenomena, such as the loss of the breast and the womb. For Jacques Lacan, castration becomes a symbolic threat which characterizes and forms human conditions; the incest taboo entails significations for human conditions which transcend the individual experience. Today, castration often possesses a significance of human limitation, an acknowledgement of lack, to give up omnipotence, to recognize the mother's relation with a third part, for both sexes. Furthermore, castration anxiety often partakes of the process of integrating and organizing more primitive anxiety.

There are psychoanalysts who ascribe a very different meaning to the boy's sex organ compared to the traditional phallic one. Birksted-Breen (1996) has introduced a difference between phallus and penis-as-link, where phallus represents an "illusory wholeness", which is a kind of defense that the boy can more easily use due to his possession of a penis. However, the penis is not exclusively an organ but can also be a symbol in its function of being a link to someone else. Concerning penis-as-link one's lack and one's need of the other are recognized. Birksted-Breen maintains that penis-as-link has a bisexual character in the sense that the masculine and the feminine are not incompatible. Yet another contribution in the attempt to create a theory about non-phallic masculinity is Karl Figlio's (2010) idea about a "seminal masculinity", which, however, I think seems speculative and fabricated. This seminal function is constructed upon the anatomy of the male, but not on account of his possession of a penis. Instead, it is the man's inner world, an inner genital phase that is referred to. This seminal and inner masculinity, in the form of the prostate, the testicles, the seminal vesicle get a similar status as the woman's reproductive ability.

As has become clear, the concept "identification" has been, and still is, extremely fundamental in order to comprehend the sex/gender development. However, in recent years, an almost opposite process to the child's identification with a parent has been used as an explanation for sex/gender development. I am referring to the adult world's, and in particular the parents', assignment of sex/gender values to the child. Laplanche (2007) is one of those psychoanalysts who have emphasized that the constitution of the sex/gender happens by dint of assignment, rather than explaining it from the vantage point of the child's identification *with* the other, such as a parent or parents. By means of the concept "assignment", Laplanche turns around the relation between the child and the other one; identification (if we stick to that word) here signifies, first of all, an identification *by* the other one/parent/parents. Hence, here we have to do with identification by the other one, and not the child's identification with the other one. Laplanche observes something important when he stresses the role of assignment in the constitution of gender, although I believe that his theorizing suffers from a certain one-sidedness. I think it is unfortunate to polarize between the child's identification with the other one and the other's assignment, identification by the child's sex/gender.

Before I delve into a discussion about the theoretical development that has taken place with respect to the many different identifications that the boy may be part of, I want to say a few words about the cultural aspect whose significance for gender development has gained more and more recognition (Aron, 1995; Chodorow, 1999; Dimen, 1991; Fogel, 2009; Harris, 1991). Here we see an obvious influence from social constructionism in that gender is conceived of as something changeable and culturally conditioned, and where there are many forms of gender identity. For example, Gerald Fogel claims that constructionism has been a great help for psychoanalysis as it "frees us [...] from rigid, categorical, or sexist biological and anatomical constraints" (2009, p. 235). Even if this adoption of constructionism thinking has had a positive influence in many respects, I am afraid that it also has contributed to obscuring the relevance of an existential dimension which goes beyond the cultural horizon in the constitution of the individual's identity (more on this in Chapter 6).

Without denying that masculinity can appear changeable and that it has many forms, one ought to be aware that sometimes different expressions of masculinity can hide a less variable and non-shifting inner problematic. The latent level that psychoanalysis may address can be contrasted to manifest levels that meanings can be played out on. If we, for example, think of phallic masculine ideas and ideals, there might be a common core between those who, for example, consider the American macho actor Sylvestor Stallone as masculine and those who find United States' ex-president Barack Obama masculine. The cultural changes which are evident reflect, perhaps, neither the existential problematic that psychanalysis discloses nor the inertia with which changes are brought about in relation to the unconscious.

A reminder in this context is social anthropologic works, which show that different cultures with very little in common, nevertheless, can display striking similarities concerning deeply rooted ideas about masculinity and masculine ideals. David G. Gilmore combines cultural materialism and psychoanalytic theories in his attempt to uncover masculine deep structures in cultures that are different from one another. A conclusion drawn from his studies is that cultures with little in common can share essential similarities under superficial differences. He stresses that unlike with girls and women, one finds with boys and men a constant recurring idea that real "manhood" is not something that develops naturally through biological development but something that must be achieved "against powerful odds" (1990, p. 11).[13]

I want to finish this presentation of, and discussion about, the reformed view of masculine development that has taken place after Freud's theorization, by bringing up the most important aspect, which I do under its own heading.

Preoedipal identification processes and masculinity development

If Freud's gender theory focused on the phallic genital and oedipal phase, the most influential post-Freudian theorization came to draw attention to the earlier stages in life. Here, there are reasons to refer to Stoller's influential contribution to the psychoanalytic theorization about sex/gender development. Fast (1999) claims that Stoller developed two different and mutually incompatible perspectives on sex development, in his two volumes of *Sex and Gender*. Unfortunately, the incompatibility between those two perspectives never became apparent to Stoller or his successors. In the first perspective (Stoller, 1968), the theory of the "core gender identity" developed as the outcome of the following three factors, which, however, are of various weights: (i) the parents' assignment of a specific sex (boy or girl) at the birth of the child and the subsequent, conscious and unconscious, attitudes and way of relating to the child with respect to its sexual belongingness from the parents and the surroundings; (ii) the child's perception of its own sex and/ or the sex of persons with another sexual belongingness and (iii) biological factors that have an impact on sexual belongingness.

Only the first of the abovementioned factors is crucial for the development of a core gender identity, while the other two contribute to such a development. In this perspective, it is the relation between parents/surroundings and the child which is crucial for the development of a core gender identity, the stage when the child possesses an own sense of gender identity and is able to begin referring to itself as girl or boy. The core gender identity is, according to Stoller, fully established between 18 and 36 months of age, "before the fully developed phallic stage" (1968, p. 30). In other words, it has come a long way before anatomic sex differences and oedipal questions are raised.

The sex organ does, however, play an important role in this respect by filling the function of being a sex marker for the parents and the surroundings in the assignment of the child's sexual belongingness. The fact that the child shows interest in their sex organ and can satisfy themselves with it already during the first year of life, does not, however, reflect a relevance for their sexual identity. The sexual identity does not require an awareness of the anatomical sex difference between girls and boys. The child has a sense of sexual belongingness before their can identify their sex organ in terms of sex (de Marneffe, 1997). Whereas the sex will function as the primary signification or marker of the sexual belongingness once the child has identified their sex organ with their sex.[14]

In the second publication, Stoller (1972) developed an entirely different perspective, in that his theorizing rested upon Ralph R. Greenson's (1968/1993) idea about a "primary femininity".[15] An essential difference between these two incompatible perspectives is that the first implies a relational point of view; the child develops their sexual identity in interaction with their parents and surroundings. In the second perspective, it is as if the child were a part in a supposedly blissful child–mother symbiosis, with the implication of a feminine development for both girls and boys. Fast (1999) argues, I believe, convincingly both the incompatibility of these two perspectives, and the invalidity of the second perspective. By support from, among others, empirical studies, the idea of a blissful child–mother symbiosis lacks evidence.

As stated above, Stoller's contribution to the tradition is associated with the idea that all children go through a primary feminine phase, a so-called "proto-femininity". And together with Greenson, Stoller has put forward the influential and contested theory that a beneficial masculine development requires the boy's disidentifying from his mother and identification with his father. One even talks about a "counter identification", which, supposedly, would help to counteract the previous identification with the mother.

Greenson maintains that men are less secure in their masculinity compared to women in their femininity, which is due to the specific problem evoked by the issue of disidentifying from the mother. Greenson states that it "is a fact that the male child, in order to attain a healthy sense of maleness, must replace the primary object of his identification, the mother, and must identify instead with the father" (1968/1993, p. 258). Quindeau claims that this disidentifying perspective has remained common in the psychoanalytic discourse and that it, to a great extent, defines the psychoanalytic understanding of masculinity today (2013, p. 168) – an opinion I find somewhat surprising. But no doubt, in a similar manner as Freud's explanation of the development of masculinity, based on the phallic–genital phase, functioned as a springboard for the ensuing theorizing and discussion, Greenson's and Stoller's theory, about the importance of the boy's disidentifying from his mother, has served as the starting point for the theorizing of recent years where their theory has been seriously criticized. Quindeau is an example of such a criticism:

> In my estimation, such a dis-identification leads to a reduced, even halved, masculinity, while integration of feminine identification, or identifying with the (representation of the) mother and her desire, is what enables a stable construction of a male gender identity.
>
> (2013, p. 169)

The criticism of Greenson's and Stoller's theory of dis-identification has, to a large degree, been concerned with the fact that the dis-identification from the mother may reflect a failed development of identity, rather than being a beneficial step towards a sound masculinity. Certainly, there are periods in the child's development when other people capture the interest of the child, resulting in the child's turning away from the mother. However, under beneficial circumstances, such a turning away is temporary and assists the child in its identity development, and should, thus, not be conceived of as a dis-identification in Greenson's and Stoller's sense. The fact that the child, in a certain sense, turns away from the physical mother, the outer mother, is not the same thing as turning away from an inner, assimilated motherly object. Unlike the idea that the child's turning away from the mother is a sign of dis-identification, it may instead facilitate an identification with important traits with the mother. The process of identification can, *under certain circumstances*, be strengthened by separation and loss (Diamond, 2004a, 2004b, 2006; Fast, 1999) – an idea which, by the way, we saw that Freud touched upon. But it is crucial to realize that a secure masculine identity does not develop on the basis of separation from the mother, but thanks to an attachment with her, which is why the traditional designation separation-individuation should be replaced by attachment-individuation (Fast, 1999).

Despite its unclear meaning, the concept "bisexuality" has accompanied the psychoanalytic theorizing. For Winnicott, bisexuality represents an inner balance in the psychical integration and makes up a creative element. Winnicott (1971/1991, p. 107ff) talks about the existence of "pure female elements" and "pure male elements" in men and women. The female elements are about the experience of *being*, a being which precedes "being-at-one-with", since the infant and the mother still are one.[16] The male element, on the other hand, is about *doing* and presupposes separation and object relating. Winnicott is of the view that psychoanalysts have tended to focus on the male elements and neglected the female ones. The feminine is, for Winnicott, a primary non-differentiation for both sexes, which implies that men have a more fragile sex identity and a greater bisexuality (for Freud the woman was more bisexual due to her relation to the mother).

The problematic of recognition and the possibility of equality between the sexes

Jessica Benjamin (1988, 1995, 1998) is one of those theoreticians who have asserted the importance of the child identifying with both parents on a pre-oedipal level, in order to foster a development of masculinity that does not base itself on sexual oppression and a subject–object relationship. Today's unequal relationship between men and women is characterized by a relation between a desiring subject (the man) and a passive object (the woman).

If this inequality is going to be overcome, it requires that the woman/mother is recognized as a desiring subject by the boy/man, which is emotionally straining for the boy, since it presupposes giving up the early dyadic relation with her.

Benjamin is, moreover, of the opinion that psychoanalytic theorizing has neglected to tackle the problematic of recognition. The theories of development have usually stressed the value of a development towards separation-individuation, while Benjamin wants to draw attention to the intersubjective, social dimension in our development. At the same time, as the child's development progresses towards individuation and autonomy, there is also a development towards the possibility of sharing one's experiences with other people. This is the kind of social dimension, which, for example, Margaret S. Mahler and coworkers' (1975) theory of separation-individuation neglects.[17]

The problematic of recognition has a central position in Benjamin's thinking. What does recognition then mean concretely in the child's upbringing? Benjamin (1988, p. 15f) lists a number of phenomena which are close to recognition, such as "affirm, validate, acknowledge, know, accept, understand, empathize, take in, tolerate, appreciate, see, identify with, find familiar [...] love". And the phenomenon "mutual recognition" between the mother and the child is described in terms of "emotional attunement, mutual influence, affective mutuality, sharing states of mind". These terms can be understood as describing mutual recognition on different developmental levels. Attunement, for example, corresponds to one of the earliest forms of mother–child relation. Hence, all these designations cannot claim to reflect a full-blown mutual recognition between two independent subjects.

It is the recognition of the other which enables one's feelings, intentions and actions to be experienced as meaningful; such a recognition empowers one, in a significant way, to realize agency. Benjamin writes that "recognition begins with the other's confirming response, which tells us that we have created meaning, had an impact, revealed an intention" (1995, p. 33). However, this requires that this recognition come from someone whom we ourselves recognize in their autonomy and subjectivity. The problematic of recognition entails a paradox; we are entirely dependent on the other in order to be recognized in our independence. The recognition of the other comprises a tension between self-assertion and mutual recognition, a tension that hopefully can be kept manageable, because if this tension breaks down, the result will be dominance and submission between individuals, according to Benjamin.

As for other psychoanalysts, so also for Benjamin, the boy's earliest development takes place in relation to the mother and with respect to the difference to the mother. The big challenge for the boy involves the capacity to handle and contain the difference to the mother. The first demand for making it possible for the boy to develop into an autonomous subject is that the mother both recognizes him in his subjectivity and is able to assert herself as a desiring subject. On the part of the mother, the awareness of a mutual recognition is required, which establishes both a connection to the child and its independent existence: a combination of togetherness and otherness. Benjamin concretizes the relation on the part of the mother in the following way: "I recognize *you* as my baby who recognizes *me*" (italics in the original) (1988, p. 15).

The boy, and later the man, is in the situation that in order to become a subject himself, he needs a recognition from the other, which, however, cannot be reached unless he himself recognizes the other's (mother's, woman's) autonomy as subject/agent. It is a difficult and painful process where the boy must give up the dyadic relation with the mother. Benjamin describes it as if the mother must have a dialogic ability in order to stimulate the child's recognition of her subjectivity, which is made attainable by her reflecting the child's own subjectivity. This reflection is assumed to develop a symbolic capability in the child; if this fails, the "father" and the "penis" will not become symbolic but will be imagined as concrete "things" "that make for difference" (Benjamin, 1998, p. 53).[18]

When the desires of the mother, her subjectivity and agency, are not recognized, a sexual development occurs where complementarity between them is expressed in the form of opposites: man as opposed to woman with the ensuing consequences, subject vs. object, active vs. passive, sadist vs. masochist and desiring subject vs. desired object. But there is another kind of complementarity: the one which Benjamin recommends, where man and woman are not each other's opposites (more on this shortly).

The father plays a significant role in Benjamin's theorizing, although the first object of identification for the boy is the mother. The boy's love for the father is described in terms of *identificatory love* and emerges during the second year of life and runs simultaneously with the love for the mother. This father is dyadic, not triadic as the forbidding oedipal father, and does not rule out a dyadic identification with the mother for the boy. The child, the boy as well as the girl, can thus identify with both parents.[19] However, these identifications address different aspects in the development. In a traditional family, the mother makes up the source of goodness during rapprochement (approximately 16–24 months), while the father represents the exciting and compelling world; "he is the figure of freedom who has access to and enjoys the world" (Ibid., p. 61).

The boy's identificatory love with the father makes possible a new kind of love, namely an ego-ideal. This love can also endorse the development towards becoming a desiring subject and is not to be restricted to being a defense against a mother regression. It is important that the father responds and that the boy be recognized in his identificatory love be like the father. However, not only the boy perceives that he can be like his father, but the father can also give expression to how it feels to be like his son: "I was once like you and I remember how that feels" (Benjamin, 1995, p. 155).

The gist of Benjamin's reasoning is that if the development is to head towards mutual recognition and equality between the sexes, then the polarization between the identification with the mother and that with the father must not grow too big. The polarization between the mother and the father begins, somehow, in the preoedipal phase and is amplified with the oedipal phase. The separation from the mother risks turning into a repudiation, which implies that the boy loses the feeling of possessing the motherly source of goodness. Benjamin's recipe for a more favored gender and masculinity development is to extend the period of bisexuality, by which is meant that both feminine and masculine identifications are to exist side by side (1988, p. 169).

The polarizing complementarity comes to the fore in the oedipal phase. But Benjamin wants to nuance this phase by distinguishing between an early oedipal phase (just before the age of 4) characterized by a rigid gender complementarity and a scornful repudiation of the opposite sex and a later oedipal phase which brings to the fore, in the case of the boy, the challenge to accept and be able to mourn that he will not be the mother, which also includes the difficulty to acknowledge the envy vis-à-vis the feminine. By referring to Fast, Benjamin (1995, p. 66) asserts that during the later oedipal phase, the rigid gender complementarity and repudiation can be soothed in that the love for the object can compensate the narcissistic loss.

The (phallic) oedipal way, for masculinity to assert itself, is by defending itself against the mother's activity, by turning and constructing it to a passive femininity. Such a masculine subjectivity implies both an absence of an identification with a containing mother, as well as not allowing her to become represented as a sexual subject. What remains is thus only a passive woman or "femininity". In this position, masculine self-assertiveness reigns at the expense of mutual recognition. This tension between self-assertiveness and mutual recognition has, in this case, failed to be contained, and instead it has led to supremacy and submission between individuals and between sexes.

However, there is also a solution, where the tension between self-assertiveness and mutual recognition becomes contained, so man and woman, masculinity and femininity do not make up each other's opposites, which can happen in the position described, by Benjamin, as postoedipal. As the name indicates, it is a position that comes after the oedipal one, but Benjamin does not advocate a linear phase thinking, that is to say, that the development unfolds by putting earlier phases behind itself. Instead, she comprehends it in the sense that a later phase reshapes earlier phases, in line with Freud's idea about deferred action (*Nachträglichkeit*).[20] More precisely, the postoedipal phase consists of an integration between the preoedipal overinclusive position when the child is, so to speak, both sexes, and the oedipal position when an articulated sex determination rules, and the child defines itself in contrast to the other sex. In this mixture of preoedipal and oedipal positions, the possibility is born of a postoedipal complementarity in which different sides or elements can be together instead of being experienced as incompatible. These are sides that, instead of being experienced as forbidden, can appear as possibilities; to move between contrasting positions can be pleasurable rather than being experienced as dangerous according to Benjamin. In other words, the postoedipal phase makes possible a certain loosening of rigid boundaries – boundaries that have polarized between identification objects and love objects, between men and women, and between hetero- and homosexuality.

Some further aspects concerning the development of a secure manliness/masculinity

Many different circumstances and aspects have been presented in the literature as crucial for a secure masculine development. I will finish this chapter by presenting some of these circumstances and aspects.

1. A viewpoint of significance is thus that a secure masculinity develops out of an identification with the mother and not by disidentifying from her. The boy constructs his psychic structure, not least, by identifying with his mother. This identification with the mother also implies an identification with how the mother relates to him as a male person, that is to say, how the mother relates to him as someone with a different sex (Benjamin, 1988; Diamond, 2004a, 2004b; Fast, 1999).

2. In the literature, the weight of the boy's identification with both parents is stressed, and that the identification also with the father takes place on a preoedipal level, is stressed. Above, I pointed out the significance of identifying with both parents. Here, I will mention some other theoreticians who likewise assert the importance of this. Diamond (2004a) talks about a "progressive differentiation" in the development of an early gender identity, rather than the mother and the father emerging as opposites. This progressive differentiation can then play out in a mutual identification with both the mother and the father or a substitute father. Hence, the boy identifies himself with the mother, and, as mentioned before, this identification also entails the mother's way of relating to him as being of the male sex. Likewise, the boy identifies himself with the father, which presupposes that the father makes himself accessible for such an identification and is himself capable of identifying with the boy.

In general, when it comes to the preoedipal father, some theoreticians emphasize the similarity between the father and the mother in their respective

attitudes to the child. Other psychoanalysts emphasize the difference between the father and the mother, in the sense that, roughly speaking, the
mother is comforting, while the father has the role of stimulating to activity.
The preoedipal father is depicted as someone who is supportive and non-
competing, but also who stimulates to activity (cf. Abelin, 1975; Cath et al.,
1982).

3. The boy's identification with his parents does not only include an identification with the parents individually but also include how the parents relate to one another and that they, together with their child, can form a triad.
For example, how does the mother relate to the father as someone of the
same sex as her son, and how does the father relate to the mother and those
qualities that she has? If the father is estranged from uniting with the mother
in the forming of a triad together with the child, this can lead to difficulties
for the son to identify himself with the mother in his gender development.

4. When talking about the father as an important identification object for
the boy (and, by all means, for the girl as well, although here I limit myself
to discuss the boy's gender development), it also concerns the preoedipal –
and not only the oedipal – father and that in an entirely different sense from
Freud's cannibalistic incorporation of the father. Diamond (2004b) differentiates between phallic and genital qualities when it comes to the question
of identifying with the father. The genital qualities, which the father can
provide, encompass protecting and holding aspects, unlike phallic qualities in the form of penetration, activity and strength. The father's genital
qualities endorse a recognition of the sex differentiation and facilitate the
acceptance that one cannot be everything, without, for that matter, implying a repudiation or a denial of qualities which belong to the other sex. The
identification with the father's genital qualities thereby facilitates an integration of motherly feminine identifications. It seems as if Diamond puts
special weight on the need for a protecting father for the boy, in comparison
with the girl's need, due to the process of separation-individuation – which
is simultaneous with the discovery of the sexual difference – being more
traumatizing for boys, since they are less cognitively and emotionally developed than girls at the time of this process. The boy is forced to struggle
with a double trauma: separation from the mother with the simultaneous
discovery of the sexual difference.

5. As is clear from the above points, in the psychoanalytic theoretical
development, the boy's identification processes have come to involve many
different objects. For Freud, the father was the object of identification and,
in particular, the oedipal father. For Greenson and Stoller, the earliest identification concerned the mother, from whom the boy subsequently was to
disidentify, in order to achieve a secure masculinity. In the abovementioned
points, the identification has had to do with the mother, the mother's relation

to the boy as a male sex, the preoedipal father and the parents' relation to one another. In this final point, I want to multiply the possible objects that could serve as objects of identification. Indeed, there is really no limit to what could function as an object of identification for a person. Both living and dead objects can be charged in a way that makes them into objects of identification.

Common identification objects, which can be disclosed in therapeutic and psychoanalytic treatment, are people who are a bit further away from the child compared to its parents. Here we have siblings, and, not least, older siblings, grandmothers and grandfathers, playmates' parents and siblings. Other, not unusual people, whose manners and way of behaving, can exert influence on the child in becoming an object of identification, are staff at preschools and schools. Further possible objects of identification are animals and pets. To give an example, the boy who identified himself with his family's big, strong dog and its protective security for its puppies, something that he himself felt missing in his upbringing.

As we have seen, the masculine ideal can be conveyed in many different ways to the child/the boy, where the identification with someone/something is an extremely significant process. The identification can also be supported by very various factors depending on the conditions one lives under. For example, the identification with a person can be facilitated and supported if the boy feels love, warmth and trust to the person in question. Here, we are dealing with positive, loving feelings that make up the basis for the processes of identification. However, other factors that do not qualify as positive and loving feelings can also play a crucial role. Power is such a factor. Not least for boys, the father's power can become a source which facilitates identification with the father.

Identifications can also occur, more subtlety, enrolled in larger contexts, in which the boy assimilates masculine values and ideals. The masculine value can, for example, be more or less assigned or taught to the boy, or that the boy assumes attitudes and manners by adapting himself to values and norms with the intention to gain, for instance, the parents' love and appreciation. The boy struggles with such questions: How am I to behave to gain my mother's/father's or some other important person's love? What is it that mother/father/another significant person thinks is important when being a boy? Such questions can arise in situations that involve many other processes than identification processes in the boy's assimilation of ideals and values. However, identification processes can, nevertheless, play a role in different ways even in such situations. The identification with the parents or with one of them lies there as a foundation to let oneself be influenced by them. Or the values and norms which they convey motivate charging and identifications with different people's expressions and behaviors. For example, a family with distinct and definite political values may motivate the son to charge and identify himself with a prominent politician who, besides, has the same name as his father.

Notes

1 Even if this chapter is primarily based on psychoanalysts' clinical experiences, extraclinical research is also a relevant source in my presentation and discussion. When it comes to the early sex/gender development, it is motivated to use both clinical and extraclinical experiences in the pursuit of understanding it, something that de Marneffe expresses her approval of: "[...] support has steadily grown for the view that a working back and forth between the clinical situation and extraclinical research provides the optimal ground for our theories" (1997, p. 4).
2 On one occasion, Freud expresses himself less assuredly that the sexual difference lacks significance for all children during the first time in their lives when he states that attributing the same male genital to both sexes counts in any case for boys (1916/1917, p. 317).
3 Jones is critical of Freud's choice of terminology:

> Freud himself does not use the word 'anxiety' in regard to the female genital, but speaks of 'horror' (Abscheu) of it. The word 'horror' is descriptive, but it implies an earlier dread of castration, and therefore demands an explanation of this in turn.
>
> (1933, p. 6)

4 The focus of this work is masculinity, but let me make some comments on Freud's contested ideas about women, which first of all has concerned penis envy. Freud understood this as the starting point for femaleness and not as a kind of defense or an obstacle for female development, which many other psychoanalysts believe (cf. Breen, 1993). I have already given examples of Freud's problematic formulations when it comes to his view of women. Here, I will provide the reader with a couple of more examples: "She acknowledges the fact of her castration, and with it, too, the superiority of the male and her own inferiority" (1931, p. 229). And in the essay on femininity, he talks about "the discovery of female castration" as an "unwelcome fact" (1932a, pp. 129–130). Another psychoanalytic experience which contributes to the questioning of Freud's reasoning concerning the dynamic of penis envy and woman's lack of a penis can be mentioned: When a person feels contempt, it is often based on a feeling of threat instigating a projection of one's own unacceptable feelings that one seeks to get rid of. But Freud's way of talking about the lack of penis gives the impression that the feeling of contempt or disdain is more or less justified. "This means, therefore, that as a result of the discovery of women's lack of a penis they are debased in value for girls just as they are for boys and later perhaps for men" (Ibid., p. 127). And in a context of male homosexuality, we read: "Depreciation of women, and aversion to them, even horror of them, are generally derived from the early discovery that women have no penis" (1922, p. 231).
5 Freud writes: "Similarly, boys regularly fear castration from their father, although in their case, too, the threat most usually comes from their mother" (1931, p. 233). Yet another example: "Usually it is from women that the [castration] threat emanates; very often they seek to strengthen their authority by a reference to the father or the doctor, who, so they say, will carry out the punishment" (1924, p. 174). And this is repeated in Freud's late unfinished

work *An Outline of Psycho-Analysis*: "Usually, in order to make the threat more frightening and more credible, she delegates its execution to the boy's father, saying that she will tell him and that he will cut the penis off" (1940, p. 189).

6 The term "bisexuality" is used in two meanings in the literature, one of which is its relation to the libidinal object choice (love towards both the mother/the woman and father/the man) and the other as a characterization of one's identity, as a mixture of feminine and masculine traits.

7 On many occasions, Freud struggles to pinpoint the difference between masculine and feminine. In his essay *Femininity* (1932a), he deals, several times, with the polarization between active and passive but treats it in an ambivalent and contradictory way. It seems obvious that he is stuck in this terminology, which he simultaneously finds unsatisfactorily.

8 In psychoanalysis, there are different forms of assimilating processes, where identification, usually, counts as the most mature one. Others, less mature forms of assimilation which have an impact on the formation of one's identity and the masculine development, are incorporation, imitation and introjection (cf. Diamond, 2004a; Laplanche & Pontalis, 1985; Schafer, 1968). The concept of identification is to be developed in the text; therefore, I will, in this footnote only, say something briefly about the other three assimilating processes. *Incorporation* is the earliest form of assimilation. It has a concrete embodied character, in the sense that the subject assimilates the object, first and foremost, through the mouth, even though other body openings can function as alternative entrances. We witness this mechanism in connection with Freud's description of the murder of the father and the ensuing incorporation of the father's strength by means of the sons' totem meal, which he put much weight on, in the development of masculinity. Another circumstance to be mentioned, which Housel (1999) has described, is from the vantage point of gender. He maintains that the bisexuality is incorporated on the level of partial objects and gives room for a fatherly partial object in the child's sucking on the breast; the nipple has the function of being a fatherly partial object, while the breast constitutes a motherly partial object. Incorporation makes up a bodily model for introjection and identification.

Imitation means that the subject behaves, thinks or feels like the object in certain respects. Schafer (1968) points out that imitation, which can be conscious although it does not need to be that, is a necessary part in identification. To imitate, mimicking is a common behavior among those children who look up to parents or other beloved objects. I also want to draw attention to the fact that imitating other's behavior may enable one, in one's inner psychic life, to capture what the other one feels. It makes it possible, so to speak, to be able to get in touch with both sides of the experience, the outer as well as the inner. It is a proven method, in body-oriented psychotherapy, to awake a person's experiences by asking the person to perform a certain sequence of movements (cf. Wrangsjö, 1987).

Introjection is a process where the subject "moves" the qualities of the object from the outside into one's own inside. It is apparently a process which resembles incorporation but without presupposing the concrete borders of the body. It may concern an introjection of the object into one's ego or ego-ideal. In the Kleinian tradition, the dynamic, between introjection (to take in) and projection (to place it outside of oneself), plays a central role in the structuring of the self. The introjected object is preserved in the subject's inner world, but not in such a way as if the subject had been transformed in accordance with the object, which makes up a difference in relation to the process of identification. The introjected object, for example, the father, appears, in a certain sense, as a foreign presence.

9 The male homosexual object choice entails, according to Freud, an identification that takes place after the end of puberty, but now it concerns an identification with the mother. The boy/man identifies with the mother and seeks a person who replaces him, whereby he can love such a man as the mother once upon a time loved him (cf. Freud, 1910)

10 In line with Freud's consistent stance that the boy's identification is with the father/the man (except when he discusses male homosexuality), it is the girl who appears in the foreground when he talks about how one's sexual object also can become one's identification object:

> (I)t is [...] possible to identify oneself with someone whom, for instance, one has taken as a sexual object, and to alter one's ego on his model. It is said that the influencing of the ego by the sexual object occurs particularly often with women and is characteristic of femininity.
>
> (1932b, p. 63)

11 Jane Flax draws attention to the fact that Freud is willing to acknowledge the importance of the preoedipal experience for the girl's development, but not for the boy's, whose personality formation is located to the oedipal period. "This masculinist bias recurs in the work of many subsequent analysts, both 'orthodox' and Lacanian" (1990, p. 79).

12 We are reminded about Horney's (1926) remark that Freud's theory of penis envy and the girl's sense of inferiority represent the thinking of the oedipal boy.

13 And, from a historical perspective, it may be of interest to take part of Hubbard's reflection on the question of the constancy of masculinity ideals:

> Although on a theoretical level acknowledging the multiplicity, contingency and social constructedness of masculinities, historically oriented scholars have nevertheless focused their gaze upon favoured themes of male sexual domination, violence, militarism, imperialism and oppression of minorities, which are treated as so historically pervasive that they almost re-essentialize the concept of masculinity
>
> (2013, p. 189)

Another quote concerning the ominous character of masculinity can be found in a work by the psychoanalytic psychotherapist Jukes: "Every major non-geological disaster in history has been man made, from climate change to credit crunch and from warfare to genocide. Masculinity is not fit for purpose if that purpose is to ensure the survival of the human race" (2010, p. 194).

14 Phenomenological research has shown that children's gender categories are acquired and practiced at very early ages. Like for (most) adults, they are dichotomized and binary, but they are based on non-biological cultural markers; for example, if someone wears barrettes in the hair, it must be a girl (see Johnson, 2000).

15 Fast (1999) points out that Stoller had used the expression "primary femininity" in another meaning earlier on, namely in the sense that the girl's gender identity is based on the relation between the parents and the daughter, and thereby the girl's gender identity cannot be considered secondary as if it were the outcome of envy and lack of a penis. In Stoller's work from 1972, a completely different meaning of primary femininity is presented, in the sense that both boys and girls allegedly begin their development in a blissful child–mother symbiosis, which is supposed to require, as we will soon see, a disidentifying from the mother on the

part of the boy, in order for the boy to achieve a secure masculinity, according to Greenson and Stoller.

16 Winnicott's exposition about "BEING" as something that precedes being-at-one-with seems to me to suffer from obscurity as he writes "(t)wo separate persons can *feel* at one, but here at the place that I am examining the baby and the object *are* one" (italics in the original) (1971/1991, p. 108).

17 According to Mahler, the child is born without being aware of the other. The first time in life, Mahler describes in terms of an *autistic stage* (0–3 months), followed by a *symbiotic stage* (until 4–5 months). Thereafter, the process of *separation-individuation* occurs (4–36 months), which consists of a number of phases: *differentiation* (i.e., the hatching from the symbiosis, approximately 5–10 months); *practice* (i.e., to physically and psychologically go away and come back, 7–16 months); *rapprochement* (i.e., reestablishing on a higher psychic level, 16–24 months); *towards increased self- and object constancy* (approximately 30–36 months). Later in her life, Mahler abandoned the idea of an initial normal autistic stage, but seems always to have claimed that the first period time of the child's life did not consist of any awareness of a difference between "I" and "not-I". She and her coworkers were focused on investigating the path from infantile symbiosis or primary narcissism to an object relation by going through a process of separation-individuation.

18 Mesterton emphasizes the importance of considering the mother's symbol creating capacity since

> psychoanalytic theory abounds with expressions that describe a polarizing thinking: the regressive mother and the liberating father, the mother represents the body and the father the law or the symbolic, the mother as attachment versus the father as liberation. With such reasoning, the struggle for recognition and separation from the mother figure is split off, and the theory creates a division between maleness and femaleness.
>
> (2005, p. 40)

19 My presentation is limited to discussing the boy's identification with the father, even though the girl's identification with him is also of utmost importance according to Benjamin. Naturally, it is just as important for the girl as for the boy to develop agency and to become a desiring subject.

20 Laplanche and Pontalis define "Nachträglichkeit" as follows:

> Term frequently used by Freud in connection with his view of psychical temporality and causality: experiences, impressions and memory-traces may be revised at a later date to fit in with fresh experiences or with the attainment of a new stage of development. They may in that event be endowed not only with a new meaning but also with psychical effectiveness.
>
> (1985, p. 111)

References

Abelin, E. (1975). Some further observations and comments on the role of the father. *International Journal of Psycho-Analysis, 56*(3), 293–302.

Aron, L. (1995). The internalized primal scene. *Psychoanalytic Dialogues, 5*(2), 195–237. Doi:10.1080/10481889509539062

Benjamin, J. (1988). *The bonds of love. Psychoanalysis, feminism, and the problem of domination*. Pantheon Books.

Benjamin, J. (1995). *Like subjects. Love objects. Essays on recognition and sexual difference.* Yale University Press.

Benjamin, J. (1998). *Shadow of the other. Intersubjectivity and gender in psychoanalysis.* Routledge.

Birksted-Breen, D. (1996). Phallus, penis and mental space. *International Journal of Psychoanalysis, 77,* 649–657.

Breen, D. (1993). General introduction. In D. Breen (Ed.) *The gender conundrum.* Routledge.

Brenner, Ch. (1979). Depressive affect, anxiety, and psychic conflict in the phallic-oedipal phase. *Psychoanalytic Quarterly, 48*(2), 177–197. Doi:10.1080/21674086.1979.11926874

Cath, S.H., Gurwitt, A.R. & Ross, J.M. (Eds.) (1982). *Father and child. Developmental and clinical perspectives.* Little, Brown and Company.

Chassegeut-Smirgel, J. (1985). *Creativity and perversion.* Norton.

Chodorow, N.J. (1999). *The power of feelings.* Yale University Press.

Corbett, K. (2009). *Boyhoods. Rethinking masculinities.* Yale University Press.

de Marneffe, D. (1997). Bodies and words: A study of young children's genital and gender knowledge. *Gender and Psychoanalysis, 2*(1), 3–33.

Diamond, M.J. (2004a). The shaping of masculinity: Revisioning boys turning away from their mothers to construct male gender identity. *International Journal of Psychoanalysis, 85*(2), 359–380. Doi:10.1516/U8XV-LG0A-WXNW-1285

Diamond, M.J. (2004b). Accessing multitude within: A psychoanalytic perspective on the transformation of masculinity at mid-life. *International Journal of Psychoanalysis, 85*(1), 45–64. Doi:10.1516/3PFY-NQMU-C95F-HH0W

Diamond, M.J. (2006). Masculinity unravelled: The roots of male gender identity and the shifting of male ego ideals throughout life. *Journal of the American Psychoanalytic Association, 54*(4), 1099–1130. Doi:10.1177/00030651060540040601

Dimen, M. (1991). Deconstructing difference: Gender, splitting and the transitional space. *Psychoanalytic Dialogues, 1*(3), 335–352. Doi:10.1080/10481889109538904

Dimen, M. & Goldner, V. (2005). Gender and sexuality. In E.S. Person, A.M. Cooper & G.O. Gabbard (Eds.) *APPI textbook of psychoanalysis.* American Psychiatric Press.

Fast, I. (1999). Aspects of core gender identity. *Psychoanalytic Dialogues, 9*(5), 633–661. Doi:10.1080/10481889909539349

Figlio, K. (2010). Phallic and seminal masculinity: A theoretical and clinical confusion. *International Journal of Psychoanalysis, 91*(1), 119–139. Doi:10.1111/j.1745-8315.2009.00215.x

Flax, J. (1990). *Thinking fragments. Psychoanalysis, feminism, and postmodernism in the contemporary west.* University of California Press.

Fogel, G.I. (2009). Interiority and inner genital space in men: What else can be lost in castration?. In B. Reis & R. Grossmark (Eds.) *Heterosexual masculinities. Contemporary perspectives from psychoanalytic gender theory.* Routledge.

Freud, S. (1900). The interpretations of dreams. *The standard edition of the complete psychological works of Sigmund Freud, 4.*

Freud, S. (1905). Three essays on the theory of sexuality. *The standard edition of the complete psychological works of Sigmund Freud, 7.*

Freud, S. (1910). Leonardo da Vinci and a memory of his childhood. *The standard edition of the complete psychological works of Sigmund Freud, 11.*

Freud, S. (1913). *Totem and taboo. The standard edition of the complete psychological works of Sigmund Freud, 13.*

Freud, S. (1916/17). The sexual life of human beings. *Introductory lectures on psychoanalysis. The standard edition of the complete psychological works of Sigmund Freud, 16.*

Freud, S. (1917). A childhood recollection from *Dichtung und Wahrheit. The standard edition of the complete psychological works of Sigmund Freud, 17.*

Freud, S. (1921). *Group psychology and the analysis of the ego. The standard edition of the complete psychological works of Sigmund Freud, 18.*

Freud, S. (1922). Some neurotic mechanisms in jealousy, paranoia and homosexuality. *The standard edition of the complete psychological works of Sigmund Freud, 18.*

Freud, S. (1923). *The ego and the id. The standard edition of the complete psychological works of Sigmund Freud, 19.*

Freud, S. (1924). The dissolution of the Oedipus complex. *The standard edition of the complete psychological works of Sigmund Freud, 19.*

Freud, S. (1925). Some psychical consequences of the anatomical distinction between the sexes. *Introductory lectures on psycho-analysis. The standard edition of the complete psychological works of Sigmund Freud, 19.*

Freud, S. (1926). *The question of lay analysis. The standard edition of the complete psychological works of Sigmund Freud, 20.*

Freud, S. (1931). Female sexuality. *The standard edition of the complete psychological works of Sigmund Freud, 21.*

Freud, S. (1932a). Femininity. *The standard edition of the complete psychological works of Sigmund Freud, 22.*

Freud, S. (1932b). The dissection of the psychical personality. *The standard edition of the complete psychological works of Sigmund Freud, 22.*

Freud, S. (1940). *An outline of psycho-analysis. The standard edition of the complete psychological works of Sigmund Freud, 23.*

Galenson, E. & Roiphe, H. (1980). The preoedipal development of the boy. *Journal of the American Psychoanalytic Association, 28*(4), 805–827. Doi:10.1177/000306518002800403

Gilmore, D.G. (1990). *Manhood in the making. Cultural concepts of masculinity.* Yale University Press.

Greenson, R.R. (1968/1993). Dis-identifying from mother: its special importance for the boy. In D. Breen (Ed.) *The gender conundrum. Contemporary psychoanalytic perspectives on femininity and masculinity.* Routledge.

Harris, A. (1991). Gender as contradiction. *Psychoanalytic Dialogues, 1*(2), 197–224. Doi:10.1080/10481889109538893

Horney, K. (1924). On the genesis of the castration complex in women. *International Journal of Psychoanalysis, 5,* 50–65.

Horney, K. (1926). The flight from womanhood: The masculinity-complex in women, as viewed by men and by women. *International Journal of Psycho-Analysis, 7,* 324–339.

Horney, K. (1932). The dread of woman: Observations on a specific difference in the dread felt by men and women respectively for the opposite sex. *International Journal of Psycho-Analysis, 13,* 348–360.

Horney, K. (1933). The denial of the vagina – A contribution to the problem of the genital anxieties specific to women. *International Journal of Psycho-Analysis, 14,* 57–70.

Housel, D. (1999). The psychoanalysis of infantile autism. Föredrag vid Svenska psykoanalytiska föreningen den 7 maj 1999. [Lecture at the Swedish Psychoanalytical Association, 7 May 1999].

Hubbard, Th.K. (2013). Athenian pederasty and the construction of masculinity. In J.H. Arnold & S. Brady (Eds.) *What is masculinity? Historical dynamics from antiquity to the contemporary world.* Palgrave Macmillan.

Johnson, A. (2000). Understanding children's gender beliefs. In L. Fisher & L. Embree (Eds.) *Feminist phenomenology.* Kluwer Academic Publishers.

Jones, E. (1927). The early development of sexuality. *International Journal of Psycho-Analysis, 8,* 459–472

Jones, E. (1933). The phallic phase. *International Journal of Psycho-Analysis, 14,* 1–33.

Jones, E. (1935). Early female sexuality. *International Journal of Psycho-Analysis, 16,* 263–273.

Jukes, A.E. (2010). *Is there a cure for masculinity?* Free Association Books.

Laplanche, J. (2007). Gender, sex, and the sexual. *Studies in Gender and Sexuality, 8*(2), 201–219. Doi:10.1080/15240650701225567

Laplanche, J. & Pontalis, J.-B. (1985). *The language of psychoanalysis.* The Hogarth Press.

Lieberman, J. (2006). Masculinity in the twenty-first century: An introduction. *Journal of the American Psychoanalytic Association, 54*(4), 1059–1066. Doi:10.117 7/00030651060540041201

Mahler, M.S., Pine, F. & Bergman, A. (1975). *The psychological birth of the human infant. Symbiosis and individuation.* Hutchinson.

Mesterton, A. (2005). Sexualteori i förändring – om Jessica Benjamin. [Sexual theory in transition – on Jessica Benjamin]. Svenska psykoanalytiska föreningens skriftserie, no. 8, 35–47. [The Swedish Psychoanalytical Association's series, no. 8, 35–47].

Person, E.S. (1986). Male sexuality and power. *Psychoanalytic Inquiry, 6*(1), 3–25. Doi:10.1080/07351698609533615

Person, E.S. & Ovesey, L. (1983). Psychoanalytic theories of gender. *Journal of the American Academy of Psychoanalysis, 11*(2), 203–226. Doi:10.1521/jaap.1.1983.11.2.203

Quindeau, I. (2013). *Seduction and desire. A psychoanalytic theory of sexuality beyond Freud.* Karnac.

Reis, B. & Grossmark, R. (2009). Introduction. In B. Reis & R. Grossmark (Eds.) *Heterosexual masculinities. Contemporary perspectives from psychoanalytic gender theory.* Routledge.

Schafer, R. (1968). *Aspects of internalization.* International Universities Press.

Stoller, R.J. (1968). *Sex and gender. The development of masculinity and femininity,* vol 1. Maresfield Reprints.

Stoller, R.J. (1972). *Sex and gender,* vol 2. Aronson.

Tyson, P. (1989). Infantile sexuality, gender identity, and the obstacles to oedipal regression. *Journal of the American Psychoanalytic Association, 37*(4), 1051–1069. Doi:10.1177/000306518903700409

Warren, B. (2003). Redaktionell inledning. In *Samlade skrifter av Sigmund Freud. Sexualiteten,* Band X. [Editorial introduction. In Collected writings of Sigmund Freud. Sexuality, Volume X]. Natur och Kultur.

Winnicott, D.W. (1971/1991). *Playing and reality.* Routledge.

Wrangsjö, B. (Ed.). (1987). *Kroppsorienterad psykoterapi.* [Body-oriented psychotherapy]. Natur och Kultur.

Three forms of masculinity with a focus on phallic masculinity

The focus of this chapter will be on phallic masculinity. The epithet "phallic" indicates that there are ideas about the existence of other forms of masculinity. The literature examined in previous chapters has made it clear that there are many different kinds of masculinities that have been discussed. Unfortunately, however, the outcome of these discussions has often presented an unclear and confused conceptual usage. Here, I will address three kinds of masculinities: hypermasculinity, phallic masculinity and demasculinized masculinity. Phallic masculinity can be seen as central in relation to the other two forms: hypermasculinity is an extreme – and sometimes very extreme – form of phallic masculinity, while demasculinized masculinity has phallic masculinity as its prerequisite.

Just a general word about these three forms before I present and discuss each of them. Whilst phallic masculinity is, to a great extent, an ideal in society, in general, for both men and women, hypermasculinity is quite the opposite. Its propensity for violence, sexism, xenophobia and religious terrorism awakes denunciation with most people and in society at large. On the other hand, there is another kind of experience of masculinity, which, after a great deal of uncertainty, I wish to preserve as a kind of masculinity, a paradoxical form of masculinity and one which I believe is most adequately captured by the oxymoron "demasculinized masculinity". The differences between these forms of masculinity can, to some extent, be described in structural, intrapsychic terms which is what I will do in this chapter. The presentation and discussion of these three forms of masculinity will, first of all, be pursued from psychoanalytic experiences and reflections.

Hypermasculinity

Before I delve into the main objective of this chapter, phallic masculinity, I would like to say a few words about the so-called "hypermasculinity", which indirectly can assist us in capturing the gist of phallic masculinity. I would like to start by reiterating something which was emphasized in the Introduction, namely that the psychoanalytic, explanatory model cannot claim

DOI: 10.4324/9781003352761-4

to be exhaustive in explaining phenomena such as masculinity, in this case hypermasculinity. Psychoanalysis can be conceived of as a science which enlightens intrapsychic and social relations in the formation of personalities. An aggravating circumstance is that persons with this type of hypermasculine personality rarely seek psychotherapeutic or psychoanalytic treatment, which is why the clinical experience of this phenomenon is relatively limited.[1]

An important distinguishing trait between phallic masculinity and hypermasculinity is the character of the preoedipal father. In phallic masculinity, the rivalry and competition between the son and the father takes place on the oedipal level, while the preoedipal father very well can be experienced as supportive for the son. As was clear from Chapter 2, the preoedipal father's important role in the child's development is stressed in the psychoanalytic theorizing. Among other things, the significance of the preoedipal father identification was pointed out, in its function to widen the sphere of the child, so as to enable the boy/man (as well as the girl/woman) to candidly and confidentially act and operate in the world. In other words, it is important to make a kind of triangulation possible on the preoedipal level, in order to enlarge the child–mother dyad to encompass a structure of three elements, child–mother (primary care giver)–father (someone outside the child–mother dyad). Roughly speaking, one can say that the struggle, the rivalry and the competition with the father, in phallic masculinity, take place on the oedipal level.

The characteristic trait for the preoedipal father in the hypermasculine constitution is a father imago which resembles Freud's primal father, that is to say, an archaic, despotic and omnipotent father – a father who demands unlimited power and subjection.[2] A triangulation between the son–mother–father is missed here; that which appears in those family constellations is, among other things, a symbiotic son–father relationship. It is a symbiosis, which is characterized by the son being subservient, submitting to the archaic and feared preoedipal father, or that which Stein calls the "archaic phallic father". However, I want to draw attention to the fact that the family constellation with a despotic and omnipotent father also can exist without the son developing an aggressive form of violent, sexist, xenophobic character. The specific circumstances can have laid the ground even for a development of, at least on the manifest level, a nonaggressive, self-effacing attitude.

The son's submission to the father is motivated by more than his fear of castration. For the son, the issue is not a struggle of surviving and overcoming the fear of being castrated by the father; here we witness a scenario of subjection, to become the father's tool, his extended arm. To quote Ruth Stein:

> Rather than the rebellious son fearing castration by the father and overcoming it, what is at stake here is the subjection to a lethal ideal,

a regression to the archaic phallic father [...] submission to the father involves more than a castration, since such submission effects wholesale investment of all of one's (and one's group's) energies in fighting *for* the father's sake, rather than fighting *the* father.

(Italics in the original) (2010, p. 57)

It is a feared father who reigns through power and dread, and it is a son who with his love seeks to reach his father by submission. The fear and the desire of the father are like two sides of one and the same thing; the fear of the terrifying father goes hand in hand with the desire to annihilate oneself by being submissive to the father's power (cf. Ibid., p. 85).

In psychoanalysis, we often hear about the mother regression, the longing that all one's needs will be unconditionally satisfied, metaphorically expressed in the longing to go back to the womb. In connection with the son's symbiosis with the preoedipal father, we have to deal with a father regression of a completely different kind than the longing for an unconditional satisfaction of needs. This regression represents an ascetic of giving up of oneself, a very fundamental absence of an experience of identity. There is room for nobody but the father. And in this kind of family constellation, the motherly, the feminine, and dependence and vulnerability are despised. What counts here is unlimited power of the father, the mother and the woman as well as one's own independence must be given up. In the void that is created in the son's relation to the mother, and in the absence of a nourishing, supportive and emotionally affirming relation, the shame grows – a shame which is hard to contain and which can be projected and be ascribed to others; the shame is, in other words, transformed to shamelessness (cf. Kjellqvist, 1993). Let us take a look at a quote from Stein:

The son [...] is taught to be dismissive, even contemptuous, toward his mother, sister, and wife, which further restricts his chance of identifying with tender intentions and relations. Deprived of identification with his mother as well, the son's shameful parts are projected onto others who are now treated with contempt, even violence.

(Ibid., p. 84)

Instead of the son's struggle with the oedipal father, the typical scenario in the phallic development of masculinity, here in the hypermasculinity we witness a father regression: submission instead of the murder of the father. This symbolic murder of the father is not performed. The son is not in a position to experience a "murder" of the father, which the father survives. What is important to consider, when it comes to the so-called "murder of the father" and the survival of the father, is that it has to do with a process of liberation, the fact that the son can grow up and become a person in his own right, and which is something that the parents, in this case the father, can accept and contain.[3]

I believe that one can consider this symbiotic father–son relation as a symbiosis between fears: the father is not only feared and desired by the son, but he is also regressive and ruled by fears of motherliness and dependence. This experienced "weakness" (because this is the way in which dependence, motherliness and femininity are comprehended) makes it more difficult for the son to take up the fight with the father, who is thus not only horrifying but can also be experienced as weak.

The above account is inspired by Stein's (2010) description of hypermasculinity, which she developed from the vantage point of the terrorist attacks in the USA on the 11th of September 2001. In her book *For Love of the Father*, she analyzes religious terrorism from a psychoanalytic perspective. Focus is on the personality of the terrorist, even though her analysis has a broader application. That which is characteristic for the religious terrorists is that their mentality, thinking and language are religious according to Stein.

In line with the above problematic, religious terrorism is about regression to an archaic father with unlimited power. The son submits to the father and his ideal by exterminating the enemies of the father and banishing everything that is connected to femininity and motherliness. The love for a primitive father imago takes place at the expense of the capacity to create loving and rewarding relationships with women. And the love for the father is channeled to the masculine figure which in their fantasy allows itself to be represented by the superior and sovereign father figure, that is to say, God. Stein notes that the religious suicide bombers very rarely get married or become fathers – they, so to speak, remain sons; sexual arousal and desire are only marginally directed towards women or other men, except for the intention of quickly relieving embodied sexual tension. The real excitement and passion are directed towards God, who is experienced as a superior, male, father figure.

Chodorow (2012) has also examined religious terrorism, ethnic cleansing and xenophobia from the vantage point of a gender perspective. It has struck her that these phenomena often are discussed as a general human problem, despite the fact that it is almost exclusively men who are involved in them.[4] She asks what kind of psychic organization is involved in ordinary masculinity, which motivates so many men to develop hatred, and when humiliated react aggressively and violently, in a manner which most women do not do (Ibid., p. 126).[5]

From a psychoanalytic point of view, Chodorow understands terrorism and other extreme forms of violence partly as a result of schizo-paranoid splitting and projective identification (see Klein, 1975) and partly from the vantage point of narcissism and the feeling of being humiliated. In Klein's theory of development, the first position has a schizo-paranoid character, where the bad and the good objects are not integrated, but the objects are either exclusively bad or good. It is not until the second position, the so-called "depressive position" (many have suggested that it should be designated as an integrating position), that the good and the bad can start to be integrated, so as to make it possible, for the child to experience the other one as both good and bad – the one that one loves can simultaneously awaken one's hatred. A mechanism operating in the schizo-paranoid position is projective identification, where the bad is placed with the other, while one's self holds all the good. However, this leads to anxiety and fear to be exposed to attacks from the (bad) other and results in further splitting. A more beneficial development takes place if the self is capable of reintegrating the bad objects and is able to contain both good and bad objects within oneself (the depressive position).

Chodorow emphasizes, in particular, that in the violent actions and fantasies the paranoid fear is not contained: the self is throughout good and is threatened from the outside by the projection of the bad on to the other. The bad which is placed outside oneself must be destroyed; it is an extreme form of "we-and-them" thinking: we are good – they are bad and must be destroyed.

Apart from the schizo-paranoid splitting, Chodorow describes a second dynamic, which has to do with the complex shame, humiliation and narcissism. Clinically, it is common that individuals who feel humiliated and shameful react with anger and grandiosity. Chodorow draws a parallel to how expansionism and ethnic cleansing justify collective violence and terrorism with reference to humiliations and defeats from the past.

After this investigation, Chodorow takes on the task of trying to link the above dynamics to masculinities concerning such phenomena as religious terrorism and ethnic cleansing – which contrasts to the fact that they are often described in terms of gender-neutral terms. Even when violence is described as being national or ethnic, men are clearly overrepresented in those contexts. Therefore, the above dynamics (schizo-paranoid position and projective identification, as well as narcissism, humiliation and shame) must be understood from the vantage point of masculine problematics. Chodorow conceptualizes the connection to masculinity and the two abovementioned operating mechanisms of, for example, terrorism as two psychical fault lines.

The first masculine fault line concerns gender and self-hood in relation to femininity and motherliness. Here, we recognize the analysis and its application also to phallic masculinity. The problematic concerns easily awakened feelings with men in relationships with women and has its origin in early relations with their mother: the fear of dependence, the fear of being abandoned, the fear of losing one's self and the fear of women's sexuality. An important element is the fear of the omnipotent mother: the feeling of humiliation and insufficiency lead to a repudiation of women and the fear of being feminized. Masculinity defines itself, to a large extent, as not-feminine and not-mother in a manner that is not the case for femininity in relationship to masculinity and the father. The important thing for men and masculinity is to not be a woman or feminine.

The second fault line, which may be more important in order to understand the present problematics, concerns the relationship between the father and the son or the relationship between men. Narcissism and a feeling of humiliation originally have to do with a father–son relationship. Thus, masculinity involves the feeling of both *not* being a woman and *not* being a boy/child in relation to an adult/father. Chodorow uses the Achilles myth to capture the man's psychology and the conflict surrounding "man against man" and superior/subordinate. Achilles is a younger man and is humiliated by the older Agamemnon, who already has a wife and children, but also demands Briseis, a captured woman in Achilles's age and his concubine. Achilles's heel is that part of his body that is vulnerable, since his mother did not succeed in protecting it when she lowered it into the river Styx in order to make him invulnerable. According to Chodorow, the Achilles's heel represents the fear of narcissistic humiliation in relation to another man. The currency in this dishonor is often conquering or monopolizing, not of the man, however, but of younger women who should belong to the younger man. In general, Greek mythology, with the exception of Oedipus, tends to be characterized by older men humiliating younger ones.

Chodorow notices that this dynamic, characterizing extreme violence, ethnic cleansing and religious terrorism, also exists in homophobia. Homosexuality figures both as submission to other men and as a challenge towards the division of man/woman; it feminizes men. Chodorow writes:

> Attraction to men from a boy identification, attraction to passivity and receptivity, feminine identifications vis-à-vis men, can all be deeply threatening to masculinity, threatening the hard-won achievement of active, aggressive, heterosexual masculinity. Characteristically, femininity and submissiveness to men have to be split off and projected outward, where these, in turn, become extremely persecutory possibilities.
> (Ibid., p. 135)

In summary, we can see that the first fault line concerned masculinity as a man, not being feminine/a woman, and the second fault line was about not being a boy/child in relationship to an adult/father, not being humiliated or defeated by another man. When these edicts or ideals are threatened, there is a risk that men react with extreme violence according to Chodorow.

It is beyond the scope of this work to discuss Stein's and Chodorow's different theoretical explications of the phenomenon of hypermasculinity. Suffice to say, I do not conceive of the differences as incompatible as much as complementing one another.

Phallic masculinity

In psychoanalysis, the concept "phallic masculinity" stems from Freud's view of psychosexual development. The phallic phase is described, by Freud, as the third phase, after the oral and anal ones, when "the male organ (and what corresponds to it in girls) attains an importance which can no longer be overlooked" (1932, p. 99). According to Freud, the child only knows about the male genitals, and the psychosexual organization is, thus, phallic for both boys and girls. Most boys enter into the phallic phase between the age of 2 and 3 years, and it has been pointed out that the father's and the son's standing position when urinating structures this process: a urethral eroticism can be noticed, a fascination with the boy at the father's urination (Tyson, 1982).[6] The identification with the father becomes prominent; Freud writes that a little boy "will exhibit a special interest in his father, he would like to grow like him and be like him, and take his place everywhere [...] he takes his father as his ideal" (1921, p. 105), and this process helps to prepare for the Oedipus complex. To be masculine means to be big, to stand up, to possess and to use penetrating weapons and to be aggressive. Women have not yet become desired objects, which is why the boy's masculinity first of all is narcissistic, as John Munder Ross points out: "It is a dance whose aim is to be applauded" (1996, p. 65). The traumatic sexual differentiation, taking place around the age of 3–5 years, causes castration anxiety for boys (the fear of losing one's penis) and penis envy for girls.

Phallic masculinity is not always called "phallic" in the literature, but often it is simply talked about as masculinity even though the meaning is phallic masculinity. It comes to expression in many different ways, and the threat to it is also expressed in many ways and should not be limited, for the boy's part, to a fear of losing one's penis. Next, I will try to draw a picture of what characterizes phallic masculinity. In the psychoanalytic literature, it is common to depict it by means of a number of traits, formulated as the opposite of femininity. As an example of this, a quote from Fogel can be given:

> I characterize masculine by outwardness, feminine by inwardness; masculine by precise boundaries, shapes, entities, and definitions, feminine by ambiguity or fluidity of boundaries, shapes, entities, and definitions; masculine by penetration, feminine by receptivity and holding; masculine by deconstruction and cutting through, feminine by construction, creativity, and synthesis; masculine by differentiation and separateness, feminine by recognition, integration, and unification; masculine by representation, feminine by space, masculine by doing, feminine by being.
>
> (2006, p. 1141)

However, the question of masculinity is more loaded than just being the opposite of the feminine. The feminine, or the woman, does not merely appear as a kind of undramatic opposite to masculinity or to the man.

As Fogel notices, the problem for most men is women: "as boys and men we are dependent upon, threatened by, vulnerable to, and envious of women – in far more conscious and unconscious ways than we ordinarily can bear" (1996, p. 9). In other words, one ought to go a couple of steps further than defining masculinity as the opposite of femininity. First, it can be claimed that masculinity is constituted by a rejecting and repudiating femininity, and, in addition, motherliness. Masculinity does not want to know about the feminine, which in our culture is represented by the infantile; "for being childish or dependent; for lacking control of appetites or emotions; for irrationality; for incompleteness, emptiness, and longing; for helplessness, passivity, greed, jealousy, and envy" (Ibid., pp. 9–10).

Second, in line with Benjamin (2004), it can be pointed out that the femininity which masculinity repudiates is not to be conceived of as some existing feminine "thing" or "essence", but is a construction of the male psyche. It is a man's construction about passivity, conditioned by oedipal loss, being excluded, vulnerability and helplessness, which are placed in something that Benjamin calls "the daughter position".[7]

In Freud, we can read of another interesting fantasy that relates to the feminine, where the angle is not that femininity is made up of such things that one does not want to know about, but, quite the opposite, it is something that gives satisfaction but also awakes fear:

> Wherever primitive man has set up a taboo he fears some danger and it cannot be disputed that a generalized dread of women is expressed in all these rules of avoidance [...] The man is afraid of being weakened by the woman, infected with her femininity and of then showing himself incapable. The effect which coitus has of discharging tensions and causing flaccidity may be the prototype of what the man fears; and realization of the influence which the woman gains over him through sexual intercourse, the consideration she thereby forces from him, may justify the extension of his fear. In all this there is nothing obsolete, nothing which is not still alive among ourselves.
>
> (1918, pp. 198–199)

Quite how far from jouissance or pleasure the masculine can move could be read about in an article from the Swedish newspaper, *Dagens Nyheter* (2014), which dealt with oil drilling in the USA. A man working with the drilling equipment in an oil company describes how he loves his job:

> It's hard and sweaty, just the way I want it. I have worked on the oil rig when it is minus 25 degrees Celsius and the snot in my nose freezes to ice and you get blisters on your hands. That's when you feel like a real man.

Examples of phallic masculinity are activity, controlling the world as well as one's own feelings, sovereign power, strength, determination, fantasies about being a hero or achieving something extraordinary, self-assertiveness in one's sexual life as in life in general and going beyond the existing. Concerning this trait – going beyond the existing or transcending – one can notice an interesting connection to Beauvoir's existential phenomenological thinking, in that the male body can be described in terms of transcendence. Transcendence and immanence are two important concepts within phenomenology, not least in Beauvoir, but have found no place in psychoanalysis. Transcendence captures a masculine way of being in the world, which is embodied in the penis "in a graspable way and it is a source of pride" (Beauvoir, 1949/2011, p. 58). The living sexual body, more precisely in this context the penis, with its urinating function and possibility of erection, is given an existential, transcendent meaning, which makes the male body privileged in relationship to the female:

> The advantage man enjoys and which manifests itself from childhood onwards is that his vocation as a human being in no way contradicts his destiny as a male. The fact that the phallus is assimilated with transcendence means that man's social and spiritual successes endow him with virile prestige.
>
> (Ibid., p. 739) (See also endnote 6 in this chapter)

In phallic masculinity, sexuality is characterized by men's satisfaction to express power and dominance over the other (Frosh, 1994, p. 100). Men can be very obsessed with their capacity to sexually satisfy their partner. There is a risk that the sexual act becomes more a matter of being able to show off one's own capacity than having a shared sexual experience with one's partner, which also involves a sense of control over one's partner. The urge to control women's sexuality, I believe, can be seen in the striking opposite attitudes to frivolous sexuality depending on if it is a man or a woman who is the agent: a man who sleeps around shows a highly esteemed masculine trait, whereas a woman with the same behavior runs the risk of being perceived as a whore. Zilbergeld, cited in Person (2006, p. 1174), has described the sexual phallic ideal as a "large, powerful, untiring phallus attached to a cool controlled male, long on experience, confident, and knowledgeable enough to make women crazy with desire [...]". However, as Person notices, this phallic ideal indicates more often underlying feelings of insufficiency than a genuine sexual self-confidence (Ibid., p. 1180). Even though men experience a variety of sexual fantasies, Person (1996) emphasizes that there seems to be some general differences between men's and women's sexual fantasies: men's fantasies are often distinctly sexual and are about dominating, whereas women's fantasies rather have a romantic character and are about submission.[8] Sexuality involves and challenges many feelings, such as aggressivity, tenderness, a movement to let go, surrendering and sharing an experience.

Heterosexuality is the apogee of the relationship between men and women, and here sexuality can be the source of many difficult problems. It is common that problems with sexuality for men have to do with ideas about what it means to be a man, something that thus concerns masculinity and ideals of masculinity. Heterosexuality as a phenomenon is interesting, since the possibility for its expression requires an alloy of many different disparate traits. The masculine macho ideal is a struggle with impulses that become extremely contradictory. On the one hand, we have everything that potentially can be expressed in the heterosexual act in the form of unity, being together, surrendering, and, on the other the potentiality of sexuality as conquering and aggressivity. The macho-inspired masculinity uses something that on a manifest level has been rejected, that is to say, the wish for recognition. Instead of affirming this wish, the woman becomes represented as "the Other" in the terminology of Beauvoir (1949/2011) – a position in which she has been deprived of her subjectivity and where she does not participate in a struggle for recognition.

The masculine project is manifest in many ways, such as an incessant striving for achievement, gaining a top position in competition with others (in particular with other men), controlling and domineering, and not least going beyond the existing conditions. A common clinical experience with men can thus be described as follows: the sense of meaning and value in one's existence tend to be limited to one's capacity to perform startling achievements. More or less concealed in one's psyche is harbored the wish and the pressure to reach a top position, to be number one and to be best. The alternative to this sought-after goal is often to be at the bottom of the ladder. With only these two alternatives at hand, there are certainly reasons for "fear of falling".[9] Confronted with such a scenario, it is understandable that the pressure to hold a top position easily yields a feeling of being alone, being exposed and being in a vulnerable position, where one's fellow human beings are experienced as threatening. In other words, it becomes difficult to affirm a dependence that can be experienced as supportive and comforting. "The others", namely other men, risk being limited to nothing but potential rivals. Such a position makes the man narcissistic vulnerable and tends to leave him with a sense of being insufficient.

The striving to assimilate such a masculine project starts early in life for boys/men and is never given up by many men (cf. Kaftal, 1991). The unreachability of the masculine project easily leads to feelings of insufficiency, worthlessness and an inner emptiness. The masculine striving can be described as a hunt for a narcissistic wholeness to seal the gap between the ego and its ideal, something which in turn has threads back to the traumatic separation from the primary caregiver/the mother. Vesa Manninen (1993) draws attention to the unconscious wish to reach unity with the now separate mother. Phallus bestows the power to transform this traumatic separation to being in control over the mother, which works as a matrix for subsequent development; "…only by conquering the world can one conquer the mother" (Manninen, 1992, p. 7).

The significance of castration anxiety

This phallic masculinity, connected to oedipal wishes, entails a tripartite: the child and two other persons, usually the mother and the father. This oedipal world is a big step for the child compared to the period with the dyadic relation between the child and the primary caregiver, usually the mother. To go from a bipartite to a tripartite relation involves the evocation of many feelings and phenomena. Strong feelings like love and hatred are shaped in their specific way in the tripartite oedipal relation: a space of conflict emerges which binds the child in love to one person and the wish that the other person would disappear. Love, hatred, disappearance and death are experienced simultaneously.

In the oedipal world, we find feelings and phenomena, such as comparing, jealousy, rivalry, competition and achieving which also imply that one can win and triumph or lose and fall. To come forth, to be seen, to assert oneself and to take up space, stand in sharp contrast to stand back, to make oneself invisible, to keep down, not to take up any space. In other words, the child's or the person's narcissistic wishes can be realized or live a more secluded existence. One can try to be admired or impress the other by triumphing or winning in competition over the other. The triumph does not only consist in defeating someone but also imply that it is achieved in front of a physically present or imagined coveted/respected other person. To receive the other one's admiration is supposed to be achieved by triumphing over the third and all others, that is to say, the fourth, the fifth, the sixth and so on. The difference between the second and the third is of a completely different kind than the difference between the third and all the others (the fourth, the fifth, the sixth and so on). This is the reason which is why we can talk about the third as representing the world. The dyad – the mother and the child – is extended to a world.

To step out of the dyad to a tripartite relation, and to embrace a world, is two-edged. It is connected with many challenges and, as stated above, many painful experiences which one must try to contain. But to embrace the world also makes it possible to open up for the reality that surrounds us in an entirely different way than before. To recognize the third (the father) is to recognize the loss: the loss of an exclusive relation with the (m)other. To enter the oedipal constellation is to recognize the other's independence, that the other is something beyond my wishes and projections.

We have seen that the father can be of help for the son in creating a triangular space: a connection is established between the parent couple. Unless such a triangular relationship is established, the relation to the other can be dominated by a closed, manipulative and calculating attitude. In such an attitude, there is no room for surprises. The fundamentally open and presumptive character of existence is replaced by calculating logic: "if I do this, the other one will do that", "if the other does so, I must do so, in order for the other to do so" and so on, since this chain can be expanded considerably. The step from a dyadic to an oedipal constellation also implies a recognition and organization of a linear timeliness. An essential trait in the linear temporality is that every "point" is there only once and never comes back. My clinical experiences with men who are stuck in a symbiotic relationship with their mothers and where the fathers are psychologically denied are that it engenders a resistance of acknowledging separation and loss, and with that comes difficulty in conforming to linear temporality.

It is important for the boy that the identification with the father does not become of a kind which implies an antagonistic relation to the mother, or as an opposite to the mother, as if the identification with the mother and the father were incompatible. The identification with the father is important as an aid to cope with the separation-individuation from the mother, at the same time as she continues to be available as someone that the boy can be like, even after the father has become a distinct object of identification.

The threatening image that the boy has to struggle with is called "castration anxiety" by Freud, and for him, this anxiety had a clear connection to the penis. As shown in Chapter 2, in the psychoanalytic theorizing, a more holistic and metaphoric kind of castration has been developed. Castration can then have many different forms, such as weaning from the breast, the experience of not being everything and the transience of existence. I believe it to be problematic to extend this concept in such a way, since it can dilute and conceal the central role which the penis has in the phallic and oedipal problematic. The phallus is the foremost symbol for phallic masculinity. To emphasize the connection of the castration threat to the penis/phallus also implies a concrete embodied anchorage and credibility in relation to the child's concrete thinking. The boy's interest in his penis is awakened, by all means, earlier than him entering the phallic oedipal phase, since already in the second half of the first year's life an intended self-stimulation is noticeable: during the second year of life, it can also be noticed that the boy feels proud of being able to control his urinating (from Person, 2006, p. 1167, which refers to observations made by P. Tyson and R. Tyson).

But even if the penis attracts the little boy's interest very early, it is in the oedipal phase that the castration anxiety becomes central and a source of the oedipal boy's inferiority feelings in relationship to his father's genital organ. This experience then makes up the basis for the teenager boy's, as well as the grown-up man's, interest in comparing his masculinity with other men, the size of his penis and his sexual behavior.

However, it would be wrong to take it for granted that the castration anxiety must focus on the fear of losing one's penis. The repercussions of castration fear can go beyond a fear of losing one's penis, such as losing one's reputation – a displacement from the penis to other experiences of oneself. My experience is that when the castration anxiety is unfolded, it has a vague and elusive character, which in no way degrades its annihilating force. It is experienced as erasement even though it does not possess the reality-dissolving character of the psychotic anxiety. The experience of castration anxiety means, first of all, a feeling that one's reputation is entirely wiped out and that the meaning of life has been lost. This kind of social annihilation can appear as absurd and elusive, when the person's sober reflecting gains a certain distance to the inordinate claims that the anxiety stems from. The claims have a colossal format – such as being sovereign, accomplishing great deeds, being boundlessly admired and being a hero: claims that appear comic, once the person has gained a liberating distance from them. Nevertheless, it can be a devastating experience to fall from this phallic and pretentious height, and sense that the meaning of existence threatens to be wiped out. The combination of the absurd and infantile claims with the experience of annihilation can be shaking: what kind of madness is it that I harbor in my inner life?

Such castration anxiety which more manifestly concerns sexual problematics can be about reputation, achievement and admiration, but also about fantasies of losing one's penis. My impression is that men, to a larger extent than women, feel threatening and unpleasant sensations in the abdomen when confronted with mutilation. Arnold M. Cooper (1996) accounts for a similar observation, when many men, at the sight of a bloody injury, feel sensation in their groin and feel how the scrotum can tighten and the penis wrinkles. Cooper seems to take these experiences as evidence for the castration anxiety to be the least feared of early worries and thereby so close to consciousness. On deeper levels, we can, for example, find anxiety which concerns the loss of the breast or of the mother's love. "Terrifying as it is, the loss of the penis is still only a loss of a part of oneself, a relatively small loss compared with still-active fears of pre-oedipal total annihilation" (Ibid., p. 119). I would like to maintain that castration anxiety awakens associations to an earlier established annihilation anxiety.

Another source of boys'/men's anxiety is the lack of control of the penis: the penis can become erect on occasions which one is not comfortable with, and the boy can, perhaps in particular in the adolescence, feel overwhelmed by sexual arousal. Person (1996, p. 82) identifies a kind of contradiction in the boy's sexual experience: a pride in the force of the penis and possibility of pleasure simultaneously with a sense that he does not really possess it and that it is not under his control.

Phallic masculinity is established early in life and then prevails throughout life. There are striking similarities between the little phallic boy and the grown-up man (and, by all means, the grown-up woman, but this is beyond the scope of this analysis), even though the phallic masculinity often is challenged when reaching middle age and thereby is offered the possibility to adapt. However, the outcome is not given: phallic masculinity may decrease, many times, in disruptive periods in life when the experience of limitations can lead to the giving up of phallic illusions, but phallic masculinity can also retain its intrapsychic grip on the person and cause pain and stagnation. Some become depressed and feel lethargic, and others can, on a manifest level, react by making great changes in their life, which can be expressed in many different ways and which stand in sharp contrast to a less active life that moves towards aging. This can be seen in divorces and starting a new family, or in projects that require strength and power, as, for example, in beginning intense workout programs.

Diamond (2004) points out the gender aspect in feelings which is awakened in middle age, and his recipe for psychic health consists of embracing sides in one's self which earlier were rejected due to their association with femininity. Earlier in life, it was more common to seek to match idealized ideas of what it means to be a man – ideas that have their source in the little phallic boy's view of his father. In middle age, the phallic character can be widened and entail identifications which usually are with the mother and which concern care and relational qualities. That which earlier on was repressed or denied, in the striving for a certain identity, now can become relevant and accepted to a greater degree. The interest in care and relations can be strengthened, unless instead the phallic defensive character is strengthened, and masculinity and femininity are further polarized, and this thereby has an inhibitory effect on personal development in middle age.

Demasculinized masculinity

I cannot suggest a better name for this form of masculinity than the oxymoron, "demasculinized masculinity", which has a paradoxical character in the sense that it is by a demasculinizing act that the person experiences himself as masculine. Demasculinized masculinity emerges from the rejection of a phallic masculine ideal in a liberating movement; it is an experience of being genuinely masculine by liberating oneself from phallic masculine ideals. The liberation consists of an experience of a (mature) masculinity. It is not a question of going beyond, transcending the structuring of sex/gender, which we will see examples of in Chapter 6, when I discuss ego-identity and authenticity. In my clinical work, when I have come across that which here is called demasculinized masculinity, I have not perceived it as a kind of inauthentic affirmation of masculinity. I feel therefore obliged to retain one form of masculinity, demasculinized masculinity, which does not possess the character of being a project, nor can be understood as an overcoming of gender categorization. Besides, I want to emphasize that demasculinized masculinity should not be understood as a kind of castrated masculinity – a misinterpretation that I have come across.

The common denominator in the experiences that entail demasculinized masculinity is abstaining from something that has been identified with being masculine, with the feeling of being a "real" man. I want to emphasize that the examples I give below on manifest behavior draw their sense from the vantage point of the meaning that the person in question endows it with. Thus, it is not a question of judging the rightness or wrongness of the behavior in question.

A typical example is a man who has identified himself as a womanizer, skilled in conquering women, which has required a courage to approach women in a self-confident way. This kind of behavior captures not only possible pleasurable experiences with desired objects but also the striving to *identify oneself* with an image of what it is to be a "real" man, a phallic masculine man. Abstaining from trying to realize possibilities is felt as devastating to one's masculinity, like a self-inflicted castration. Being a masculine man then is to go beyond that which is, and to realize possibilities or, in the existentialist language of Beauvoir, to transcend oneself. It can be seen as an expression of inauthenticity, in which one's acts are based on an idea of what it is to be a man/to behave as a real man, rather than acknowledging and taking responsibility for one's lived subjectivity, experiences and feelings. This manifestation of phallic masculinity undergoes a radical change when the man *chooses* to abstain from affirming behaviors that have hitherto been considered masculine. In the example of being a sexual conqueror, it may express itself by abstaining from a possible conquest to affirm a relationship with one's partner, which often implies a relief of anxiety of not "needing" to pretend to be someone/something. The earlier masculine ideal has gone through a considerable change, but not, by primarily constructing or creating a new ideal to live up to, but rather by abstaining from trying to fulfill the earlier masculine ideals, which yields the feeling of having come home. It is like "coming home in one's manly belongingness" is synonymous with a masculinity without masculine ideals.

Another example of this kind of demasculinized masculinity is the man who succeeds, to his own surprise, in abstaining from struggling with a man with whom a constant rivalry has been experienced in the past. Also, in this case, male patients can relate how they suddenly decided not to bother arguing or competing with, for example, their male friends. And this new and unfamiliar behavior is not due to resignation or a feeling of having been defeated, but rather due to a feeling of growing up and being able to overcome a childish need for confirmation.

A common denominator in both these examples is the experience that masculinity entails a connection with a mature masculinity by abstaining and by giving up previous sensations, desires, fancies and wishes. The demasculinized masculinity receives its character in the contrast that emerges between an infantile masculinity and a grown-up man's ability to overcome his infantility. That which makes this kind of masculinity essentially different from hypermasculinity and phallic masculinity is, among other things, its non-dilutional character. That which is expressed in these actions, characterized by demasculinized masculinity, is not charged with grandiose fantasies and wishes, but gives satisfaction in being in that which is.

Apart from my own clinical experiences, I have, in the psychoanalytic literature, found one example that basically represents that which I have labeled demasculinized masculinity.[10] Diamond gives an example of a man who reported a situation in which he watched his wife and daughter playing with each other. It was difficult for him to just stand by and watch, and he felt an urge to actively participate and do something, "maybe toss his daughter in the air or tickle her". However, he managed to refrain from breaking into their game, which made him feel happy, and he related the following to Diamond: "That evening, I noticed that I felt 'older and heavier,' not so 'light and spry.' But you know, I felt more like a man that night than I ever have" (1997, p. 461).

How is one to understand the conditions of the demasculinized masculinity? As stated, it has a paradoxical character. The phallic masculinity functions both as a springboard for, and that which is abolished through, the movement of the demasculinized masculinity. There is no straight trajectory to demasculinized masculinity; it needs to go through a phase of phallic masculinity. An essential trait in the liberation achieved in demasculinizing phallic masculinity concerns the ability to abstain from transcending in order to open oneself up for the experience of receiving, affirming that which exists. In all the examples that I have described as demasculinized masculinity, it is a matter of giving up something that can be described as phallic masculinity. I think it is this abstaining which makes it possible to capture the experience of demasculinized masculinity as coming home, as an affirmation of immanence. I have earlier pointed out that the concepts "immanence" and "transcendence" do not exist in the psychoanalytic literature, but are common, with various meaning, in phenomenology (in Chapter 6 I will come back to the relevance of these concepts in order to understand phallic masculinity). Another important aspect of this demasculinizing is the change from a narcissistic attitude to a world consisting of individuals other than myself. There is space for others; one's view is extended so as to consider one's existence against the background of other people's needs and wishes. I become less trapped in my own world and more receptive and open to other people.

How is one to psychoanalytically explain that which I have tried to capture with the oxymoron demasculinized masculinity? In the article that describes how the father felt more like a man than he ever had done due to his abstaining from interrupting in his wife's and his child's common play, Diamond (1997) discusses how a healthy adult masculinity requires an integration of masculine and feminine identities. This is an explanation that we recognize from other psychoanalysts' theorizing about the development of a mature masculine identity. In this context, one should also point out that de-masculinized masculinity not only displays the feminine–masculine dichot-omy but also small boy–adult man in the tension between the narcissism of the infantile boy and the adult man's overcoming of his infantile narcissism.

A psychogenetic explanation for demasculinized masculinity, as it has been depicted above, may have to do with the preoedipal father as an object of identification for the son. In Chapter 2, I referred to Diamond's (2004) distinction between genital and phallic qualities. The genital qualities that the father can provide concerns protecting and containing aspects as op-posed to phallic qualities in terms of penetration, activity and strength. The identification with the father's genital qualities facilitates an integra-tion of motherly/feminine identifications, since the father's genital qualities bring about an acknowledgment of sexual differentiation and its inevitable restrictions (one cannot be everything), without implying a repudiation or denial of qualities that belong to the opposite sex.

Notes

1   The discussion of the meaning of hypermasculinity will be carried out by the aid of Stein's (2010) and Chodorow's (2012) ideas. For a summary of psychoanalytic views of religious terrorism, see Jones (2006).
2   Stein maintains that Freud's phallic and archaic preoedipal father (the primal father) has disappeared in psychoanalytic theorizing: "Notions of a phallic 'primal' father have curiously not received much attention in psychoanalysis in comparison to the figure of the phallic mother" and she asks: "Could it be that the notion of father-fusion as the desire to merge with the archaic father imago arouses too deep a dread to contemplate?" (2010, p. 74).
3   Stein quotes Loewald concerning how to understand this symbolic murder of the father:

> by evolving our own autonomy, our own superego, and by engaging in non-incestuous object relations, we are killing our parents. We are usurping their power, their competence, their responsibility for us, and we are abrogating, rejecting them as libidinal objects. In short, we destroy them in regard to some of their qualities hitherto most vital to us.
>
> (2010, p. 86)

4   Chodorow writes:

> Terrorism, suicide bombing, the violence of nationalism and ethnic cleans-ing, all, it would seem, involve desire to humiliate a male enemy. This mascu-line desire to humiliate defeated men and to shore up male identity intersects further with misogyny, such that cases of ethnic cleansing often include the mass rape of women and girls, and that political torture usually includes, specifically, the sexual torture of both men and women, as if the perpetrators are enacting male dominance as well as political or ethnic dominance.
>
> (2012, p. 124)

5   Jukes (1993, 2010) claims that men live in a perpetual enmity and hatred to-wards women, and that this is expressed either overtly or covertly in order to establish and maintain control of women; "misogyny is as natural to men as the

possession of a penis – its development is inevitable" (1993, p. 11). His theory of the construction of masculinity is founded on the connection between the traumatic separation and loss of the maternal primary object and the phallic narcissistic defences on the oedipal level.

6 In Beauvoir's (1949/2011) feministic magnum opus, *The Second Sex*, in which an analysis of the woman's situation is carried out from an existential-phenomenological tradition, she uses contributions from biology, psychoanalysis and historical materialism. Psychoanalysis is thus an aid to explain the privileged situation of the man. In this context, she gives the penis a significant role in the life of the little boy; the penis works as a kind of "double", as it is both a foreign object and himself. It is simultaneously a plaything and his own flesh. Parents treat it like a person. Beauvoir also attaches importance to the urinating function for his self-esteem:

> Because the urinary function and later the erection are midway between voluntary processes and spontaneous processes, because it is the impulsive, quasi-foreign source of subjectively experienced pleasure, the penis is posited by the subject as himself and other than himself; specific transcendence is embodied in it in a graspable way and it is a source of pride; because the phallus is set apart, man can integrate into his personality the life that flows from it. This is why, then, the length of the penis, the force of the urine stream, the erection and the ejaculation become for him the measure of his own worth.
>
> (p. 58)

7 Benjamin writes:

> I have been suggesting that the very norm of femininity was constructed to hold unwanted experiences of vulnerability and helplessness, and that this occurs through the defensive splitting of activity and passivity. This view of the feminine corresponds to the classic image of the daughter, the one who, Freud insists, must switch to the father [...] I have termed this construction of femininity the 'daughter position' because its transmission is encoded in the shift to the father, the role of passive container, caretaker, or incest victim such as we saw in the hysterical daughters of Freud's famous cases.
>
> (2004, pp. 157–158)

8 In Person, we can read the following from a study that she was part of carrying out:

> It was apparent [...] that some male fantasies were designed so as to cover over, or deny, men's sexual fears, some of them pervasive. With regard to performance, men sometimes worry about getting it up, keeping it up, and satisfying their partners, because there is a fundamental difference in sex: a man cannot hide his failure to achieve an erection, whereas there is no certain way to gauge a woman's sexual arousal or orgasm. Thus, it is difficult for a man to be sure he is a good lover. That men frequently ask their partners 'Did you come?' is evidence of this. Sexual anxiety is also manifest in the obsession some men have with their partner's past lover: 'Was he better? Did you have more orgasms? Better orgasms?'
>
> (2006, pp. 1176–1177)

9 Academic research has been carried out from the vantage point of the experience of unmanliness, showing that one sign of unmanliness is to lose self-control in terms of all sorts of falling: fear of falling in tears, fall to nothing, fall asleep and fall from a great height. Falling symbolizes the opposite of self-control,

and according to Lowen's experiences of body-oriented psychotherapy, men are supposedly more afraid of falling than women (see Ekenstam, 1999, 2006).

10 In academic research on masculinity, there is one study which, to some extent, resembles the paradoxical character of demasculinized masculinity, namely Wetherell's & Edley's (1999) analysis of masculinity in relationship to Connell's idea about hegemonic masculinity. They found in interview studies that men comparatively rarely related to a so-called "heroic positioning", a designation that corresponds to the norm of hegemonic masculinity, in terms of toughness, courage, control and power. Instead, the men portrayed themselves, to a surprisingly high degree, as "ordinary" in relation to macho ideals which were rejected as extreme stereotypes and signs of immaturity. They conclude that a subtle form of masculinity is to distance oneself from hegemonic masculinity. If one switches hegemonic masculinity to phallic masculinity, there is a certain similarity between Wetherell's and Edley's paradoxical description of an ordinary form of masculinity and demasculinized masculinity.

References

Beauvoir, S. de (1949/2011). *The second sex.* Vintage Books.

Benjamin, J. (2004). Revisiting the riddle of sex: An intersubjective view of masculinity and femininity. In I. Matthis (Ed.) *Dialogues on sexuality, gender, and psychoanalysis.* Karnac.

Chodorow, N.J. (2012). Hate, humiliation, and masculinity. In her *Individualizing gender and sexuality. Theory and practice.* Routledge.

Cooper, A.M. (1996). What men fear: The facade of castration anxiety. In G.I. Fogel, F.M. Lane & R.S. Liebert (Eds.) *The psychology of men.* Yale University Press.

Dagens Nyheter (2014). Det här stället är som Kalifornien under guldrushen. 4th January, 2014. ["This place is like the California gold rush". 4th January, 2014].

Diamond, M.J. (1997). Boys to men: The maturing of masculine gender identity through paternal watchful protectiveness. *Gender & Psychoanalysis. An Interdisciplinary Journal, 2*(4), 443–468.

Diamond, M.J. (2004). Accessing multitude within: A psychoanalytic perspective on the transformation of masculinity at mid-life. *International Journal of Psychoanalysis, 85*(1), 45–64. Doi:10.1516/3PFY-NQMU-C95F-HH0W

Ekenstam, Cl. (1999). Rädd att falla: gråtens och mansbildens sammanflätade historia. [Afraid to fall: The intertwined history of crying and the male image]. In A.M. Berggren (Ed.), *Manligt och omanligt i ett historiskt perspektiv.* [Manly and unmanly in a historical perspective]. Forskningsrådsnämnden, Rapport 99:4, 157–173. [Swedish Council for Planning and Co-ordination of Research. Report 99:4, 157–173].

Ekenstam, Cl. (2006). Mansforskningens bakgrund och framtid: Några teoretiska reflektioner. [The background and future of men's studies: Some theoretical reflections]. *NORMA (Nordisk tidskrift för maskulinitetsstudier), 1,* 7–23. [NORMA (Nordic Journal of Masculinity Studies].

Fogel, G.I. (1996). Introduction: Being a man. In G.I. Fogel, F.M. Lane & R.S. Liebert (Eds.) *The psychology of men.* Yale University Press.

Fogel, G.I. (2006). Riddles of masculinity: Gender, bisexuality, and thirdness. *Journal of the American Psychoanalytic Association, 54*(4), 1139–1163. Doi:10.1177/000 30651060540040801

Freud, S. (1918). The taboo of virginity (contributions to the psychology of love III). *The standard edition of the complete psychological works of Sigmund Freud, 11.*

Freud, S. (1921). *Group psychology and the analysis of the ego. The standard edition of the complete psychological works of Sigmund Freud, 18.*

Freud, S. (1932). Anxiety and instinctual life. *The standard edition of the complete psychological works of Sigmund Freud, 22.*

Frosh, S. (1994). *Sexual difference: Masculinity and psychoanalysis.* Routledge.

Jones, J.W. (2006). Why does religion turn violent? A psychoanalytic exploration of religious terrorism. *Psychoanalytic Review, 93*(2), 167–190. Doi:10.1521/prev.2006.93.2.167

Jukes, A. (1993). *Why men hate women.* Free Association Books.

Jukes, A.E. (2010). *Is there a cure for masculinity?* Free Association Books.

Kaftal, E. (1991). On intimacy between men. *Psychoanalytic Dialogues, 1*(3), 305–328. Doi:10.1080/10481889109538902

Kjellqvist, E.-B. (1993). *Rött och vitt. Om skam och skamlöshet.* [Red and white. On shame and shamelessness]. Carlssons.

Klein, M. (1975). *Love, guilt and reparation and other works 1921–1945.* The Hogarth Press.

Manninen, V. (1992). The ultimate masculine striving: Reflexions on the psychology of two polar explorers. *The Scandinavian Psychoanalytic Review, 15*(1), 1–26.

Manninen, V. (1993). For the sake of eternity: On the narcissism of fatherhood and the father-son relationship. *The Scandinavian Psychoanalytic Review, 16*(1), 35–46. Doi:10.1080/01062301.1993.10592287

Person, E.S. (1996). The omni-available woman and lesbian sex: Two fantasy themes and their relationship to the male developmental experience. In G.I. Fogel, F.M. Lane & R.S. Liebert (Eds.) *The psychology of men.* Yale University Press.

Person, E.S. (2006). Masculinities plural. *Journal of the American Psychoanalytic Association, 54*(4), 1165–1186. Doi:10.1177/00030651060540041501

Ross, J.M. (1996). Beyond the phallic illusion: Notes on man's heterosexuality. In G.I. Fogel, F.M. Lane & R.S. Liebert (Eds.) *The psychology of men.* Yale University Press.

Stein, R. (2010). *For love of the father. A psychoanalytic study of religious terrorism.* Stanford University Press.

Tyson, P. (1982). The role of the father in gender identity, urethral erotism, and phallic narcissism. In S.H. Cath, A.R. Gurwitt & J.M. Ross (Eds.) *Father and child. Developmental and clinical perspectives.* Little, Brown and Company.

Wetherell, M. & Edley, N. (1999). Negotiating hegemonic masculinity: Imaginary positions and psycho-discursive practices. *Feminism & Psychology, 9*(3), 335–356. Doi:10.1177/0959353599009003012

4

The man's three challenges

In Chapter 3, I discussed three different forms of masculinity with a focus on phallic masculinity. In this chapter, I will continue to focus on phallic masculinity but will structure the presentation and discussion somewhat differently. This chapter and the previous one complement each other. Here, I will discuss the boy's/man's gender formation in terms of three developmental psychological challenges, in order to explain phallic masculinity from a psychoanalytic perspective. Then, to illustrate certain thoughts, I will finish the chapter by referring to a couple of events that Knausgård (2014) describes in his *My struggle. A Man in Love.*

The three challenges concerning the boy's/man's identity development which have to do with gender problematics are (i) challenge concerning the human being's existential conditions in terms of helplessness and dependence, (ii) castration threat in relation to the preoedipal mother and (iii) castration threat in relation to the father. I will primarily discuss the first of these challenges, since it is less developed in the literature and deserves more attention than it has received. The remaining two got more space in Chapter 3. Since the objective of this chapter is exclusively phallic masculinity, I will sometimes just refer to it as "masculinity" in order to be more reader-friendly.

The distinction between the three challenges are theoretic explications and, as such, deficient as mirrors of reality. Even if one can talk about a certain linearity, there are not unequivocal boundaries between them. They are connected with each other in an intertwined way, something which has been stressed by many psychoanalysts when it comes to describing a child's sex/gender development (Brenner, 1979; Person, 1986; Tyson, 1989).

(i) A challenge concerning the human being's existential conditions

Let us begin with that which concerns the existential dimension and the human being's original predicament in the state of total helplessness and total dependence. Without the adults' care, the newborn infant's biological life would soon be over, and without a psychological and emotional readiness

DOI: 10.4324/9781003352761-5

to receive, contain and confirm the infant's existence, it would meet a psychic death, and sometimes even – as experiences from orphanage testify – a biological death.

In order to understand the development of masculinity, we must thus start with the helpless human being and the helpless body, and not the phallic body or the capacity to perceive similarities and differences between one's own body and of the others. There is a risk of missing the infant's predicament in life and of viewing the infant as better equipped than it actually is. This helpless body is the originally living/experienced body for both the girl and the boy. The fact that the child's life begins in a state of helplessness and dependence is, by all means, no news and was pointed out many times by Freud, even though its significance for the gender development was not given adequate consideration.

This original existential dimension is something that the human being has always been forced to deal with, regardless of historical and cultural affiliation, and something that follows her throughout life: it reveals the vulnerability of existence, transience and dependence. Our dependence on others is most apparent at the beginning of life, but remains a condition throughout our entire life. And even if our personal development entails a striving towards autonomy, and in a certain sense independence, it is intertwined with and dependent on others' recognition (Benjamin, 1988, 1995, 1998). Psychological theories of development and clinical experiences also testify that a vital emotional life demands the containment and care of others (Anzieu, 1989; Bion, 1962; Hollway, 2006; Winnicott, 1960/1965). An early experience of having been well contained is a good ground for the development of a capacity to care and a mutual exchange between equal subjects, a subject–subject relation instead of a subject–object relationship.

Here, the primary aim is not to investigate and discuss all the various and complex consequences of different experiences of early containment. What I want to emphasize is that one of the attitudes which this existential situation, characterized by helplessness and dependence, creates is the attitude characteristic of the masculine project/ideals. In other words, in so far as the person attempts to embrace the masculine ideal, this stands in contrast to affirming a motherly containment. And this struggle to embrace masculine ideals begins early in our culture and accompanies many men until the grave: indeed, there are even different, gendered ways to die, whereof some are associated with masculinity:

> Death has often been considered a trial, a test, a definitive event in life that often flirted with fatalities. In Homeric ethics, notably, the mode of a man's death was considered a definitive mark of his character. To die bravely in battle was virtuous. To die of the flu or pneumonia was – not to be too unkind – pathetic [...] To die of old age was commendable, but only if one had the full background of battle-scars and near

misses. In classical cowboy ethics, to jump thirty centuries, it was considered essential "to die with one's boots on". Death was a ritual, and if it meant that you lost the fight, it also signified that you put up a good one. (Being shot "in the back" meant not only cowardice on the part of your assassin. It also deprived you of your chance for an honourable death). Southern American dueling rituals and contemporary urban gang fighting maintain similar codes of honour, loyalty and death, where death is not only a part of life but also its ultimate test. How one dies means everything [...] In much of the Christian tradition, the aim is to die with a clear conscience, whether by reason of right behavior or by way of a well-timed confession [...] A woman's death, through much of the same history, was thought to be a simpler thing, preferably quiet and uncomplaining, or tragically in childbirth [...] Only rarely was a woman's death an exceptional act of honour, heroism or patriotism.

(Solomon, 1998, p. 160)

Both the helplessness and the dependence of the motherly containment are present in the masculine project. More precisely, the phallic masculine ideals which are characteristic for the boy's upbringing entail a repudiation of femininity/the motherly containment. And this repudiation is first and foremost a repudiation of *a way of being*, which is tied to the motherly containment. This containment is manifested in, for example, the mother's and the child's mutual tactile touching, the caregiver's lap as a containing boundary and protecting ground and the bodily warmth and softness which the child is held in and spoken with. Here, we are dealing with something like an atmosphere or mood, rather than a visual world of different body parts (breast, penis) or specific capacities (give birth, breastfeed). An atmosphere that corresponds to feelings and sensations of, for example, warmth–coldness, soft–hard and smoothness–friction.

This atmosphere or mood has a global and indivisible character, rather than a selection of one or several outer objects which are perceived. It makes up a kind of background and original way of being in the world. It is from this background or atmosphere that we focus on certain objects in the world. For example, when I feel a nagging worry or anxiety, I will tend to become more aware of unkind, hard looks or persons that speak to me in a superior and cold way.

The motherly containment can be described as a continuity, which is both of pre-semiotic and pre-erogenous character, and which Francois Gantheret (1983) talks about as a "substantial continuity". The substantiated adjective "the motherly" is not to be understood as the mother as an object, but it is a determination (adjectivization) of the mother in her property as, or function of making up, a protecting continuity or as a substance according to the principle: "nothing is lost, nothing is newly created" (Ibid., p. 25). The maternal as substance "carries in its semantic being the idea of the diffuse, of the undivided, of the omnipresent support, of the connective tissue" (Ibid., p. 8). And it is important to notice that the relationship to this form of maternal body is described as pre-erotic (Ibid., p. 19).

The motherly reminds Gantheret about Winnicott's "the pure female element". In this formulation, "the pure female element", we can discern an incorporation of the mother, in that "the female element" does not refer to the breast and the mother as an object of drive satisfaction. Instead, this element relates to the breast or the mother in an entirely different way: *"the baby becoming the breast (or mother), in the sense that the object is the subject"* (italics in the original) (Winnicott, 1971/1991, p. 107). Winnicott connects the female element to the capacity to be or being, which precedes the capacity to do. The capacity to be presupposes exactly a holding surrounding,[1] whereas the capacity to do is associated with the male element and this object presupposes separateness; the male element is brought to the fore in the child's struggle to separate the ego from the nonego. When the separation has been achieved, the child can relate to others as objects, and thereby also experience drive satisfaction (in Winnicott's terminology also "id satisfaction"). It should be pointed out, to clarify, that the female and male elements are theoretical concepts, and exist, in normal cases, to varying degrees in both girls/women and boys/men.

This figure of thought, concerning the motherly containment as a background or a ground, resembles, to some extent, Matthew Ratcliffe's (2008) "existential feelings", which are based on earlier phenomenologists' thoughts, such as "mood" (Heidegger, 1927/1980) and "horizon" (e.g., Husserl, 1913/1962, 1920–1926/2001). Existential feelings are about feelings of belonging to the world and about the different ways in which we can belong to the world: the existential feelings stake out or constitute a "space of possibilities". And my perception of objects in the world takes place against the background of this emotionally constituted space of possibilities. According to Ratcliffe, the existential feelings are, in a certain sense, pre-intentional, and they are feelings that precede object intentionality. When we direct ourselves towards (intentional) objects, we are already in a situation or in a world in a specific way; the existential feelings are thus not objects *in* the world, but they are the horizon of significance from which intentional objects can be experienced. The intentional objects can be all sorts of perceptions, feelings and thoughts which are directed towards a certain object *in* the world, such as the fear of a certain phenomenon or the grief of the loss of a beloved person. But, as Ratcliffe says,

> before one feels afraid, one already has a sense of belonging to the world, of being in a situation *in* which one is afraid [...] In other words, one is attuned to the world in such a way that experiences of object-directed fear are possible.
>
> (italics in the original) (Ibid., p. 49)

The existential feelings are also experiences. They are felt, but not as objects which one directs oneself towards; they have a global character, and the distinction between self and world is more difficult to establish than what is the case for intentional objects. One way to describe the difference between the existential feelings and the intentional objects is that the former, by all means, are experienced, but they are not experienced *objects*. Thus, one must differ between experiencing, feeling, and the experienced object which becomes felt. For example, the feeling body must be distinguished from the experienced body/the body that is exposed to be felt. In other words, our body possesses the possibility to present itself both as a feeling body and as something that is felt; it is the feeling body that forms the existential feelings. In this context, it may be worth noting the importance of tactile sensations and the skin, which tends to be neglected in favor of the visual perception that often counts as the most important sense. However, to begin with, it is important to point out that there is not one particular sense which structures the existential feelings, but it is rather the human body in its wholeness that brings this about. The senses do have a synthetic character; they are intertwined with each other, in such a way that I can see the fragility of the glass or hear a person's cold and hard words. Ratcliffe writes: "Regardless of whether we see, touch, smell, taste or hear something, all our perception is structured by a background bodily orientation" and, he adds with the words of Merleau-Ponty, "I perceive in a total way with my whole being; I grasp a unique structure of the thing, a unique way of being, which speaks to all my senses at once" (Ibid., pp. 100–101).

Nonetheless, we find traits in the tactile sense which make it better equipped to capture the intimate relation between the human being and the world than what the visual sense, with its more objectifying character, is able to do.

> Touch [...] serves to illustrate something important about our relationship with the world: it is a matter of belonging and connectedness, rather than of full-scale confrontation between body and object [...] The intimate connection between existential and tactile feeling also indicates that there will be a variety of existential feelings, given that there are many different kinds of tactile experience.
>
> (Ibid., p. 97)

Psychoanalytic theory formation has also tended to be characterized by ocular centrism, in that it is the sight of, for example, the phallus, which has provided the foundation for understanding identity development. But there is one exception, and when it comes to the view of the importance of tactility for human beings and the psychic life, Ratcliffe's ideas are well in line with those of Anzieu. In his concept of the "Skin Ego", Anzieu (1989) developed a model that gives an original function to a containing, protecting envelope, before something like the pleasure principle/libidinal discharge begins to function. The two most important elements in the constitution of the Skin Ego are the skin's function and the early care of the infant. The function of the Skin Ego is to maintain the psyche in tandem with the skin's function to support skeleton and muscles. Furthermore, the Skin Ego entails an assimilation of that which Winnicott labeled "holding" and which involves the primary caregiver's concrete, physical and psychical care (e.g., Winnicott, 1960/1965, p. 49). Anzieu's idea is that the primary caregiver in the act of holding provides the infant/child with a kind of outer envelope, and thereby, it is possible that a fantasy of a common mother/child envelope is created. The optimal is if this fantasy about a common skin is of such a kind that it can keep the primary caregiver and the child together, and simultaneously notify their mutual separation. If the Skin Ego is not sufficiently containing, sexuality can be too traumatic: "[...] genital or even auto-erotic, sexuality is accessible only to those who acquired a minimum sense of basic security within their own skins" (Ibid., p. 39). And another illuminating quote is the following: "The Skin Ego fulfils the function of providing a surface for *supporting sexual excitation*" (italics in the original) (Ibid., p. 104).

The protecting envelope that the Skin Ego exerts can be structured in many ways. Anzieu mentions many forms of envelopes, such as the olfactory envelope, the sound envelope, the thermal envelope, the second muscular skin and even an envelope of suffering according to the motto "I suffer therefore I am" (Ibid., p. 201), which is to be understood as a way of recreating the containing function of the skin by inflicting on one's own body a real envelope of suffering. But of all these different envelopes, the skin is the structurally most important one, according to Anzieu: it is the skin that functions as a kind of basic reference point for the other senses, and it is not difficult to note similarities between Anzieu's and some other phenomenologists' views.[2]

And if we situate ourselves in a Kleinian frame of reference, we find an emphasis on touch and skin as the operative senses. One example is Thomas H. Ogden's (1992) suggestion that the autistic-contiguous position makes up the primitive psychological organization. This position concerns a sensory-dominated, pre-symbolic generation of experience. The term "autistic" is not to be understood in a pathological sense, but intends to depict "normal autism", designating isolation and disconnectedness. The term "contiguous", in this context, connotes the sensory connections, for example, the touching between the infant and the mother. It is in this original position that a rudimentary "I-ness" arises according to Ogden.

For Anzieu, the Skin Ego is a container, which, however, is not to be interpreted solely as something concrete. Here, I want to highlight that the body and the body experience is a dimension which does not mark a clear boundary to something outside the body, outside the concrete body surface area.

When the body experience functions in an adequate containing way, it is global; the feeling of being contained does not end, so to speak, at the boundary of the body, but a feeling of being contained does not differentiate between me and the world, between my body and that which, strictly speaking, lies outside my body. The experience of being contained deviates from a body experience which does not fulfill its containing function, when the body, for example, can feel attacked or poisoned. Apart from the body as a containing container/envelope or as something which is not containing, there is also the erogenous body: the body as content, to speak to Anzieu, for example, in the sense of the sexually stimulated body.

When the motherly function, which serves as continuity and provides a kind of background to more objectifying experiences, breaks down, this can be apparent in psychotherapeutic or psychoanalytic treatment. The motherly function in the primary caregiver's care of the child corresponds with the patient's relationship towards the frame of the psychotherapeutic/psychoanalytic treatment. The psychoanalytic situation includes both an outer and an inner frame. The outer frame refers to the regularity of the treatment: one meets at the same place, at specific times and for the same length each time. The inner frame is about the attitude and relationship of the psychoanalyst, which is to be characterized by an emotional stability and an engaging and open listening, with the purpose of alleviating the suffering by understanding the patient's inner world.

The psychoanalytic frame can evoke very different feelings with the patients (or with one and the same patient, depending on which problematic is uppermost for the time being), which reflect early experiences of motherly containment. With some, the frame can be experienced as a protecting shield, an existing continuity which is there as a silent background, against which the psychoanalytic work takes place, and which makes it possible to approach difficult and painful experiences, thoughts and fantasies. Other patients have a history where they have not been able to feel sufficiently contained or held: they have been forced to the defense of "self-holding" in Winnicott's words. For those patients, the frame and its nature can – consciously or unconsciously – easily come into focus. Painful questions are raised: What is it one is doing? What's the point with this? What meaning does it have? The psychoanalytic project can be experienced as deeply meaningless, and "meaningless" often has a confusing character. Instead of instilling an experience of continuity, constituted by the reoccurring sessions, each session in the psychoanalytic treatment is experienced as new and yields a feeling of separation and meaninglessness. I want to stress that this kind of anxiety, separation and feeling of meaninglessness, can be very deep and involves a feeling of existential desolation. It is a desolation which deprives life of its meaning, and here, "the meaning of life" is not a philosophical, intellectual question which can be answered in different ways, but in this case, it is a deeply lived meaninglessness, permeated by anxiety and desolation – this is what separation from the mother and difficult breaks in the motherly containment can signify. A personal history of not having felt contained does not, however, need to appear in such an open way in the psychoanalytic work in relationship to the psychoanalytic frame. One can defend oneself in many different ways: one can be very detached towards the psychoanalytic treatment, be indifferent to it, and experience breaks in it (e.g., the rather long summer break) as something irrelevant, or one can stick to the sessions as something one slavishly submits to, where a late arrival to a session can awake deep anxiety and worry that this process will end due to the late arrival.

On this existential level, one can talk about the infant's identification with the motherly containment. The identification is with the mother's way of containing the needs and feelings of the infant/child, not least feelings which are painful, anxiety-ridden and worried by nature. Thierry Bokanowski (2010) suggests that the child's primary identification with the motherly and feminine dimension includes two phases. The initial phase of this primary dimension is more often described as motherly rather than as feminine in its character, in the sense that the mother is completely preoccupied with the care of her child. In the second phase, the feminine aspect comes more to the foreground, and this phase is about the mother's libidinal, sexual attachment to the father. Bokanowski emphasizes that this transition from the first phase to the libidinally charged second phase can be experienced traumatically by the child. We recognize Bokanowski's thoughts from what was said above, in connection with Gantheret, Winnicott and Anzieu, that is to say, the importance of the motherly containment before one is able to handle such matters as sexually charged objects, for example, the mother as a sexually desirable object.

To meet helplessness with phallic masculinity

The core of the masculine attitude, the ideal, or what I here want to call a project, is the negligence of the foundational existential conditions, such as helplessness, transience and dependence. As I have emphasized earlier on, I refrain from talking about a masculine identity, since it is more appropriate to conceive of it as a project. The term "project" indicates that masculinity is a coveted but not yet realized possibility, as opposed to the term "identity" which describes an existing being.

Masculinity attracts here as a possibility, but one that will not be realized since the project essentially can be said to be about transcending the fundamental existential conditions: to ignore helplessness, transience and dependence implies a rejection of the motherly containment. It is, of course, a great challenge not only for the boy/the man but for each one of us to relate to these fundamental existential conditions, and my point is that the masculine project represents one of these attitudes.

Masculinity as a project becomes an unreachable dream of such a compelling character that it seems to throw one's identity as a man into (constant) crisis. Perhaps this circumstance gives us a clue to understanding the
many discussions about modern men being in a crisis, which we have heard
during recent years. In research on the history of masculinity, the turn of
the 19th century is often cited as a period of crisis, and in England at the end
of the 17th century. The historian David Tjeder, however, concludes, on the
basis of, among other things, advisory literature, that there was a concern
for masculinity during the entire 19th century; indeed, he questions whether
there has been any period without concern for masculinity. "Men were always assumed to have been more masculine before" (Tjeder, 1999, p. 179). If
we try to understand that assumption from a psychoanalytic perspective, we
can pose the question if it may rest on the child's projected father's imago, a
fantasy about masculinity as rescue.

How is one to understand that the existential conditions, such as helplessness and dependence, are handled by repudiating femininity/motherly
containment in the development of masculinity? The most important circumstance should be the traumatic separation from the primary caregiver/
the mother. An important psychogenetic factor in the construction of masculinity is the difference between the little boy and the mother. In Chodorow's (1978/1999) epoch-making work, *The Reproduction of Mothering*, a
number of aspects are mentioned in connection with this difference, such
as the length of the preoedipal period being shorter for boys than for girls,
that the identification between the boy and the mother does not have the
same mutual quality as the one between the girl and the mother. The boy
appears as the opposite to the (heterosexual) mother, and oedipal matters
like sexuality and masculinity are intertwined with preoedipal strivings for
separation and individuation. One difficulty for the boy, which easily leads
to a splitting of the relation with the mother, is that the mother is the first
and uniquely important object as caregiver, at the same time as a sexualiz-
ing and oedipalizing of her unfolds (Ibid., p. 188).

Adam Jukes (1993, 2010) stresses the profound traumatic experiences of
the infant's separation from the primary object/the mother, that is to say, the
separation from mother–infant dyad; a life-threatening event for the infant's
psyche which constitutes a "gendered psychosis". Masculinity is constituted
by how the separation and loss of the mother is dealt with in the oedipal
phase. It is as if this profound pain of separation, and in a certain sense the
loss of the mother, receives gendered meaning as a deferred action in the
Oedipus complex. This encapsulated gendered psychosis consists, later on
in life, of a splitting of men's expectations of women: one part based on the
idealized, life-giving mother and the other based on the boy's phallic masculine resolution of the Oedipus complex, where the castrated woman is the
inferior sex. The basis of misogyny in terms of the fear of the omnipotent
mother and the more or less hidden hatred towards women is a universal

phenomenon for men, with wide societal implications: "society needs men to have unresolved Oedipus complexes; that we continue to live with the fear of the father (the Law). A truly free man would represent a real threat to social organization" (Jukes, 1993, p. 114).

To be, so to speak, a "real" man, that is to say, a man who gives off the correct masculine signals, is not the outcome of a natural process of development but an achievement, something that is created or conquered. Masculinity is conquered and constructed in a manner which lacks a counterpart in the development of the girl to a woman. In the work of Diamond, we can read: "Basically boys do *not* grow up experiencing themselves as masculine by dint of being male; masculinity has to be typically proven repeatedly" (italics in the original) (2013, p. 15). Chodorow (1978/1999) describes masculinity as more unreachable and idealized than femininity is for girls. Masculinity is conquered by a negation; it is defined as *not* being femininity but as an experience of "otherness" (Kaftal, 1991). In many cultures, the transition from being a boy to becoming a man is done by means of different rituals, where the boy, sometimes very brutally, is separated from the mother and from women. In Sweden, it was used to be said that "the military service makes men of boys". But the construction of masculinity can also be discerned in how boys are educated when they participate in football teams (see Fundberg, 2003). What is essential is to break with boyishness and a boy's longing for his mother. What matters is to "stand up for himself", to not be a "milksop".[3]

Furthermore, many boys have to deal with a double burden vis-à-vis possible identificatory objects. With respect to mothers/women, as we have seen, we can talk about a negative identification, in the sense of their repudiation of motherly care, and with respect to fathers/men, we know they are often absent. Instead of having the opportunity to identify with a real father/man, boys are often left out to identify with cultural, sexist ideals (cf. Layton, 2004).

It is difficult to acknowledge the loss of the closeness to the mother as a loss, not least since the cultural norm is to distance oneself and reject dependence on the mother. Masculinity is highly rated in our culture, perhaps because it conceals the ground on which it rests, our vulnerability and our dependence. The difficulty in mourning the loss of the mother does not become less, when considering that masculinity is, to such a high degree, associated with initiative, activity and control – thus, the opposite to what mourning requires. It is telling, and not at all rare, that men express an inability to mourn by saying: "I don't know how to do!".

The masculine ideal certainly also contains a selfless generosity: one sacrifices oneself for one's country, one supports one's family, one indulges in an important social task or one goes all out for one's football team. Therefore, one may claim that there is a kind of giving in the masculine ideal which has its counterpart in the giving of the motherly containing. However, what does not fit in with masculinity, which may be the most important trait in the containing, both when it comes to the child–mother relation and the therapist–client relation, is to share an experience. It is a sharing that is about the mother/the therapist being able to feel and feel what the child is experiencing – a description which reminds us about the communicative meaning in projective identification. Masculinity is a reaction to such a sharing: it wants to feel free from the containing force; it wants to be self-sufficient. This is often played out in the therapeutic situation with male patients in the transference, when the therapist symbolizes the motherly containing function; the therapist's containing is then experienced as something sticky, viscous and frightening. An example from everyday life of one basically enjoyable experience, but which often stirs up deep discomfort with men, is a kind of unreserved exhilarated joy. The model here is when the mother and the child engage each other in a joint babbling. Such a situation can be described as an exclusive intersubjective sharing where all objective states of being are absent.

This kind of early intersubjectivity can be described as a "sharing" and an emotional attunement. In psychoanalysis, it has been common to describe the early mother–child relation in terms of activity and passivity. One of the great discoveries that came after Freud, concerning the boy's preoedipal phase, is the difficult task to cope with passive strivings in relation to the mother (Breen, 1993, p. 24). The terminology passive/active continues to be used in the literature, despite the fact that it has often been found to be problematic and unsatisfactory. A more adequate conceptual pair in this context could be receiving versus controlling. It is possible that the emotional difficulty to receive often is experienced as (inhibitive) passivity, but to use the passivity in order to describe psychological strivings runs the risk of concealing their emotional meaning.

Another aspect of the character of masculinity is the resistance to receive, in favor of the initial movement to go beyond, to transcend. In so far as this early mother–child relating has the character of being a mutual sharing, it does, indeed, involve an intersubjective experience of a more qualified kind than a mutual giving and taking.[4] It is a receiving that both the mother and the child experience as a receiving. Such a receiving can be difficult to contain, in particular for many men who experience that the possibility of a meaningful existence depends on individual sovereign achievements and going beyond one's existing conditions. The character of masculinity can be described as the opposite to the subjective attitude which opens itself for the receiving. One is unable to enjoy the natural pulse of life when the value of life is restricted to achieving. Thus, the masculine project tends, to a large extent, to deprive the person of the ability to experience the existence as a gift (more on this in Chapter 7).

So far, the focus has been on the primary caregiver/the mother, but some words should be said about the relation to the person who is outside the mother–child dyad, represented by the father. During this early phase in the child's life with the primary caregiver/the mother, the father comes in, first of all, as a possible support for the mother–child relation. But as was apparent in Chapter 3, the father also eventually forms a dyadic relation to the child. Benjamin (1995) has formulated a theory about the boy's *identificatory* love to the father, which can be developed in different ways. Here, I will limit myself to one scenario in this relationship, namely when the boy's identificatory love to the father provides a source for the idealizing of masculine power. This kind of polarizing identification with the father (the father vs. the mother) begins often in the preoedipal phase in order to reinforce in the oedipal phase, in which the polarization between masculinity and femininity comes into the foreground.

The boy's identification with the father is doubtless an important source for the construction of masculine ideals. In particular, it becomes important in the polarizing oedipal phase with the father as an object of identification and where the boy's penis is narcissistically charged. But the boy harbors a humiliation: his penis is small compared to his father's. Thus, the boy struggles with a challenge not only about sexual differences but also about the generation difference. The erect penis becomes a symbol which represents strength, initiative, capacity, dominance and independence. The narcissistic charge of the erect penis is, as Ruth Lax (2003, pp. 132–133) points out, not the same as the sexual pleasure that a penis can give, but is to be understood as a compensation for the boy's narcissistic humiliation of not being like his mother.

I have hitherto emphasized the existential challenge that the human being has to handle when it comes to her helplessness, vulnerability and dependence, and which constitutes the ground on which the masculine project rests. I will now move on to briefly discuss the two remaining challenges, whose hub is the boy's body, not least his penis, and his experience of shortcomings concerning sex development and sexual capacity.

Let me point out that the problematics that these later challenges bring about should be seen in light of helplessness and the dependence that the boy struggles with as his first challenge. It can be formulated as if the outcome of the first challenge forms a kind of background feeling to that which meets him as he approaches, and eventually enters, the oedipal situation.

(ii) Castration threat in relation to the pre-oedipal mother

If I, concerning the first challenge, emphasized the significance of the mother's containing function for the totally helpless and totally dependent child, I here, under this point, highlight other aspects of the preoedipal mother, especially those which are present in a somewhat later period of the preoedipal phase. An important event during this period is the boy's explicit discovery of the sex difference, which occurs sometime between the age of 18 and 30 months. The discovery of the sex difference breaks with the earlier undifferentiated and all-inclusive identity, and constitutes the crucial condition for the construction of masculinity (and, of course, for gender in general). Here, we are dealing with a mother who possesses abilities and body parts which the boy by nature lacks.

It is common to understand the discovery of this difference as a trauma, which evokes a number of very painful feelings for the boy. He can be neither his mother nor her sex. His wishes to identify with his omnipotent mother, to become like her, lead to shame. He feels envy towards her ability to give birth and her both nourishing and sexually exciting breast, a breast which also is big, "bigger than his penis", which is pointed out by Lax (2003, p. 132).

These feelings of inferiority and insufficiency towards the mother and women can be conceived of as a kind of preoedipal castration complex which the boy faces and which involves an extension of Freud's Oedipus complex. In earlier chapters, I mentioned that psychoanalysts have argued for an extension of the classic castration complex.[5] Castration anxiety has, among other things, been linked to the vagina, the big, unknown and dangerous hole, which the little boy's penis is too small for: the boy's inability to satisfy the mother or to give her a baby (cf., Brenner, 1979; Chassegeut-Smirgel, 1985; Horney, 1932; Jones, 1933; Person, 1986). Person pays attention to the fact that the anxiety of having been rejected by the mother, due to his insufficient genital equipment, is something that some men never get over, and therefore, one can say that these men "are destined to suffer lifelong penis envy" (1996, p. 80). Apart from the little boy's sexual inadequacy, the preoedipal castration anxiety has been connected to the separation from the mother, disturbances in the relation between mother and child and the omnipotence of the mother (Galenson & Roiphe, 1980; Person, 1986; Tyson, 1989).[6]

In line with an extended castration complex, Fast (1984, p. 65) has suggested a differentiation between two kinds of castration anxiety for men. An early version stems from questions which have to do with the sex difference, and then the castration refers to a loss of feminine qualities. The second and later versions of castration anxiety have to do with the oedipal rivalry with the father, and here castration refers to masculine qualities.

(iii) Castration threat in relation to the father

The third challenge facing the boy/the man is the classic Freudian castration anxiety, where the threat comes from the father as a reaction to the boy's sexual wishes and activities. It is this castration threat which puts an end to the Oedipus complex, in which the boy wishes to replace the father and be the mother's lover. When the boy meets the threat to lose his penis, he usually gives up his oedipal wishes in favor of the identification with the father.

Such an oedipal outcome means the establishment of the incest taboo and the constitution of the superego. Freud lets us know that the Oedipus complex requires more than an ordinary repression unless it is to have pathogen impact. What is required for an ideal dissolution is "a destruction and an abolition of the complex" (Freud, 1924, p. 177).

When working psychotherapeutically with a neurotic, heterosexual man, the oedipal castration complex often appears in the form of the rivalry, the competition and the comparison with the therapist, as well as, in particular, with male persons in the everyday life. On the surface it may look like it is a game with only men involved, but underneath these masculine expressions, women are to be found and ultimately even the mother. Chodorow notices that boys "turn their lives into search for success that will both prove their independence and win their mother" (1978/1999, p. 188).

Let me summarize this discussion about the masculine project. We have been able to see that the description of, in particular, the first challenge, the one which concerns the existential conditions of being a human being, applies for both men and women. Masculine ideals and the masculine project are certainly embraced first of all by men, but then also by women, and are in general highly esteemed ideals in our part of the world. Bokanowski (2010) notices the fact that men who show feminine tendencies experience them with shame and castration anxiety, whereas women do not seem to have any difficulties to come to terms with phallic strivings and masculine tendencies. This causes Bokanowski to wonder if the exclusively negative attitude to the feminine dimension has to do with the fact that for men this dimension is too intimately interconnected with the primary mother identification.[7] Such a denial of motherly containment and identification with the motherly dimension correspond, according to Birksted-Breen (1996), with an identification with the phallus – an identification which is also described in terms of a denial of lack and feelings which are associated with the lack, such as need, envy, fear, guilt and helplessness. Identification with the phallus partly explains the inequality between the sexes.

> It is this phantasy of penis as phallus which confers to masculinity its coveted position, and if we think of this phantasy as ubiquitous, it goes some way towards explaining social phenomena which have given men greater power and status.
>
> (Ibid., p. 651)

Even if the masculine project is highly esteemed both by women and men, nevertheless it is not coincidental that it is designated as a masculine project, and that we therefore somehow tie it to the male sex. But the connection between the male sex and the masculine gender should not be understood in terms of biological essentialism, as if masculinity were a natural and essential result of belonging to the male sex. The connection between the male sex and the masculine gender should be understood neither as merely an empirical generalization nor as a statistical connection between facts. I suggest that the masculine project can be described as *meaningful tendencies* which are manifested in the conditions under which the helpless boy is usually born and raised: ejected from a woman's body and thereafter with the mother/a woman as the primary caregiver, and a man as the third element in a family constellation, surrounded by a patriarchal structure. In other words, the masculine narcissistic defense allows itself to be used easier by a boy/man than by a girl/woman, given the masculine cultural ideal ascribed to an individual with a male body: a boy whose primary caregiver is the mother/a woman, and who identifies with the father/a man, who is also equipped with a penis.

Karl Ove Knausgård's *My struggle: A Man in Love*

I will round off this chapter by using Knausgård's (2014) enthralling struggle with himself in his novel *My struggle. A man in love* (Book 2 in his series of six books), in order to illustrate, in a speculative spirit, certain thoughts about phallic masculinity. In this second volume, we find a section where Knausgård feels humiliated and reduced in his masculine strivings. The two situations, from which I take my point of departure, are the one that takes place at children's party and the one in which Knausgård attends Rhythm Time class with his 8-month-old daughter.

Knausgård describes very well how he experiences situations of care to be very incompatible with being a man. Both at the children's party and at the Rhythm Time class, this expresses itself, among other things, as a strong feeling of estrangement vis-à-vis others: here are children and other adults, both women and men, with whom no community is shared. It is the others who laugh, chat about everyday things and socialize with one another. Knausgård's candid way of describing the situations reveals a person who distances himself from the others, something that he has done in his whole adult life since he has been prepared to be rejected. As a reader one takes part in a man's contempt for, and ridicule of, these situations, and between the lines, and one gets a glimpse of a human being who feels outside and who places himself outside.

Knausgård's readiness to be rejected indicates that this experience has been a pattern established (far back?) in the past. Naturally, the feeling of being rejected could have been experienced in many different situations. It is an inevitable experience owing to the impossibility that all the child's needs and wishes can be satisfied. Seen in light of the problematic which was revealed in connection with "the man's first challenge", we find a form of rejection that the boy often experiences in relation to his surroundings. Not rarely, the boy's expressions of vulnerability, smallness and need of consolation are met with detachment just because he is a boy. As we saw above, Chodorow mentions a number of circumstances in which the girl and the boy are met differently by the mother and the surroundings. For example, the preoedipal period is shorter for boys than for girls, and the identification between the boy and the mother tends to be of less mutual quality. The separation from the mother may be more difficult and more problematic for the boy, when oedipal and sexual aspects are more easily drawn into the boy's development towards separation and individuation.

If we move on to the so-called "second challenge", we can see how humiliating it can be to feel rejected by the mother due to one's insufficient genital equipment. We are reminded of Person's observation that this is something that some men never get over, which caused her to state that there are men who are "destined to suffer lifelong penis envy" (1996, p. 80). Hand in hand with the experience of being rejected, we find a feeling of inadequacy and emptiness, which seeks compensation by assimilating the masculine project, and as Emmanuel Kaftal (1991) points out, the assimilation of the masculine project begins early and many men never give it up.

Knausgård describes his relationship to his parents very differently. In relation to his mother, in the comparatively slight extent that she appears in the series of novels, there is closeness and warmth, whereas his relation to his father is particularly vulnerable and there is no room for being affirmed in his vulnerability and his dependence. As we have seen, the psychoanalytic theorizing has paid more and more attention to the importance of the father coming across as a good object of identification, where the father/masculinity does *not* represent the opposite to the motherly containment.

His existence as a caring father for, in the first place, his daughter Vanja, is a task that almost evokes a feeling of meaninglessness for Knausgård. His extremely extensive novel project (not to mention phallic with its six thick volumes!) has tarnished his relationship with Linda, his wife, and Vanja. But now it is Knausgård's intention to take responsibility for the family and the relationship, which does not turn out to bring any joy, but boredom instead: "A lot of effort was spent getting her to sleep so that I could read" (2014, p. 81). The early motherly containment seems to be a form of care, which, to say the least, makes Knausgård feel bored. I will discuss the conditions for the capacity to care in Chapter 6.

At the children's party and at the Rhythm Time course, the mothers of the children appear mostly as an anonymous mass, whereas the men are paid attention to in their individuality, although throughout in a feminized and negative way. One can describe the mothers as inoffensively foreign: they do not appear as rivals or competitors for something sought-after. Nor does he conceive of them as persons that could help him in his sprained situation, in that which gets the features of "hell", that is to say, "gentle and nice and full of mothers you didn't know from Eve with their babies" (Ibid., p. 87). I think this is an excellent description of an experienced atmosphere, a background feeling which is experienced as something threatening which one may be drawn into. An experience of hell quite reasonably makes us want to withdraw; in hell, the possibility to share an experience as something rewarding does not arise.

That which is foreign for the masculine project, and in Knausgård's description, is an equal subject–subject relation to others, not least to women (Benjamin, 1995; Karlsson, 2014). In Knausgård's description, the woman becomes neither rival nor potential asset, but becomes rendered "the Other" to use Beauvoir's (1949/2011) terminology – a position in which her subjectivity is deprived her, and where she is not involved in a struggle for recognition. In line with such a positioning, there is the possibility for her to appear as something almost mysterious: when Knausgård has returned home from his hellish experience, in connection with the Rhythm Time class, and explains his abhorrence about what he has experienced to Linda, the contrast between them is sharp. Linda becomes like an indulgent mother towards him and is capable to show a care for Vanja which was "so different. It was all-embracing. And completely genuine" (Knausgård, 2014, p. 97). This observation can also serve as a good illustration of Benjamin's analysis of a deficient mutual recognition of the other: Linda does not become another desiring subject, but rather something mystified, something quite different, where the complementarity between them takes the form of opposites.

Knausgård's text provides descriptions that make one think of a splitting between a (repudiated) containing motherliness and a sexually charged woman. An example of the latter is the young woman who is in charge of the Rhythm Time course, but who is reduced to an attractive sexual object. The only thing which Knausgård is attracted to, apart from her being young, is that she is extremely beautiful ("attractive young woman", "she really was attractive", "her smile was so attractive", "(h)er breasts were well formed, her waist narrow, her legs, one crossed over the other and swinging, were long and still clad in black boots", "stamping her attractive foot"). Such an inspection that Knausgård's evaluation reveals of the person in question, we can imagine from someone who, in his thought, has conquered the woman, who is in control of her. If we allow ourselves to speculate freely, such a wish can be about a striving of achieving a unity with the now separated mother (Manninen, 1993).

We get to know nothing about the young woman's capacity to lead the complex activity to implement baby rhythmicity in a group consisting of small children and parents. We may ask ourselves if this beautiful young woman also leads the activity in a containing and competent manner – and if this does not evoke problematic feelings. The whole situation is experienced as utterly disgusting and seems to awake castration feelings. Now Knausgård cannot feel superior and domineering, but quite the opposite:

> By sitting there I was rendered completely harmless, without dignity, impotent, there was no difference between me and her, except that she was more attractive, and the levelling, whereby I had forfeited everything that was me, even my size [my comment: here it is of course

hard avoiding not to associating to castration anxiety in different shapes], and that voluntarily, filled me with rage.

(Ibid., p. 86)

It is interesting to notice that his feeling that "there was no difference between me and her" simultaneously reveals that being a woman/feminine is "being harmless, without dignity, impotent". The only thing that stands out in a positive way has to do with possible attractiveness. We see an obvious splitting and polarization between seeing oneself in a subject position as a man/masculine and the inferior object position of being a woman/feminine. Furthermore, our feelings are overdetermined and stem from many sources; when it comes to this sequence, it may also reflect a splitting of the object: one senses a difficulty in uniting a containing motherliness with the woman who evokes desire and sexual lust.

Knausgård's description of the Rhythm Time course illustrates, furthermore, I believe, how an intimate intersubjectivity evokes deep disgust: it is also depicted in a ridiculous way when he speaks to his friend Geir. The situation is also exacerbated by the fact that the beautiful woman, who was in charge of the Rhythm Time course, is sexualized. This is how it sounds when Knausgård relates his experience for Geir (Ibid., p. 92):

> She was the teacher in charge of a Rhythm Time class for babies, so I had to sit there clapping my hands and singing children's songs in front of her, with Vanja on my lap. On a little cushion. With a load of mothers and children.
> Geir burst into laughter
> I was also given a rattle to shake.
> Ha ha ha
> I was so furious when I left I didn't know what to do with myself, I said. I also had a chance to try out my new waist line. And no one was bothered about the rolls of fat on my stomach.
> No, they're nice and soft, they are. Geir said, laughing again.
> Karl Ove, aren't we going out tonight?

Knausgård describes an episode which, first of all, evokes anger and which, in my simplified and schematic structure, perhaps illustrates that which above was described as the second challenge. "What the *fuck* had that got to do with me" (italics in the original) (Ibid., p. 54) – Knausgård asks, after a woman at the children's party had confided in him that she was hoping for a sibling to her only son. We can imagine a man who has felt attacked by an improper seduction, where a "no" may stir up both guilt and a feeling of not being able to manage a sexual challenge.

In the description of the contact with other men, we can take part in an initial ranking, where the other one becomes either something inferior, despised and feminine or something threatening masculine; to share experiences with the other one is not considered a possibility. It should be part of the logic of ranking that it easily leaves one lonely and vulnerable. The host father at the children's party seeks contact and asks if everything is fine, which stirs up feelings: "If he'd had a pronounced or strong character, that might well have bothered me, but he was dithery in a weak-minded, irresolute kind of way, so whatever he might be thinking didn't worry me in the slightest" (Ibid., p. 29). Men who take care of children, who are with their children at Rhythm Time classes or go around with buggies, are devoted to "feminized" activities, which yields a two-edged contempt, since he as a father feels captivated in this parenting microcosm where no value can be found.

The only person who stood out at the children's party is a man with a large face and scarred cheeks, coarse features and intense eyes. He is dressed in 50s style and has a typical slicked-back hairstyle, including side burns. He does not say much but stands out and is different in his charisma. I do not think that it is too audacious to guess that this charisma indicated strength and independence, something that in this context personified phallic masculinity. This man evokes the memory of a man, a boxer, who at a party had made Knausgård feeling inferior and not energetic enough, since it was the boxer who kicked open the toilet door that had become stuck for Linda, highly pregnant at the time, so she could come out. In this description, there are elements of comparison and competition between men, and simultaneously of shame in front of women, for example, in front of the hostess who suggested that the boxer and not Knausgård should kick open the toilet door. Here the contempt has uncovered self-contempt and shame, not least by the fact that women are turned into dangerous subjects, in a dynamic that is made up of a subject–object, and not subject–subject relationship.

Let me finish the reflections on Knausgård's novel by again referring to his relation with his friend Geir, who, of course, did not attend the children's party or the Rhythm Time class, but with whom he shares his experiences. It is, admittedly, a friendship with a distinctly "boyish" character, where undisguised vulnerability is conspicuous by its absence. It also seems to exclude the presence of children, as when Geir wants Knausgård to come by his workplace without Vanja. It is with Geir who Knausgård talks on the phone an hour every day and with whom he has rewarding and educated conversations, in sharp contrast to all the everyday routines in the "small world".

Notes

1 Winnicott writes:

> Either the mother has a breast that *is*, so that the baby can also *be* when the baby and the mother are not yet separated out in the infant's rudimentary mind; or else the mother is incapable of making this contribution, in which case the baby has to develop without the capacity to be, or with a crippled capacity to be.

(italics in the original) (1971/1991, p. 110)

2 Anzieu writes:

> Even supposing that it is not chronologically anterior, the skin possesses a structural primacy over all the senses and this is true for at least three reasons. Firstly, it is the only sense organ that covers the whole body. It itself also contains several distinct senses (heat, pain, contact, pressure…) whose physical proximity entails psychical contiguity. Lastly […] touch is the only one of the five external senses which possesses a reflexive structure: the child who touches the parts of its body with its finger is testing out the two complementary sensations, of being a piece of skin that touches at the same time as being a piece of skin that is touched

(1989, pp. 61–62)

Not least the last reason is identical with, for example, Husserl's and Merleau-Ponty's analysis of the tactile sense and which they make a big point of.
3 A question may be raised concerning how the idea that masculinity is not the result of a natural development, but something that, to an even higher degree than femininity, must be conquered, harmonizes with Beauvoir's most famous statement from *The Second Sex:* "One is not born, but rather becomes, woman" (1949/2011, p. 293). I think that the views are compatible, but that the becoming of femininity and masculinity, respectively, is done in different, but symptomatically, ways for these, to a large extent, opposite gender constructions. Beauvoir's idea about the feminine becoming deals with how the girl and the woman are constituted and are ascribed a passive character, which in no way is biologically given, but the outcome of education and the surrounding's impact. As has been pointed out by several theoreticians, neither the boy's development to a (masculine) man comes about in a natural way, but must be conquered. In contrast to the development of femininity, to become a (feminine) woman, the boy's path to become a (masculine) man is lined with the challenge to conquer masculinity, for example, in the form of activity or to endure tough trials in environments that mothers/women have no access to.
4 The meaning of the term "relating" is, of course, quite different from its connotation with Winnicott in his discussion about "object-relating" and "the use of an object" (see Winnicott, 1971/1991, ch. 6).
5 Chasseguet-Smirgel is one of those psychoanalysts who have argued for an extension of the castration complex:

> I propose that we add to the castration complex, as an intrinsic part of it, the painful feeling of inadequacy of the pregenital child unable to satisfy mother and to give her a child. The castration complex thus understood enables us to link it to what precedes it: separation anxiety.

(1985, p. 86)

6 Person points out that the man's fear of the woman stems from different levels of development:

> The male's fear of the female, of his inability to please her (and his anger at her) stem from different development levels: fear of the preoedipal mother who abandons/engulfs, of the anal mother who intrudes/indulges, of the phallic-narcissistic-level mother who falsely seduces/denigrates masculinity, of the oedipal mother who cannot be fulfilled, rejects, falsely seduces.

(1986, p. 20)

7 How psychoanalysis tends to relate to this motherly containment is pointed out by Monique Schneider: "Generally, psychoanalysis doesn't want to know anything about this enveloping power because it reactivates a sort of deep feminine and maternal identification" (from Breen, 1993, p. 33).

References

Anzieu, D. (1989). *The skin ego.* Yale University Press.

Beauvoir, S. de (1949/2011). *The second sex.* Vintage Books.

Benjamin, J. (1988). *The bonds of love. Psychoanalysis, feminism, and the problem of domination.* Pantheon Books.

Benjamin, J. (1995). *Like subjects. Love objects. Essays on recognition and sexual difference.* Yale University Press.

Benjamin, J. (1998). *Shadow of the other. Intersubjectivity and gender in psychoanalysis.* Routledge.

Bion, W.R. (1962). *Learning from experience.* Karnac.

Birksted-Breen, D. (1996). Phallus, penis and mental space. *International Journal of Psychoanalysis, 77,* 649–657.

Bokanowski, T. (2010). Vicissitudes of the feminine dimension in men and bisexuality in the analytic situation. In L.Glocer Fiorini & G. Abelin-Sas Rose (Eds.) *On Freud's "femininity".* Karnac.

Breen, D. (1993). General introduction. In D. Breen (Ed.) *The gender conundrum.* Routledge.

Brenner, Ch. (1979). Depressive affect, anxiety, and psychic conflict in the phallic-oedipal phase. *Psychoanalytic Quarterly, 48*(2), 177–197. Doi:10.1080/21674086.1979.11926874

Chassegeut-Smirgel, J. (1985). *Creativity and perversion.* Norton.

Chodorow, N.J. (1978/1999). *The reproduction of mothering.* University of California Press.

Diamond, M.J. (2013). Evolving perspectives on masculinities and its discontents: Reworking the internal phallic and genital positions. In E. Ester Palerm Mari & F- Thomson-Salo (Eds.) *Masculinity and femininity today.* Karnac.

Fast, I. (1984). *Gender identity.* Analytic Press.

Freud, S. (1924). The dissolution of the Oedipus complex. *The standard edition of the complete psychological works of Sigmund Freud, 19.*

Fundberg, J. (2003). *Kom igen, gubbar! Om pojkfotboll och maskuliniteter.* [Come on chaps! On boy's soccer and masculinities]. Carlssons.

Galenson, E. & Roiphe, H. (1980). The preoedipal development of the boy. *Journal of the American Psychoanalytic Association, 28*(4), 805–827. Doi:10.1177/000306518002800403

Gantheret, F. (1983). L'impensable maternel et les fondements maternels du penser. *Nouvelle Revue de Psychoanalyse, 28,* 7–27.

Heidegger, M. (1927/1980). *Being and time.* Basil Blackwell.

Hollway, W. (2006). *The capacity to care: Gender and ethical subjectivity.* Routledge.

Horney, K. (1932). The dread of woman: Observations on a specific difference in the dread felt by men and women respectively for the opposite sex. *International Journal of Psycho-Analysis, 13,* 348–360.

Husserl, E. (1913/1962). *Ideas. General introduction to pure phenomenology,* vol. I. Collier Books.

Husserl, E. (1920–1926/2001). *Analyses concerning passive and active synthesis. Lectures on transcendental logic.* Kluwer Academic Publishers.

Jones, E. (1933). The phallic phase. *International Journal of Psycho-Analysis, 14,* 1–33.

Jukes, A. (1993). *Why men hate women.* Free Association Books.

Jukes, A.E. (2010). *Is there a cure for masculinity?* Free Association Books.

Kaftal, E. (1991). On intimacy between men. *Psychoanalytic Dialogues, 1*(3), 305–328. Doi:10.1080/10481889109538902

Karlsson, G. (2014). Mannens tre utmaningar. [The man's three challenges]. *Psykoterapi, 2,* 16–25.

Knausgård, K.O. (2014). *My struggle. A man in love.* Book 2. Vintage Books.

Lax, R. (2003). Boy's envy of mother and the consequences of this narcissistic mortification. In A.M. Alizade (Ed.) *Masculine scenarios.* Karnac.

Layton, L. (2004). *Who's that girl? Who's that boy? Clinical practice meets postmodern gender theory.* Routledge.

Manninen, V. (1993). For the sake of eternity: On the narcissism of fatherhood and the father-son relationship. *The Scandinavian Psychoanalytic Review, 16*(1), 35–46. Doi:10.1080/01062301.1993.10592287

Ogden, T.H. (1992). *The primitive edge of experience.* Karnac.

Person, E.S. (1986). Male sexuality and power. *Psychoanalytic Inquiry, 6*(1), 3–25. Doi:10.1080/07351698609533615

Person, E.S. (1996). The omni-available woman and lesbian sex: Two fantasy themes and their relationship to the male developmental experience. In G.I. Fogel, F.M. Lane & R.S. Liebert (Eds.) *The psychology of men.* Yale University Press.

Ratcliffe, M. (2008). *Feelings of being. Phenomenology, psychiatry and the sense of reality.* Oxford University Press.

Solomon, R.C. (1998). Death fetishism, morbid solipsism. In J. Malpas & R.C. Solomon (Eds.) *Death and philosophy.* Routledge.

Tjeder, D. (1999). Konsten att blifva herre öfver hvarje lidelse. [The art of becoming master of all suffering]. In A.M. Berggren (Ed.), *Manligt och omanligt i ett historiskt perspektiv.* [Manly and unmanly in a historical perspective]. Rapport 99:4, Forskningsrådsnämnden. [Swedish Council for Planning and Co-ordination of Research].

Tyson, P. (1989). Infantile sexuality, gender identity, and the obstacles to oedipal regression. *Journal of the American Psychoanalytic Association, 37*(4), 1051–1069. Doi:10.1177/000306518903700409

Winnicott, D.W. (1960/1965). The theory of the parent-infant relationship. In his *The maturational processes and the facilitating environment. Studies in the theory of emotional development.* The Hogarth Press.

Winnicott, D.W. (1971/1991). *Playing and reality.* Routledge.

5

Ego-identity and the possibility of emancipation

Let me roughly recapitulate the ground we have covered so far. We are, to some extent, back in the problematic that was dealt with in Chapter 1, that is to say, the question of how the sex/gender question is to be conceptualized. We could look at many theoreticians' views of how complicated, tangled and confused the area is. It has been difficult, in a satisfactory way, to define the concepts "sex and gender". Opinions differ widely concerning the relevance and validity of these concepts as well as the meaning of the possible relation between them. In Chapter 1, I claimed that the phenomenological philosophy, with its concept of intentionality, could be of help in order to clarify the structure of the sex/gender area. The concept of intentionality implies that there is always a correlation between subject and object, between the subject pole and the object pole. Phenomenology rejects both objectivism (the postulation that the object has a certain property independent of the subject) and subjectivism (the object is reduced to something that is confined in the subject). The objective/the object is given from a subjective horizon, and the subjective meaning bestowing/constituting is directed towards, and presupposes, the object. My epistemological and ontological positioning was to take a first-person perspective, from which the structure of sex and gender should be described.

A common way of conceptualizing sex and gender has been to differentiate them in the sense that sex is determined by the person's biology, while gender involves cultural and psychological meaning. The designations "woman and man" are used when sex is referred to, while gender refers to the feminine and the masculine. In the tricky and difficult discussion about sex and gender, there are many ways in which the relation between them is described. Two common opposite positions can be represented in terms of a biologistic and a poststructuralist view. From the biologistic viewpoint, cultural and psychological meaning (gender) are reduced to sex in the sense of the natural, scientifically defined biological body. Within poststructuralism, gender is conceived of as a social construction: gender represents social and cultural interpretations of sex. In a radical version, it is claimed that even biological sex is a construction: there is no given, non-constructed

DOI: 10.4324/9781003352761-6

sex on which a cultural and social interpretation of gender rests. The phenomenological alternative – to biological essentialism, which maintains an objective nature independent of a meaning bestowing subject, as well as to poststructuralism where the body exclusively is a representation – is to affirm a bodily natural being in light of a meaning bestowing subject.

Within psychoanalysis, the concepts "sex and gender" are often treated in an unclear way. Often the term "gender" is used when "sex" would probably have been more adequate and vice versa. Often, no distinction is made between those terms, but a clear position that I describe in Chapter 1, and which most likely is representative for many psychoanalysts' view, signifies a middle path between biology and culture: gender is a kind of construction with connections to the human being's biology. But this kind of the third path between biologism and poststructuralism has been criticized for adopting a body-mind dualism.

In Chapter 1, I defended a position entailing a distinction between sex (woman/man/intersex) and gender (feminine/masculine) without being trapped in body-mind dualism. In line with Bigwood's (1991) thinking, it is necessary, I believe, in a certain sense, to renaturalize the body by means of Merleau-Ponty's explication about the subjective, the so-called "living body". Here, the body gets a more constant character in relation to a cultural, language-determined gender. Bigwood stresses that this is not to be understood in terms of a causal relation between body and gender, but that the body has an "indeterminate constancy" in its indissoluble intertwinement with cultural and personal layers of meaning. The natural and the cultural body are born simultaneously, even if it is important to analytically separate them. To formulate the distinction between sex and gender in this way constituted a theoretical vantage point in this work, from which the analysis of phallic masculinity could be carried out. In other words, gender can be seen to represent the individual's relation to the sexually cultural-conditioned meaning: all historical, social and cultural meaning that has been identified with one's sexual identity/sexual body calls for *an answer*, for a position on existing masculine ideals. And in this chapter, I want to, among other things, discuss the implications of such an answer in the form of either striving for a gender identity or a rejection of the idea that there is something as a gender identity, that is to say, the claim that there exists a specific meaning attached to one's sex.

The masculinity which has been in the foreground in previous chapters is the phallic one, which traditionally has been described in terms of control, dominance, strength, sovereignty, independence, etc. In the literature, there is no lack of voices which claim that masculinity can express itself in different ways, even in ways which traditionally can be conceived of as feminine. There is reason to issue a warning here, since the terminology risks becoming unnecessarily obscure if the masculine values and qualities are the same as the feminine. The difference between femininity and masculinity then loses its significance. Naturally, gender research should make it possible to discover similarities and identical traits between women and men, but without conceptualizing femininity and masculinity as identical. Apart from this semantic reason for differentiating femininity and masculinity, I want to, like some other psychoanalysts, maintain that that which constitutes masculinity is essentially a repudiation of femininity/motherliness.

When it comes to the view of gender, the psychoanalytic thinking has been influenced by social constructionism and its emphasis on gender being something changeable and culturally conditioned, and that there are several forms of gender identity. As has been apparent, I do not use the designation identity in relation to gender, but reserve the concept of identity for a person's experience of their sex. However, it is undoubtedly the case that masculine ideals vary over time and place, even though one also ought to consider that different expressions of masculinity may conceal a non-shifting inner problematic. The development within psychoanalysis and other disciplines, such as gender studies, has nevertheless been to acknowledge a more multiple significance with the gender categories, and that the meaning of masculinity is more comprehensive than it was assumed to be in the past. In Chapter 3, I discussed three forms of masculinity: hypermasculinity, phallic masculinity and demasculinized masculinity. But in this chapter, I will go beyond the insight that masculinity is changeable and multiple, by enriching the sex/gender discussion with the concept of ego-identity. By introducing ego-identity into the discussion, I believe that a more stringent conceptual apparatus can be obtained within sex/gender research and that we can more easily liberate ourselves from stereotypical gender ideals. Besides, it also shows the relevance of the concept of authenticity in the sex/gender discussion.

The necessity of introducing ego-identity into the sex–gender discussion

Today's discussion about gender opens up for a multiplicity of gender forms and a crossover of gender identities. These ideas can be seen as a development of Freud's idea of bisexuality. A contemporary influential theoretician is Benjamin who argues for the significance of a crossover of femininity and masculinity in an individual. Such an integration of femininity and masculinity is, in particular, a task to be accomplished in the postoedipal phase that follows after the polarizing oedipal phase in which the opposite sex is repudiated (Benjamin, 1988, 1995). Benjamin suggests two different complementary forms:

> The earlier oedipal form is a simple opposition, constituted by splitting, projecting the unwanted elements into the other; in that form, what the other has is "nothing". The postoedipal form is constituted by

sustaining the tension between contrasting elements so that they remain potentially available rather than forbidden and the oscillation between them can then be pleasurable rather than dangerous.

(Benjamin, 1995, p. 73)

In *The Bonds of Love*, Benjamin ambiguously describes the possibility of going beyond the gender dichotomy. On the one hand, she argues that gender and gender identity cannot be eliminated and that individuals should integrate femininity and masculinity. On the other, she asserts the existence of "a genderless subject", when she concretizes her ideas: "Thus a person could alternately experience herself as 'I, a woman; I, a genderless subject, I, like-a-man' A person who can maintain this flexibility can accept all parts of herself" (Benjamin, 1988, p. 113).[1] Diamond follows the idea that a healthy adult masculine gender identity presupposes that one attains Benjamin's postoedipal phase with its integration of femininity and masculinity. This is also a deconstruction which is limited to gender categories: "Notions of what is masculine and feminine can thereby more comfortably destabilize, as finite categorization of gender identity is superseded by the complexity of one's multiple, differently gendered identifications" (Diamond, 1997, p. 456). I, for my part, want to go one step further than the idea of a crossover of feminine and masculine traits in one and the same person, by arguing for the validity of an ego-identity seen from a first-person perspective, which is neither feminine/masculine nor a kind of mixture of these gender categories.

Within academic masculinity research, Richard Howson has talked about the need to take a step back from gender momentarily, deconstruct the asymmetry between femininity and masculinity (which characterizes the hegemonic masculinity; see Chapter 1, endnote 4) and analyze the identity "human". And human "is a thing whose matter expresses both gender expressions" (2009, p. 15) – a contradictory existence of both femininity and masculinity. This idea reminds us, to a certain degree, of Benjamin's overinclusive position of being both feminine and masculine. I think that the same critique, in principle, can be launched against Howson as against Benjamin: he does not go far enough in the deconstruction. The conceptualization of the human seems still to be confined to the gender dichotomy.

So, what I would like to bring up is an old idea from the 1950s which Harry Stack Sullivan touched upon by his so-called "one genus postulate", in the sense that "we are all more human than otherwise" (from Kaftal, 1991, p. 319). I believe that this phrasing "we are all more human than otherwise" indicates an important point that transcends gender and cannot be understood based on bisexuality or some kind of crossover of femininity and masculinity. This line of thought is also found in the work of Mariam Alizade (2010, p. 199) when she expresses the importance of not restricting focus to sex and gender, but paying attention to the simple fact that we are first and foremost human, something that she thinks that psychoanalysis has not dealt with in sufficient depth.

In other words, the constitution of human identity requires a conceptualization that is not locked in a gender dichotomy: we need to reserve a place for an ego-identity beyond the femininity and masculinity genders. It concerns ego-identity that both precedes gender and is developed beyond the gender dichotomy, as a kind of humanizing that is an inherent possibility for the human being to strive for authenticity.

There are a number of arguments for emphasizing the priority of the ego-identity in relationship to gender.[2] Below, I will develop the following four arguments: (i) a structural argument, (ii) a developmental psychological argument, (iii) an ethical argument and (iv) an existential, experiential argument.

i) Let us begin with the structural argument that gender structure presupposes ego-identity. Before I can experience myself as gendered, as gender constituted, I must be an ego ("I"). Thus, in all determination of gender, there is an ego presupposed. The constitution of gender (femininity, masculinity) is based on a generalized idea of what it means to belong to a particular sex. For example, masculinity becomes the de-individualized idea of what it means to be a man. Here one can also reiterate the point Alizade has made: "In the beginning, before having been classified as male or female, a human being is born" (2010, p. 203).

In this context, one could also refer to Ricoeur's (1992) discussion about identity in terms of *ipse* (identity as self-hood) and *idem* (identity as sameness), where *ipse* concerns a self-constancy that is not dependent on some unchanging core of the personality. By means of *ipse*, continuity can be made comprehensible in spite of change, variation and discontinuity on the side of *idem*. These two identity limits sometimes more or less overlap one another, but *ipse* can also appear without the aid or support of *idem* (cf. Lundin, 2003). Ricoeur quotes *The Man without Qualities* by Robert Musil (1930/1996), as an example of *ipse* without the support of *idem*. Here, we have a self-hood (*ipse*), but without the support of something that can be described in terms of the same properties over time (*idem*). If *idem*/the same answers the question "what are you?", *ipse*/the self is concerned with the question "who are you?". As an illustration of Ricoeur's idea of identity as self-hood (*ipse*), we can imagine the changes that a person experiences going through a therapeutic process: the person can look at himself ("I") as always having been so keen on being courageous, a behavior that he no longer feels is necessary to manifest. From these thoughts, we may conclude that even after a radical change that a person may undergo in a therapeutic process, an identity, in terms of *ipse*, is still to be reckoned with. In other words, there is an ego that binds together the person before and after the changed behavior.

ii) In line with the above structural point of view, the earliest identity formation is about ego-identity. We encounter this ego-identity in, for example, Anzieu's (1989) so-called "Skin Ego" and Ogden's (1992) idea about the "autistic-contiguous position" as the psyche's most primitive organization in which a rudimentary "I-ness" emerges. The ego on this rudimentary level can be specified as body-ego, which does not entail explicit self-awareness. It is not only clinical psychoanalytic experiences that corroborate the existence of such an early body-ego. This ego-identity is oneself in the first-person perspective and is given as an innate, direct experience of oneself from the very beginning of one's life long before one has the experience of being sexed. If the ego-identity inherently and necessarily belongs to one's experiential streaming, one's sexual identity is something secondary. Thus, if one is faithful to an infant's first-person perspective, it is hardly reasonable to assume that its experiences involve a sexual dimension. Consequently, the original source of identity formation is the differentiation between I and others and not the differentiation between different sexes.

iii) An ethical argument for the priority of ego-identity in relation to the gender constitution concerns the capacity to acknowledge responsibility. To acknowledge responsibility, in a psychoanalytic context, means to acknowledge and own up to one's subjectivity, not only ones overt actions, but also ones inner life in terms of feelings, fantasies, dreams, etc.. In other words, in the psychoanalytic ethic concerning taking responsibility, there is an effort to feel and acknowledge one's subjectivity, where possible gender-based actions and determination of gender can be conceived of as being the outcome of an inauthentic attitude. For example, trying to live up to a masculine ideal may comprise an alienation from one's predicament. The idea of gender can thus be an impediment in the striving for authentic psychical development and increased acknowledgment of one's subjectivity. I am thinking of an experience that is not uncommon with male patients, namely the wish to control painful feelings and their expressions, not least sorrow and crying, which is nourished by the idea that crying is unmanly, girlish and wimpish. When the man feels freer to express his feelings, in this example, sorrow and the need to cry, he will not consider these feelings in light of the gender dichotomy.

iv) Finally, I want to formulate an existential, experiential argument. There are experiences in life that cannot be reduced to reflect a cultural determining horizon. I would claim that both with respect to ourselves and others, there is the possibility of a transcendent movement away from conceptualizing our experiencing based on objective categories. Merleau-Ponty has expressed this de-categorizing experience that is rooted deep in humankind:

Consciousness can never objectify itself as sick-consciousness or as disabled-consciousness; and, even if the man complains of his old age or the disabled person of his disability, they can only do so when they compare themselves to others or when they see themselves through the eyes of others, that is, when they adopt a statistical or an objective view of themselves; and these complaints are never wholly made in good faith: in returning to the core of his consciousness, everyone feels himself to be beyond his particular characteristics and so resigns himself to them.

(1945/2012, p. 458)

Even if Merleau-Ponty's examples concern disability and age, his principal argument can be extended to all sorts of categorizing of the human being, for example, in terms of sex and gender. Merleau-Ponty's reasoning can also be extended to apply to my relation to the other. When I genuinely open myself to the other human being, I see someone beyond objective determinations. I see a unique being independent of comparison and calculation. Intense existential situations, such as love or a vigil at someone's deathbed, may awaken such an experience and attitude. Furthermore, I am sure that many animal owners, in their interaction with their beloved pet, have seen a unique You that goes beyond the mere perception of a cat or dog.

I think that some of Buber's (1923/1970) reflections in his book *I and Thou*, where the *I-You* relationship is unveiled, can be of help in describing an intimate intersubjective situation in which an ego-experience transcends a relationship based on an attitude of categorizing the other, a so-called "I-It relationship".[3] Buber talks about the human being's "twofold attitude", in accordance with the basic words that can be spoken. These basic words are word pairs: I-You and I-It. They are never a single word, never just an "I". From the beginning, there is a relation and the basic relation or, in other words, the basic word pair is I-You, which is exclusively "spoken with one's whole being" (Ibid., p. 54).[4]

The difference between these two-word pairs is that I-You is a subject–subject relationship, whereas I-It is a subject–object relationship. Buber lets us know that He or She can replace it without changing the meaning. In I-You, there is presence and openness for the relation. Indeed, "(t)he basic word I-You establishes the world of relation" (Ibid., p. 56). The relationship between I and You is unmediated, whereas the word pair I-It depicts something mediated and remote from You. As I interpret Buber, I-You captures the uniqueness of a genuine relationship. This relationship is not obscured by seeing the other one in terms of categories or certain qualities. Buber states poetically:

When I confront a human being as my You and speak the basic word
I-You to him, then he is no thing among things nor does he consists of
things.

   He is no longer He or She, limited by other Hes and Shes, a dot in the
world grid of space and time, nor a condition that can be experienced
and described, a loose bundle of named qualities.

(Ibid., p. 59)

Buber's prioritizing of the I-You relationship should not be understood as if
one could do without I-It; this kind of attitude is inevitable. The I-You relationship can never last forever, and You turns into It, since one cannot only
live in the present. Nevertheless, I-You is the basic word pair, and only that
word pair captures what it means to genuinely be a human being. We learn
that whoever lives only with It "is not human" (Ibid., p. 85).

   In my clinical work, I am struck by how traumatizing and painful it is to
have felt unloved by one's parents. Buber's description of the I-You relationship captures the core of love. Love is, no doubt, difficult if not impossible
to intellectually grasp and to put into words. However, one characteristic
of love is that it reflects a relationship and that love contains the person
who is in love. Love is more than feelings: the one being able to love is also
contained. I think that Buber has expressed this in a pithy way: "Feelings
one 'has'; love occurs. Feelings dwell in man, but man dwells in his love"
(Ibid., p. 66).

   By introducing the ego-identity in the discussion about gender, I believe
that we (i) gain a clearer and more cogent conceptual apparatus within sex/
gender research, (ii) facilitate the possibility to free ourselves from stereotypical gender ideals and (iii) are able to take help of the authenticity dimension in the gender discussion.

Gender and authenticity

As we have seen, sex and gender have undergone a significant deconstruction in many respects during the last few decades. Examples can be given in
the form of the existence of a multiplicity of identities, crossover of femininity and masculinity, the intersectional character of gender or an unconscious
meaning which rules under the so-called "afterwardness" or "deferred action" (*Nachträglichkeit*; Chapter 2, endnote 20). In Chapter 4, I suggested
another kind of deconstruction, namely that masculinity as a project is
doomed to failure. I break with tradition here, not least the psychoanalytic
one, which conceptualizes gender in terms of identity.[5] Besides, I have argued for the concept "ego-identity" as something irreducible in relation to
sex/gender, and I think that authenticity has an important role to play within

this field of research. Furthermore, one can notice that many psychoanalysts emphasize the transformation of the meaning of sex/gender during one's whole life, in terms of, for example, the concept "afterwardness". Here, I want to highlight another factor which is much too absent in the theorizing around sex/gender, namely the human being's self-reflecting capacity, which can transform the meaning of gender-masculinity in a very far-reaching way by questioning its validity as grounds for one's actions and experiences. I am here referring to a self-reflection that thus says no to one's character being determined by ideas about one's sex. The capacity of self-reflection has bearing on one's ability to take a critical stance to conventions and traditions, and thereby constitutes a resource in the development of self-identity.

My point of departure has been to discuss the sex/gender area from a subjective perspective by means of psychoanalysis and phenomenology, and not from a third person perspective. In other words, statistical correlations of typical male behaviors as masculine and typical female behaviors as feminine are irrelevant in this context. This kind of research, from a third-person perspective, has definitely a function, but here it is of no relevance since it neither addresses a phenomenological first-person perspective nor a psychoanalytic (subjective) perspective.

By situating the discussion within a subjective perspective, we can bring to the fore an emancipatory dimension in the form of authenticity, that is to say, the possibility for a subject to take responsibility for its subjectivity. By introducing the concept ego-identity as something beyond the gender dichotomy, it is possible to bring in authenticity as a relevant dimension. In my view, the idea of authenticity presupposes an ego-identity, which does not allow itself to be reduced to the gender categories.

Another factor, maybe not a presupposition but which nevertheless makes it easier to bring in the concept of authenticity in the field of sex/gender, is *not* to conceive of gender in terms of identity. The concept identity is legitimate when discussing sex, but not when it concerns a possible striving for gender identity. There are many circumstances which make it problematic to talk about gender as an identity.[6] For the possibility of possessing a gender identity, it is necessary that one is a specific gender, which I find not to be the case due to this striving's negative character. By negative character, I do not primarily mean something destructive or damaging, but that the striving for a gender identity has a compensatory character. The masculine project's negative character entails different aspects. The masculine project or ideal is a narcissistic defense against our existential conditions and painful experiences, and thereby fundamentally an act of estrangement (Karlsson, 2012). It is not uncommon that men in therapy/psychoanalysis initially describe their masculine strivings in positive terms, in order to later discover that these strivings are the outcome of feelings and self-images, which are the opposite of what the masculine ideal prescribes.

Masculinity defines itself as *not* feminine/motherly, the boy as the opposite of the mother, his first object of identification. In line with this, Benjamin (1995, p. 61) talks, for example, about gender as only "partly attainable", and Chodorow (1978/1999, p. 176f) describes masculinity as unattainable. Owing to this complicated character, it is not surprising that men have always felt worried about their masculinity (Tjeder, 1999). Masculinity as a project is doomed to failure since it basically is about a denial of existential conditions. And we can add that masculinity does not only imply a denial of the existential conditions; it even "makes claims" to embrace their opposites: the existential condition of vulnerability is turned into the masculine trait of invulnerability, the existential condition of dependence is turned into the masculine trait of independence. It seems to me to be more adequate to talk about masculinity as being the crisis instead of that masculinity is in a crisis.

Another interesting observation, which can be made with respect to masculinity and its lack of being able to form an identity, is its contradictory appearance. In order to be experienced as an identity, the different appearances/sides of an identity need to harmonize to make up a gestalt. However, judging from a study on the appearances of masculinity in the psychotherapeutic situation, as experienced by therapists and patients (Ulenius, 2022), masculinity appeared as a very contradictory experience. To give one example: masculinity could be seen as polarized vis-à-vis femininity as well as non-polarized vis-à-vis femininity. When considering all the different appearances that were connected to the experience of masculinity in Jakob Ulenius's study, I was struck by the incoherence of the phenomenon. To illustrate it with a perceptual metaphor, it reminded me of a false front in the Hollywood, in the sense that something that looks like a house when you are standing in front of it reveals itself to be only a mere façade when you try to walk around it.

Here, I repeat what was said before about the relation between sex and gender: one way of formulating the relation between the sexual identity and gender as project is to say that gender represents the individual's relation to the sexually, culturally conditioned meaning. What in my opinion makes the introduction of gender necessary is that all historical, social and cultural meaning that has been identified with one's sexual identity/sexual body calls the individual to *answer*. And such an answer takes the form of either a striving for gender identity or a rejection of the idea that there is something like gender identity, that is to say, the claim that there exists a specific meaning tied to one's sex.

In Chapter 1 (p. 22), I illustrated how a problematic can exist concerning the experience of male sexual identity. Here, I briefly want to illustrate a difference between the striving for a masculine identity (masculinity as project) and an attitude to, or an experience of, oneself where the weight of the gender dimension decreases. Here, we have an example of a man who does not feel any doubt about his sex that he is a man, while a change is discernable during the psychotherapeutic/psychoanalytic treatment when it comes to gender/masculinity, in the sense that even though a striving for phallic masculinity keeps living on, it diminishes in strength. Such a change can be traced concerning his wish to be a successful womanizer, expressed by his many and unexpected sexual conquests, which, however, will be considered in a different light: they go from being experienced as something entirely unproblematic to something which is experienced as compulsively necessary in order not to feel discouraged and unattractive. Important features in such conquests can be that a "real man" can conquer women sexually, is not afraid of taking the initiative to approach and conquer women, and can impress them with one's sexual potency and skill. To be restrained, to lack courage to initiate contact and approach women he finds attractive can evoke a strong feeling of humiliation, to the extent that even if a sexual invitation is hopeless, it is still better to have shown courage to have tried than not having the guts to try such an initiative. In spite of everything, it may feel comforting to still have shown oneself that one dares even if it is hopeless. Eventually, the attitude and relationship to masculinity can change and the pressure to be a "real man" tones down, which can be manifested in many different ways, for example, to come to understand, in a thoughtful way, that certain masculine ideals are repressive and oppressive. Another way can be bodily lived, in that sexuality is something that can give pleasure and joy together with another, rather than being a question of achievement.

What I want to draw attention to in this context is that the changed experience with respect to sexuality and masculinity need not mean that the man, in his identity, feels more feminine than before, as if the mixture of gender has changed proportions, but here are occasions which must rather be understood as that the gender dimension (masculinity and femininity) has lost its importance and perseverance. Clearly, albeit subtly, one can comprehend that feelings and experiences come closer the subjective living, rather than ideas about masculinity ideals rule strivings and actions.

The risk with the phenomenon of gender is that one conceals the individual's choice, by letting their actions be legitimated from a presumed gender identity. I cannot perceive that any behavior (for instance, aggressivity, care, determination and sensitivity) should be valued differently depending on the individual's sexual identity. It is just as wrong for a man as for a woman to commit violent acts and just as wrong for a woman as for a man to be passive if the situation calls for resolute actions. The crux of the matter is when behaviors which are statistical typically for the different sexes are reified to designate allegedly inherent gender characteristics.[7]

An individual's striving for a presumed given identity, on the basis of a specific sex, can, in a Sartrean sense, be said to be an expression of inauthenticity (*mauvaise foi*) (cf. Sartre, 1942/1956). The inauthenticity lies in the fact that I escape my freedom by legitimizing my behavior in terms of my sexual being. It is as if I say that "I am male, and I should therefore act resolutely since resoluteness is a trait of masculinity". In such a case, it is as if I choose to transform myself into an idea instead of accepting my own subjectivity. I act as a (phallically masculine) man, try to be something, something in-it-self, and find narcissistic pleasure in, for example, being described as "a real man". In other words, it is a way of essentializing and reifying oneself at the price of abstaining from one's freedom.

The notion of authenticity applied here does not focus upon the content of one's actions or feelings; authenticity does not equal valuable feelings and actions, such as, for example, feeling sympathy for someone, being resolute in helping someone in distress and aiding someone in financial hardship. These may all be praiseworthy feelings and actions, but do not have anything to do with authenticity. The distinct meaning of authenticity in this context is the subject's acknowledgment and readiness to admit, not rarely, painful, diffi-cult, conflictual feelings and actions as one's own, as being part of oneself. To describe it within the framework of the psychoanalytic project: the authentic state is an act of responsibility, acknowledging one's subjectivity by making denied, foreclosed, split and repressed sides of oneself one's own.[8]

Let me, to finish this chapter, quote Gayle Rubin's dream of a genderless, but not sexless society.[9]

> I personally feel that the feminist movement must dream of even more than the elimination of the oppression of women. It must dream of the elimination of obligatory sexualities and sex roles. The dream I find most compelling is one of an androgynous and genderless (though not sexless) society, in which one's sexual anatomy is irrelevant to who one is, what one does, and with whom one makes love.
>
> (1975, p. 204)

And I believe that we find the same hope with Beauvoir:

> When finally it is possible for every human being to place his pride above sexual differences in the difficult glory of his free existence, only then will women be able to make her history, her problems, her doubts and her hopes those of humanity; only then will she be able to attempt to discover in her life and her works all of reality and not only her own person. As long as she still has to fight to become a human being, she cannot be a creator.
>
> (1949/2011, p. 767)

We have to keep coping with different gender ideals, but we can try to reveal their structures in the purpose of liberating ourselves from them.

Notes

1 In Chapter 3, I described Diamond's (2004) observation about feelings that are evoked in middle age can make possible, in the best-case scenario, an integration of feelings that previously had been rejected because of their associations with femininity and motherly containing. And in a later text, Diamond (2013, p. 19) claims that the aging man is forced to undergo changes with respect to gender ideals. Phallic ideals, previously associated with becoming a man, have to give way to less grandiose ideals associated with becoming a person. However, Ambrosio (2013) contests the idea that aging should necessarily signify such a development and the idea that the possibility of becoming a person belongs to aging.

2 My arguments are sometimes shaped on the basis of the priority of ego-identity in relationship to sex and not gender. However, if ego-identity is to be conceived of as prior to the sexual identity, this implies that it is also prior to possible strivings for gender identity. What is important to keep in mind when reading these arguments concerning the relationship between ego-identity and sex is that the priority of ego-identity concerns a logical relationship from a *first-person perspective*.

3 In a new translation of Buber's work, *I and Thou* from the German title *Ich und Du*, Kaufmann translates Du in the Ich–Du relationship to You and not Thou, which is closer to the German original and connotes something "spontaneous and unpretentious, remote from formality, pomp and dignity" as opposed to the high-flown Thou (Kaufmann, 1970, p. 14). I comply with Kaufmann's translation in my discussion of Buber's work.

4 Stoltenberg (2000, p. 304ff) uses Buber's different relational ways of being. He describes the socially constructed masculinity, manhood, as the paradigm of injustice, which is characterized by the word pair I-It. The authentic self, the selfhood, which breaks with and liberates itself from masculinity, is capable of seeing the other according to the unmediated word pair I-You.

5 Quindeau writes: "Since the 1970s, at the latest, the question of masculinity and femininity has largely been addressed in terms of identity in the psychoanalytic discourse" (2013, p. 75).

6 Goldner (1991, p. 249) thinks that the idea about gender identity reflects a normative ideal which psychoanalysis has absorbed uncritically. Instead of gender identity, she conceives of gender as a necessary fiction. See also Stoltenberg (2000) who problematizes a socially conventional constructed hierarchizing gender identity (manhood) and advocates an authentic selfhood.

7 Moi remarks that to use the terms "feminine" and "masculine" as descriptive positive features risks fostering sexual-based stereotypes, which she claims is in line with Beauvoir's thinking:

> "Feminine" and "masculine" are excellent terms of critique, but I would hesitate to use them positively, to take them as guidelines for my own work [...] Beauvoir's denunciation of femininity as a patriarchal concept is a critique of ideology. As such it is still as valid as when it was written. Regardless of whether we believe that masculinity and femininity are manifestations of deep sexual essences or the products of dazzling discursive performances, the very fact of continuing to label qualities and behaviours as "masculine" and "feminine" will foster sex-based stereotypes.
>
> (2005, pp. 106–107)

8 Weir asserts that "(t)he self-identity of the adult depends on the ability to 'take over and be responsible' for integrating all of the different, often conflicting,

positions one takes, into a narrative that is meaningful to others and to oneself" (2012, p. 274).

9 Moi joins Rubin and writes: "Ultimately, I think we should follow Gayle Rubin's suggestion and stop thinking in terms of gender altogether. To me, that means trying to produce a society without sexist ideology or gender norms, without oppressive myths of masculinity and femininity" (2005, p. 112).

References

Alizade, M. (2010). Femininity and the human dimension. In L. Glocer Fiorini & G. Abelin-Sas Rose (Eds.) *On Freud's "femininity"*. Karnac.

Ambrosio, G. (2013). Discussion of "Evolving perspectives on masculinity and its discontents: Reworking the internal phallic and genital positions". In E. Ester Palerm Marí & F. Thomson-Salo (Eds.) *Masculinity and femininity today*. Karnac.

Anzieu, D. (1989). *The skin ego*. Yale University Press.

Beauvoir, S. de (1949/2011). *The second sex*. Vintage Books.

Benjamin, J. (1988). *The bonds of love. Psychoanalysis, feminism, and the problem of domination*. Pantheon Books.

Benjamin, J. (1995). *Like subjects. Love objects. Essays on recognition and sexual difference*. Yale University Press.

Bigwood, C. (1991). Renaturalizing the body (with the help of Merleau-Ponty). *Hypatia, 6*(3), 54–73. Doi:10.1111/j.1527-2001.1991.tb00255.x

Buber, M. (1923/1970). *I and Thou*. Charles Scribner's sons.

Chodorow, N.J. (1978/1999). *The reproduction of mothering*. University of California Press.

Diamond, M.J. (1997). Boys to men: The maturing of masculine gender identity through paternal watchful protectiveness. *Gender & Psychoanalysis. An Interdisciplinary Journal, 2*(4), 443–468.

Diamond, M.J. (2004). Accessing multitude within: A psychoanalytic perspective on the transformation of masculinity at mid-life. *International Journal of Psychoanalysis, 85*(1), 45–64. Doi:10.1516/3PFY-NQMU-C95F-HH0W

Diamond, M.J. (2013). Evolving perspectives on masculinities and its discontents: Reworking the internal phallic and genital positions. In E. Ester Palerm Mari & F. Thomson-Salo (Eds.) *Masculinity and femininity today*. Karnac.

Goldner, V. (1991). Toward a critical relational theory of gender. *Psychoanalytic Dialogues, 1*(3), 249–272. Doi:10.1080/10481889109538898

Howson, R. (2009). Deconstructing hegemonic masculinity: Contradiction, hegemony and dislocation. *NORMA (Nordisk tidskrift för maskulinitetsstudier), 4*(1), 6–24.

Kaftal, E. (1991). On intimacy between men. *Psychoanalytic Dialogues, 1*(3), 305–328. Doi:10.1080/10481889109538902

Karlsson, G. (2012). Maskuliniteten som projekt. [Masculinity as a project]. *Divan, (1–2)*, 15–25.

Kaufmann, W. (1970). I and You. A prologue. In M. Buber (Ed.) *I and Thou*. Charles Scribner's Sons.

Lundin, R. (2003). *Identitet och beslutsfattande. Konstitution, relation och kreation*. [Identity and decision making. Constitution, relation and creation]. Stockholm University, Department of Education, Doctoral dissertation.

Merleau-Ponty, M. (1945/2012). *Phenomenology of perception.* Routledge.

Moi, T. (2005). *Sex, gender, and the body. The student edition of "What is a woman?".* Oxford University Press.

Musil, R. (1930/1996). *The man without qualities,* vols. 1 and 2. Vintage.

Ogden, T.H. (1992). *The primitive edge of experience.* Karnac.

Quindeau, I. (2013). *Seduction and desire. A psychoanalytic theory of sexuality beyond Freud.* Karnac.

Ricoeur, P. (1992). *Oneself as another.* The University of Chicago Press.

Rubin, G. (1975). The traffic in women: Note on the "political economy" of sex. In R.R. Reiter (Ed.) *Toward an anthropology of women.* Monthly Review Press.

Sartre, J.-P. (1942/1956). *Being and nothingness. A phenomenological essay on ontology.* Simon & Schuster.

Stoltenberg, J. (2000). *The end of manhood. Parables of sex and selfhood.* Routledge.

Tjeder, D. (1999). Konsten att blifva herre öfver hvarje lidelse. [The art of becoming master of all suffering]. In A.M. Berggren (Ed.), *Manligt och omanligt i ett historiskt perspektiv.* [Manly and unmanly in a historical perspective]. Rapport 99:4, Forskningsrådsnämnden. [Swedish Council for Planning and Co-ordination of Research].

Ulenius, J. (2022). *Maskulinitetens mening. En fenomenologisk undersökning av den psykoterapeutiska situationen.* [The meaning of masculinity. A phenomenological investigation of the psychotherapeutic situation]. Department of Education, Stockholm University. Doctoral dissertation.

Weir, A. (2012). Toward a model of self-identity. Habermas and Kristeva. In J. Meehan (Ed.) *Feminists read Habermas. Gendering the subject of discourse.* Routledge.

6

The character of care and what phallic masculinity neglects

Phallic masculinity is grounded in a defense against existential conditions, such as helplessness, vulnerability and transience. It also stands as well as in opposition to any course of action which could soothe these threatening feelings, namely an affirmation of dependence and care. The meaning of care exists more or less as an explicit antidote when it comes to phallic masculinity. In this chapter, I will put the spotlight on care with its origin in an intersubjective relation permeated by, among other things, helplessness and dependence.

I have repeatedly stated, in this book, that phallic masculinity does not want to recognize the motherly containment. The expressions "the motherly containment" and "care" are not synonymous; the motherly containment can be conceived of as an essential element in, at least, some forms of care. The care that I refer to here entails a subject–subject relation. And an important trait in the motherly containing subject–subject relation is a sharing of experience. To share experiences encompasses an *emotional* opening up to the other, something that goes under the ego's controlling radar.

A spontaneous reaction to the word "care" is often the feeling that it connotes something burdensome and self-sacrificing (which in our society tends to exclusively be understood negatively). Jeff Hearn maintains that to be a man has traditionally meant an avoidance of care (from Elliott, 2016, p. 244). Karla Elliott (2016) propagates for a caring masculinity which is a more satisfying and nourishing model of masculinity than hegemonic masculinity (see Chapter 1, endnote 4). More precisely, she describes caring masculinities as masculine identities free from supremacy and domination in favor of emotional, relational qualities and an affirmation of mutual dependence.

The fact that care can be experienced and understood as something rewarding, and which does not need to be connected with a deprivation for the self, is brought forth by Wendy Hollway:

> The idea of a primary or necessary opposition of interest between self and others not only derives from an individualistic ontology, it also renders invisible the profound pleasure of the kind of caring that is woven

DOI: 10.4324/9781003352761-7

into the fabric of daily life [...] From an intersubjective perspective, a
virtuous circle of care can be established whereby a person can take
pleasure in another's pleasure who also reciprocates.

(2006, p. 12)

The deep pleasure to be found in care can involve a higher degree of intimacy, more than that found in the outcome of a mutual giving and taking.
Hollway talks about the existence of care and pleasure "in the same act"
(Ibid., p. 104). I believe that in some respects it is difficult to distinguish between giving and receiving care. In an analogy with Buber's analysis of love
(see this volume, Chapter 5, p. 109), one can claim that care/containment is
not so much a case of something that one has but more something that one
dwells in. To express it in a concise way, one can say that when one cares, one
simultaneously dwells in, or is contained in, care.

The capacity to care

Hollway (2006) develops her theory of the capacity to care in a relationship
within an ongoing discussion between a feminist care ethic and a Kantian
ethic of justice. Feminist theoreticians have launched a critique against a
Kantian model of ethics based on values such as autonomy, abstract thinking and rationality, which has been identified as typically masculine (cf. Gilligan, 1982).[1] The care provided by mothers has been a controversial topic,
since it can easily be considered as a (conservative) preservation of sexual
roles. However, I believe it would be a mistake to interpret Hollway as a conservative thinker. Instead of talking about mothers, it would be more appropriate to say motherly containment, which does not necessarily presuppose
that it is a mother or a woman who represents this kind of containment.
Consequently, Hollway differentiates between sex and gender:

Here I want to be explicit about the distinction between sex differences
and gender differences (a distinction that unfortunately has been lost
with the dominance of a social constructionist paradigm on identity
that claims that all differences are socially produced and therefore gender differences) [...] Gender differences are much more complex, open-
ended and unpredictable.

(2006, p. 36)

In line with my earlier argument concerning the relationship between sex
and gender, one is to expect that certain experiences and behaviors are represented to varying degrees by a particular sex owing to, among other things,
gender ideals. Hollway gives expression for such an expectation, when she
asserts that, generally speaking, girls and women, to a larger extent, adopt an
ethic of care in relation to others in comparison with what boys and men do,

despite the complexity, open-endedness and unpredictability, apparent in the above quote, and the "seismic" changes that the relationships have gone through in society.

The point of departure for Hollway's theorizing is that human beings all relate to one another, but that the capacity to care is not innate, even though such a capacity can be developed, provided that one has received good enough care in one's own infancy. She maintains that the capacity to express care to oneself, to others, to nonhuman beings and to the environment/surroundings corresponds to one's own experiences of an early motherly containment.[2] Hollway's point is that an infant's incapacity to care partly depends on its incapability to put itself in the other's predicament and partly does not have an experience of a self.

Hollway consults psychoanalysis in order to understand the unconscious processes of significance for the capacity to care. The original situation of utmost importance which calls for care is the child–mother relation, which is asymmetric: a helpless infant who needs the care of the mother in order to survive physically and psychically. The child's dependence on the mother cannot be exaggerated, a fact that Winnicott has captured in the sentence: "There is no such thing as an infant", with which he meant that "whenever one finds an infant one finds maternal care, and without maternal care there would be no infant" (1960/1965, p. 39, note 1). However, care presupposes both separation and connectedness to the other, according to Hollway, who is critical of viewing them as incompatible as is often the case in the literature of care.

To endure separateness requires psychical work; it means to giving up an omnipotent, controlling way of being. This can only be achieved if the mother has the capacity to receive anxiety and emotional suffering and be able to contain and give it back in a "digested" way, a favorable form in terms of so-called "projective identification". If this unconscious intersubjective communication – projective identification – does not work, the development can bring about that which Bion has called "nameless dread". The experience of nameless dread might be a consequence of a mother's incapability to contain a child's fears, for example, a sense of dying:

> If the projection [i.e., the infant projects into the mother that it is dying] is not accepted by the mother the infant feels that its feeling that it is dying is stripped of such meaning as it has. It therefore reintrojects, not a fear of dying made tolerable, but a nameless dread.
>
> (Bion, 1967, p. 116)

Another way of describing this terrifying experience of the non-contained infant is by referring to Winnicott's description of psychotic anxiety as *unthinkable*. This kind of unthinkable anxiety can sometimes express itself in a feeling of falling, to fall forever, and where the defense is exerted by a *self-holding*, that is to say, a holding which the individual uses when the surrounding's holding is insufficient. To fall, and the fear of falling, was a theme that I touched upon, in Chapter 3, as a masculine expression of unmanliness – the anxiety which is connected with appearing unmanly in light of masculine ideals. In the work of Winnicott (1963/1989), it is a fear of *breakdown* described as a universal phenomenon in the sense that everyone can empathically grasp how it feels, when a patient expresses this feeling in a clear way. While some patients suffer from it, but not others, it is nevertheless understood by all.

Winnicott's thesis is that this fear of a future breakdown goes back to a breakdown that has already been experienced. More precisely, we are dealing with the breakdown of a defense organization, of the establishing of a somewhat unified self, which has to do with defending oneself from unthinkable anxiety. The idea that the breakdown, so to speak, already has happened is due to a traumatic early experience, where neither the ego development nor the surrounding's containing/holding was adequate to prevent the experience from becoming traumatic (Winnicott, 1963/1989). Like Bion, in connection with nameless fear, Winnicott also talks about death – an annihilation which the infant was not sufficiently mature in order to experience and where the surrounding's containing was insufficient. Winnicott describes how patients do not fear death but *fear of dying* when "there is no one there, that is to say with nobody there who is concerned in some way that derives directly from the very early infant-parent relationship" (1965/1989, p. 124).

In a strict sense, I think it is unfortunate to use the term "experience" for these early breakdowns. I believe that here we are talking about a breakdown that could not be experienced, which now motivates the individual to seek the experience of this kind of non-experienced state, or, more precisely, non-experienceable state. Winnicott (1965/1989) discusses whether it is possible to experience complete breakdown of the defense organization, and his conclusion seems to be that the infant lacks a sufficient ego-organization in order to be able to do it.

As mentioned, Hollway drew attention to the gender factor in the motherly containment. Among other things, she discusses the boy's development with respect to loss, separation and be a boy/a man, and leans heavily on Benjamin's theory of development. A crucial question is whether the boy in a defensive manner repudiates the motherly and the feminine, or if he will be able to keep the good and bad feminine, as well as the masculine, sides in himself and in the other, and thereby be able to identify himself with the mother's capacity to care. I will not go on to discuss different possible developing scenarios for the boy, but instead say something briefly about Hollway's view of the importance of gender for the capacity to care.

If I have understood Hollway correctly, her basic view is that there are many aspects that are relevant when it comes to providing a beneficial care of the infant. It would be a mistake to interpret her as a representative of biologism in the sense that only the mother has the capacity to care for the infant or is the one who is naturally the most adequate, or that a woman necessarily is more appropriate than a man to provide care. The capacity of the mother, the woman, the father and the man depends on many personal circumstances and experiences, which is why one cannot reduce the capacity to care to the question of sexual belongingness. On the other hand, Hollway believes that certain aspects of sex and gender character should be considered.[3]

From a structural point of view, it is of significance to be the first, primary care giver, in comparison with taking over as the second. The second is also called the third (in relation to the first caregiver and the child), as well as being the first who comes from the outside, while the mother and the infant constitute a combined psyche–soma unity, according to Winnicott.

The conditions for the primary caregiver are different, depending on if it is the mother or another person, and this is for many reasons. One such reason is, in reference to Winnicott's notion, that psyche–soma makes up a unity between the mother and the child. The early combined psyche–soma between the mother and the infant, in which the infant is a part of the mother's body, also colors the child's later experiences, and contrasts to the later person's (coming from the outside, often the father's) entry, into the child's world.[4] Holllway believes that the father thereby represents separation in a way that the mother will never do (for simplicity we assume that it is the father who is this person coming from the outside). The child's separation from the mother is done under very different conditions than is the case with the separation from the father. The fact that the child comes from the mother's body has a specific significance: at best it facilitates the child's self-development in the separation from the mother; however, depending on the mother's psychical constitution, it can also make up an obstacle. In other words, even if the mother and the father, in principle, can perform the same functions (motherly and fatherly), one cannot rule out that in the child's inner world these functions, nevertheless, to some degree, are of different significance, in that the child is born from the mother's body.

> Perhaps we can conclude that, while fathers can perform the maternal and paternal functions (and mothers both these factors too), in the internal world of the child, these will never be entirely interchangeable as long as the infant is born out of the mother's body.
>
> (Hollway, 2006, p. 90)

Another reason that sex and gender norms play a role in the experience and understanding of care is the phenomenon of deferred action, or afterwardsness (*Nachträglichkeit*), and existing sex/gender structures within culture and society. Even if the infant does not have any sense of sexual differentiation until about 18 months of age, it can still subsequently ascribe meaning from the point of view of the sexual aspect. Such a deferred action can, for example, imply that even in families that do not hold to traditionally sexually differentiated care of the child, the child can still live with traditional ideas: "even if qualities of the real family act in the direction of dissolving traditional gender differences, this does not guarantee that a child will grow up associating care with both sexes" (Ibid., p. 84).

Above, I have described the significance of the motherly containment, regardless of whether it is represented by a woman or a man, in order to transform that which is difficult to endure to something which is an endurable experience and thereby make life feel meaningful. If the motherly care is responsive enough and adapted to the physiological and psychological needs, such as containment of anxiety and frightening experiences, then this painful, problematic and difficult process can be turned into something positive and life affirming.

The care and the motherly containment are necessary not only to keep away psychic illness but also to give room for the possibility of joy of life. With Winnicott, we can observe that a good, holding surrounding represents the difference between an experience of chaos and a development towards a creative life. "Creativity" is an important concept for Winnicott and does not denote anything like artistic creativity or some kind of achievement, but rather the capacity, or perhaps it is more appropriate to say the possibility to experience the world as meaningful, which to Winnicott equals health: "It is creative apperception more than anything else that makes the individual feel that life is worth living" (1971/1991, p. 87).

Creativity is to be understood not as a capacity which can be acquired but as a kind of driving force to health which is inherent in human beings. One does not need to possess a special talent in order to live creatively: Winnicott claims, for example, that one can look at a tree in a creative way. If one were to be bold enough to combine Winnicott's language with the notions of immanence and transcendence, I do not think it is too farfetched to say that creativity belongs to immanence and that it is the foundation for transcendence.[5] The following can be read in the work of Winnicott:

> To be creative a person must exist and have a feeling of existing, not in conscious awareness, but as a basic place to operate from.
>   Creativity is then the doing that arises out of being. It indicates that he who is, is alive. Impulse may be at rest, but when the word "doing" becomes appropriate, then already there is creativity.
>
> (1986, p. 39)

Authentic meaning creation, creativity, to feel real and alive, and health are different sides of one and the same phenomenon. Winnicott developed several concepts in order to explicate this kind of creative living, such as the spontaneous gesture, transitional phenomena, true self and playing: they make up innate possibilities which demand a good enough relationship between a child and a caregiver in order to be developed. It is this early and original intersubjective predicament which can instill a sense of joy in our everyday existence.

The value of immanence

The terms "immanence and transcendence" are not used in the psychoanalytic theorizing about gender but have been applied in feminist theorizing ever since Beauvoir's (1949/2011) description of masculinity and femininity in *The Second Sex*. Beauvoir links masculinity to transcendence in that it captures the human character of going beyond itself, creating and constructing new things, whereas her description of the woman's situation in terms of immanence is to "maintain the species and care for the home" (Ibid., p. 455). Beauvoir's exclusively negative view of immanence as endless and repetitive housework has been challenged by Young (1997) who has argued for another potential that the idea of a home can carry. No doubt, Young agrees that, to a large extent, the home has historically functioned in an oppressive way for women, but Beauvoir's unequivocal negative image is a mistake:

> Beauvoir is right to link her account of women's oppression with domestic work, but not entirely for the reasons she has. A sexual division of labor that removes women from participation in society's most valued and creative activities, excludes women from access to power and resources, and confines women primarily to domestic work is indeed a source of oppression. Much of typically women's work, however, is at least as fundamentally world-making and meaning-giving as typically men's work... preservation is ambiguous; it can be conservative and reinterpretive, rigid and fluid.
>
> (Ibid., pp. 155–156)

Beauvoir fails to see the creative aspect which can also be a part of traditional household work and which Young names as *preservation*. Preservation can be seen as a kind of support for personal identity and meaning maintenance: preservation and the traditionally male-sounding construction are both necessary. Young argues for a feminist policy which articulates the positive values that a home can be connected with and which could demand that these values were extended to be embraced by all. She specifies the following four normative values that a home can have: *safety*, in the sense that it is a place where everyone can feel safe; *individuation*, in the sense that home is necessary in order to develop an individual existence and that a home is an enlargement of one's body; *privacy*, in the sense of the function of the home as a place where the person herself decides and has control; and, finally, *preservation*, which was mentioned above and which points towards the function of the home as building and rebuilding one's self.

I would like to connect Young's description of the (positive) possibilities that a home has to the notion of "immanence". Roughly speaking, in Beauvoir's *The Second Sex*, a dichotomy is built up between immanence and transcendence, which I believe is in line with the phallic masculine project. Immanence and transcendence become incompatible: only transcendence is recognized as valuable, in that it goes beyond the existing and creates something new. The phallic masculine (transcendent) character implies a rejection of values connected to immanence.

I would like to argue for the value of immanence. My suggestion is that this, in a certain sense, primary level of experience not only entails vulnerability, anxiety and feelings of helplessness, but can also entail the possibility of a positive existence. In support of this idea, I actually want to refer to Beauvoir, but this time from another viewpoint than the above. As a matter of fact, in *The Ethics of Ambiguity*, Beauvoir (1947/1976) depicts two different ways of being in the world: one of which is "wanting to be" (which I connect with phallic masculinity) and the other one is "wanting to disclose being" (which I connect to an openness for our existential conditions, such as vulnerability and immanence). This "wanting to be" is striving for an identity which is not a possibility for human beings, but which one can persevere in, in a self-deceptive way, in bad faith (*mauvais foi*). We can imagine the attitude: "I'm a man and therefore it is my task to be in control of the situation". Human beings are not destined to be in a certain way but are, so to speak, thrown out into the world in freedom, one can "want to be" something specific in the hope of escaping existential anxiety: human beings want to be something "in-oneself", one strives for a definitive existence, away from freedom, anxiety and responsibility. What I find reassuring in Beauvoir's analysis is that such a project, to be something "in-oneself", which is doomed to failure, is not our original way of being in the world. "There is an original type of attachment to being which is not the relationship 'wanting to be' but rather 'wanting to disclose being'. Now, here there is no failure, but rather success" (Ibid., p. 12).

Beauvoir points to the possibility of converting the human failure to a joyful and liberating existence. What is demanded is a change of attitude. We cannot be this aspired in-oneself, we cannot escape our lack of being, but by recognizing this lack of being, as our predicament, we can affirm ourselves as "a positive existence" (Ibid., p. 13). Beauvoir notices similarities between this changed attitude, from "wanting to be" to "wanting to disclose being", and the Husserlian reduction or epoché ("suspension of judgement"). In this context, it could mean that we, so to speak, refrain from maintaining our ordinary commonsense attitude in our daily life (which can be described as a kind self-objectification). Instead of just being drawn into this commonsense attitude, there is the possibility of adopting a reflective, phenomenological attitude, which can enable us to discover our intentional subjectivity. This "(e)xistential conversion" means that "man put his will to be 'in parenthesis' and he will thereby be brought to consciousness of his true condition" (Ibid., p. 14). Hence, it is by parenthesizing our wish to "wanting to be" that we get in touch with our subjectivity and thereby open ourselves for our subjective and, not least, our emotional life, where safety and joy of life can prevail over anxiety and splitting. We let go from a self-objectification and get hold of the motions of inner life. It means putting our subjectivity into play, into motion. We can imagine that the self-deceptive, inauthentic attitude "I'm a real man with control of the situation" can be transformed into an authentic attitude by affirming our subjectivity. The wish to be someone who personifies control and who can get in touch with an original longing for community with others, and yet who is always beyond my control, which is why it simultaneously can feel both risky and vulnerable. However, if the vulnerability no longer needs to be felt as something dangerous and annihilating, the longing for community can give a sense of life and joy.

Care and the experience of being contained facilitate the possibility of opening oneself for one's subjectivity. This does not mean that we deny our spontaneous, transcending movement, but we are not getting lost in it, but is instead able to get hold of in the dynamic between immanence and transcendence. It is the phallic masculinity's one-sided focus on transcendence which becomes problematic, when the contact with the deeper aspirations and longings is cut off.

In other words, one is prevented from experience the natural pulse of life, in that the value of life is constrained to a compulsory achieving whose identity-forming function is "wanting to be something". Furthermore, one's achieving or doing easily leaves oneself feeling empty, when the dialectic between immanence and transcendence is cut off. The optimistic tone that Beauvoir lends the description "wanting to disclose being" should not lead us to underestimate how difficult and psychologically demanding it can be to realize such a will. Beauvoir's ethic to live authentically is worth affirming and implies freedom for both men and women: "To want existence, to want to disclose the world, and to want men to be free are one and the same will" (Ibid., pp. 86–87).

The patriarchal, oppressive society is alienating for both women and men, and this view is clearly expressed also in *The Second Sex*.[6] Let me provide a quote, from Eva Lundgren-Gothlin, about how the alienating patriarch affects both women and men:

> Because of his subject position, man tends to alienate himself in woman set up as an object, or in things he possesses, whereas because of her object position, woman tends to alienate herself in herself as object or in man as subject [...] the behavior of both is inauthentic [...] The tendency towards alienation has its foundation in the desire of being.
>
> (1996, p. 201)

In Chapter 7, I will try to deepen the sense of immanence by considering the existential meaning of death. Death has, then, as much the function of deepening the experience of existence as being the inevitable possibility that it ends.

Notes

1 Freud clearly gives voice to the idea that ethical deliberations demand an attitude that does not involve the emotional life:

> I cannot evade the notion (though I hesitate to give it expression) that for women the level of what is ethically normal is different from what it is in men. Their super-ego is never so inexorable, so impersonal, so independent of its emotional origins as we require it to be in men.

(1925, p. 257)

2 There is certainly a kind of psycho-logic in the relationship between one's own experience of having received care and one's capacity to care. Still, I would issue a warning against simplistic reasonings and underline how difficult, not to say impossible, it is to predict an individual human being's character on the basis of how life was once upon a time for this person.

3 Hollway writes:

> The development of the capacities to care that I am collecting together under the term 'maternal subjectivity' is not guaranteed by becoming a mother, but the infant does communicate a demand for them and good-enough conditions (external and internal) make their development likely in those who are positioned to receive them. While some men find it more difficult to find creative identifications with a helpless, dependent and ruthless infant, because of the history and biography of masculinities as other than the maternal, some men can and do.

(2006, p. 80).

4 Winnicott's (1949/1958) "psyche-soma" concerns the integration of the psyche and the body, a process of personalization which is made possible because of the mother's complete identity with her infant.

> For Winnicott, in healthy development, psyche and soma are not distinguishable as far as the infant and developing child are concerned. The healthy individual takes it for granted that his sense of self is part and parcel of his body.

(Abram, 1996, p. 237)

Hence, psyche–soma can be said to integrate both the early mother–infant and the infant's and growing child's integration of psyche and body.

5 As a matter of fact, it is possible to find an idea about bisexuality connected to the question about creativity in Winnicott (see this volume, Chapter 2, p. 46).

6 A couple of illuminating quotes from Beauvoir's *The Second Sex*:

> Man even requires her to playact: he wants her to be the *Other*; but every existent, as desperately as he may disavow himself, remains a subject; he wants her to be object: she *makes* herself object; at the moment she makes herself being, she is exercising activity; this is her original treason; the most docile, the most passive woman is still consciousness; and it is sometimes enough to make him feel duped by her for the male to glimpse that in giving herself to him she is watching and judging him [...].

(italics in the original) (1949/2011, p. 669)

And yet another quote:

> We have seen why men originally enslaved women; the devaluation of femininity was a necessary step in human development; but this step could have brought about a collaboration between the two sexes; oppression is explained by the tendency of the existent to flee from himself by alienating himself in the other that he oppresses for that purpose; this tendency could be found in each individual man today: and the vast majority give in to it; a husband looks for himself in his wife, a lover in his mistress, in the guise of a stone statue; he seeks in her the myth of his virility, sovereignty, his unmediated reality.

(Ibid., p. 772)

References

Abram, J. (1996). *The language of Winnicott. A dictionary of Winnicott's use of words.* Karnac.

Beauvoir, S. de (1947/1976). *The ethics of ambiguity.* Kensington Publishing Corp.

Beauvoir, S. de (1949/2011). *The second sex.* Vintage Books.

Bion, W.R. (1967). *Second thoughts. Selected papers on psycho-analysis.* William Heineman Medical Books Limited.

Elliott, K. (2016). Caring masculinities: Theorizing an emerging concept. *Men and Masculinies, 19*(3), 240–259. Doi:10.1177/1097184X15576203

Freud, S. (1925). Some psychical consequences of the anatomical distinction between the sexes. *Introductory lectures on psycho-analysis. The standard edition of the complete psychological works of Sigmund Freud, 19.*

Gilligan, C. (1982). *In a different voice: Psychological theory and women's development.* Harvard University Press.

Hollway, W. (2006). *The capacity to care: Gender and ethical subjectivity.* Routledge.

Lundgren-Gothlin, E. (1996). *Sex and existence. Simone de Beauvoir's The Second Sex.* Athlone.

Winnicott, D.W. (1949/1958). Mind and its relation to the psyche-soma. In his *Collected papers: Through paediatrics to psycho-analysis.* Tavistock Publications.

Winnicott, D.W. (1960/1965). The theory of the parent-infant relationship. In his *The maturational processes and the facilitating environment. Studies in the theory of emotional development.* The Hogarth Press.

Winnicott, D.W. (1963/1989). Fear of breakdown. In Cl. Winnicott, R. Shepherd & M. Davis (Eds.) *Psycho-analytic explorations.* Karnac.

Winnicott, D.W. (1965/1989). The psychology of madness: A contribution from psycho-analysis. In Cl. Winnicott, R. Shepherd & M. Davis (Eds.) *Psycho-analytic explorations.* Karnac.

Winnicott, D.W. (1971/1991). *Playing and reality.* Routledge.

Winnicott, D.W. (1986). *Home is where we start from. Essays by a psychoanalyst.* Edited by Cl. Winnicott, R. Shepherd, M. Davis. Penguin Books.

Young, I.M. (1997). House and home: Feminist variations on a theme. In her *Intersecting voices. Dilemmas of gender, political philosophy, and policy.* Princeton University Press.

7

Death as a most reliable counselor

Tem Horwitz describes a feeling of astonishing relief and liberation in his everyday life after a death struggle, which he calls his "mini-death", due to an anaphylactic shock that he had suffered. He writes:

> I had witnessed how my life could end at any moment. It was this fact that gave pleasure to my daily life filled with its trivial actions [...] I was alive and living my life. I needed no more [...] Death adds a potency and concentration to life. It is a most reliable counselor.
>
> (1998, p. 15)

We will have reasons to return to Horwitz's experiences later on. I have, in this book, discussed the relationship of the masculine project with the foundational conditions of existence – helplessness, vulnerability, transience and dependence. In Chapter 6, I discussed how an adequate containing of difficult, anxiety-filled experiences can bring about a feeling that life is meaningful and rewarding. In this chapter, I will, first of all, highlight our mortality, which has a special significance in our transience and which functions as a determining horizon in our valuation of life.[1]

It may be surprising that a book that deals with gender and masculinity takes death into account. Death is very absent in the theoretical sex/gender discussion. An objective of this chapter is to show that even if death has not been central in previous chapters, it is, nevertheless, indicated and implicit in the attempt to try to understand phallic masculinity. This chapter, on death, also ends in a discussion about a kind of liberating self-experience, which the masculine project misses.

It is not only in the theoretical sex/gender discussion that death is conspicuous by its absence. As a matter of fact, the existential death is, by and large, also absent in the psychoanalytic theorizing, which must be considered odd. By all means, death does exist in the psychoanalytic literature, but rarely in the sense of the existential death.[2]

What can one then mean by "the existential death"? Existential aspects concern our temporality, transience, freedom and responsibility. Liran Razinsky (2013, p. 135ff) characterizes the existential death in some points:

DOI: 10.4324/9781003352761-8

First, death implies a negation of life. It means the termination of life and constitutes the opposite of life.

Second, death is arbitrary. It is in and of itself inevitable, but it is arbitrary in three respects: (i) it seems arbitrary concerning when and under what circumstances it will occur; (ii) it is unmotivated, there are no good reasons for it (except within any specific religious beliefs), it cannot be arranged in any rational way in life, we do not know why it occurs, but we beat ourselves up to try to understand it in an ordinary, rational way; (iii) death is indifferent, and it affects everyone, not just some who, for example, because of their way of living, could be assumed to receive it as a punishment – no one escapes death.

Third, death assaults us as something coming from the outside. Something external, in the form of illness or accident, can befall us: it is not, so to speak, from within the subject itself that death is created. Razinsky claims that these last two points – the arbitrariness of death and that it comes from the outside – can be summarized in terms of it being out of control for us.

Fourth, we know nothing about death, which is frightening for us. We do not know what death is, which state it brings us to. Emmanuel Levinas asserts that philosophers have neglected to draw attention to that which is most characteristic for death, which is not the negativity of death but its absolute inaccessibility:

> I even wonder how the principal trait of our relationship with death could have escaped philosophers' attention. It is not with the nothingness of death, of which we precisely know nothing, that the analysis must begin, but with the situation where something absolutely unknowable appears. Absolutely unknowable means foreign to all light, rendering every assumption of possibility impossible, but where we ourselves are seized.
>
> (1947/1987, p. 71)

Death does not allow itself to be represented, and it is not on the basis of knowledge of death that we dread it, but precisely the opposite: it is completely unknown to us. Among psychoanalysts, this has been expressed in the following ways: Freud describes it, among other things, as "the painful riddle of death, against which no medicine has yet been found, nor probably will be" (1927, p. 16). Franco De Masi (2004, p. 109) talks about death as a "bewilderment" or as something that is signified as an absence in our thinking, which makes a full-fledged self-integration impossible. Jerry S. Piven (2004, p. 33) describes death as "an undiscovered country", which constitutes "an affront to reason", and for human meaning, "and people have trouble believing that such a horrific destruction and victimization could simply terminate something so alive, so meaningful, and so precious" (Ibid., p. 33).

Fifth, death is terrifying in that it erases our individuality and our personality: feelings and thoughts are lost when we die, and everything disappears into nothingness. If this fifth point does not run the risk of contradicting the previous one, it should be qualified as death means the total loss of our personality, where everything disappears into nothingness because we feel that our personality and our existence are connected to each other in our lives.

Sixth, death means the end. Death is that which is after life, beyond life and outside life. And this is absolutely unique. There may be reasons to reserve against this language "what death is". If death takes us out of day and out of time, then we *are* not dead or *have been* dead so and so long. One can only state that X died at a certain point of time: there is no difference between having died one second ago and having died 100,000 years ago.

It is the existential character of death that, to such a great extent, is conspicuous by its absence within psychoanalysis. Razinsky argues for the importance of taking death seriously and argues that an existential attitude to death implies that one does not reduce it or transform it into other phenomena: what is required is instead to stress its inevitability, arbitrariness and significance for the mental life. Before I move on and venture into a discussion about possible meanings of the existential death for the psychic life, I will make a digression about how existential death has found, or rather not found, a place within psychoanalysis.

Digression: Psychoanalysis and death

By the negligence of the existential meaning of death in the psychoanalytic theorizing, there is also the risk that this is absent in the psychoanalyst's countertransference and is not taken seriously enough in the psychoanalytic practice. Death as an existential fact is also usually missing as a topic in psychoanalytic education or psychoanalytically oriented therapy educations. It may occur that it is not until a psychoanalyst is confronted with a patient, suffering from an incurable disease, that the meaning of death hits the psychoanalyst and also brings about a sense of how important an accepting attitude to our mortality is. Viviana Minerbo is a witness of that, when she describes how a psychoanalysis with a patient who was dying of cancer evoked insights that she had not had before: "I also became aware of the fact that her approaching death was also making me conscious of my own vulnerability and mortality as never before" (1998, p. 84). And this was without doubt an important experience for Minerbo: "I learned with her that dignity and courage are possible even in the most adverse situations. Perhaps this is what maturity is all about: accepting one's fate and mortality" (Ibid., p. 92). In that the existential death is neglected, there is a risk that the patient's fear, anxiety or horror for death is met by silence in the psychoanalytic clinic by, for example, reducing death anxiety to castration anxiety (more on this later). Jussi Kotkavirta (2015, p. 76) points out that psychoanalysts often have interpreted the death anxiety of patients, instead of meeting it.

There may be many possible reasons for the absence of the existential death in psychoanalysis, and here I will mention a few of them. We should not underestimate Freud's impact on subsequent psychoanalysts' view concerning the meaning of the existential death for psychic life. In his most important theoretical works, there is a denial of the importance of the meaning of death for the psychic life. But if other, theoretically less important works are taken into account, the picture is not as univocal. And in his personal life, he occupied himself a lot with death: he is supposed to have thought of it every day. Besides, he had a controlling attitude to death, in that he constantly tried to calculate when he would die. The discrepancy between the importance that death had in his private life and the place it was given in his writings, Razinsky describes as "nothing less than astonishing" (2013, p. 44).

Freud's theoretical view is that in the unconscious there is no death, but in the unconscious, we are immortal:

> What, we ask, is the attitude of our unconscious towards the problem of death? The answer must be: almost exactly the same as that of primaeval man [...] Our unconscious, then, does not believe in its own death; it behaves as if it were immortal. What we call our "unconscious"-the deepest strata of our minds, made up of instinctual impulses-knows nothing that is negative, and no negation; in it contradictories coincide. For that reason it does not know its own death, for to that we can give only a negative content. Thus there is nothing instinctual in us which responds to a belief in death.
>
> (1915, p. 296)

Since Freud put so much emphasis on the unconscious for the psychic life, death has thereby not any real significance for human beings. Here, we could present a number of arguments against Freud's attitude. A first objection is that even if there is no death in the unconscious, death can nevertheless be of utmost importance in our lives, in that death is determining for our conscious life.[3] I myself am no stranger to limiting the character of the unconscious in a manner that excludes death from it. However, there is reason to direct critique against Freud's and psychoanalysis' unfair treatment of consciousness, which hampers an adequate existential understanding of the human being's predicament.[4] Razinsky also draws attention to the contradictions in Freud's view that a religious belief in a life after this is infantile and neurotic, simultaneously as he claims that we are immortal in the unconscious. How can a belief in immortality become an illusion or a wish if there is no fear of death (Razinsky, 2013, pp. 155–156)?

Freud's idea about the timelessness of the unconscious is also assumed to entail the impossibility that death is represented in the unconscious.

That mortality, but not immortality, would entail time is a logic that can be questioned. However, I do think that Freud has a point in his conviction that one's own death is impossible to imagine[5]:

> It is indeed impossible to imagine our own death; and whenever we attempt to do so we can perceive that we are in fact still present as spectators. Hence the psycho-analytic school could venture on the assertion that at bottom no one believes in his own death, or, to put the same thing in another way, that in the unconscious every one of us is convinced of his own immortality.
>
> (1915, p. 289)

However, Freud's reasoning about the impossibility of imagining one's own death rather concerns consciousness than expressing a condition for the unconscious; neither does it say anything about the significance of death for the psychic life. Like Levinas' (1947/1987, p. 71) observation, we cannot picture an image of death or nonbeing, in that our relation to death, first of all, is characterized by its absolute unknowability. But the thought that death does not have any significance for us, just because it is impossible to picture an image of it, is untenable. Irwin Z. Hoffman (1998, p. 46) points out that such an image is hardly required in order for anxiety in the face of death to have a profound and unique meaning for us.

What is to be said about Freud's theory of the death drive in "Beyond the pleasure principle" (1920), which received the status of an important theoretical contribution to psychoanalysis? In this essay from 1920, the death drive is presented in a contradictory way, and it can be disputed whether the death drive in this version is about death at all and not its opposite, that is, existence (see Karlsson, 1998, 2004, 2010, ch. 7). However, even if one were to accept Freud's idea that his version of the death drive is about death, it is still not a description of an existential death that comes from the outside and can attack you at any time, something uncontrollable, beyond and outside of life. Freud rather describes death in his death drive as an inherent organic striving to go back to an inorganic state out of which life originally grew forth. A further problem with this theory of the death drive is the description of death as a drive, an energy or a force (cf. Razinsky, 2013).

Freud tends to reduce the death anxiety to castration anxiety: "The fear of death, which dominates us oftener than we know, is on the other hand something secondary, and is usually the outcome of a sense of guilt" (1915, p. 297). And in *The Ego and the Id*, we can read: "I believe that the fear of death is something that occurs between the ego and the super-ego" whereupon the final reduction follows: "These considerations make it possible to regard the fear of death, like the fear of conscience, as a development of the fear of castration" (1923, p. 58).[6]

However, as is often the case with Freud, the picture is not univocal. In some of the theoretically less important works, we can notice a more affirmative attitude to the existential meaning of death. In "Thoughts for the times on war and death", life and death are linked together: "If you want to endure life, prepare yourself for death" (1915, p. 300). In "On transience", Freud (1916) disputes a poet's view that the beautiful loses worth because of its transience. Freud's view is the opposite: it increases instead the joy of life over the beautiful, and there is an increase of worth due to our transience. And in spite of his conviction that death can find no room in the unconscious, there are occasions in which he illuminates our tendency to reduce the significance of death: "Our habit is to lay stress on the fortuitous causation of the death – accident, disease, infection, advanced age; in this we betray an effort to reduce death from a necessity to a chance event" (Freud, 1915, p. 290). Likewise, he shows that this reduction has a strong impact on our life: "Life is impoverished, it loses interest, when the highest stake in the game of living, life itself, may not be risked" (Ibid., 1915, p. 290).

Diane Jonte-Pac (2001) maintains that death exists as a counterthesis to Freud's "masterplot", which is the oedipal conflict. For different reasons, Freud was too attached to his conviction that the oedipal conflict was the ruling conflict in human beings' life. Behind this plot, there is an undeveloped counterthesis which Freud never addressees directly, but which remains in the form of images and metaphors. In the oedipal conflict, we have a clear patriarchal order, with the father as the holder of tradition mediation and the son as the next generation's tradition mediator. Death wishes are directed towards the father and sexual desires towards the mother. But, in the counterthesis, the death of the mother is included: the mother is no longer limited to being a sexually desirable object. The mother figures as the dead mother and thereby breaks with the oedipal paradigm. Freud is not capable of fully affirming the dead mother, but she is transformed into the sexually desired mother, which is discernable in several of his works (Freud, 1913, 1919, 1928). One example of this is his anxious childhood dreams, in which anxiety for his mother's dream is not interpreted as a fear of losing her but as the anxiety related to incestuous sexual wishes (Freud, 1900, p. 584). In other words, Freud's masterplot, the Oedipus complex, transforms death to sexuality, something that, by the way, Pontalis has observed: "In my view, the theme of death is as basic to Freudian psychoanalysis as the theme of sexuality. I even believe that the latter has been widely put forward so as to cover up the former" (1978, p. 86).

The psychoanalytic tradition has, unfortunately, not been better, but rather worse than Freud in considering the significance of death and death anxiety. Freud's tendency to treat death anxiety as something secondary in relation to castration anxiety has had consequences for the psychoanalytic tradition mediation, which has tended to turn away from death and death anxiety in favor of psychosexual conflicts, such as castration anxiety, which have been assumed to lie behind death anxiety (Lifton, 1996, p. 48). Razinsky discusses several theoreticians (e.g., Klein, Erik H. Erikson, Lacan) who seem, to some extent, to consider death, but he finds that this is done in a distorted manner (2013, ch. 10). However, there are some psychoanalysts who have treated death in an interesting and productive way. Before I delve into these, I will discuss some psychoanalytic figures of thought that can function as obstacles to a serious investigation of the question of the existential death.

Death befalls us now or in the future, whereas the psychoanalytic investigation, to a large degree, is about the past. The figure of thought for psychoanalysis is to go back to childhood. Furthermore, the unconscious has not only been conceived of as a main area; psychoanalysis also has had an unfortunate tendency, which I touched upon above, to neglect the weight of consciousness. And death has to do more with consciousness than with the unconscious. A third figure of thought is that psychoanalysis is a "talking cure", as the so-called "first psychoanalytic patient" – Anna O – expressed it.[7] However, death can be difficult to approach by means of speech. Harold F. Searles notices that the abstract character of language makes death more difficult to access: "[...] our culture's whole emphasis upon the use of *verbal communication* may serve to shield us from the reality of death" (1961, pp. 648–649, italics in the original).[8] These figures of thought, which so characterize psychoanalysis, can make it more difficult to be responsive to the significance of death. In order to avoid misunderstanding, I want to underline that I am not criticizing these figures of thought nor do I want to downplay their crucial role in psychoanalysis; psychoanalysis should naturally be interested in the unconscious, in the significance of the childhood for the adult life, and the treatment is made up of a dialogue between two persons. Nonetheless, it can be important to widen and mobilize more responsiveness than is often evident in the psychoanalytic situation by considering the significance of the definite termination of life, something that definitely will occur, if not now, then at some time in the future. One also needs to realize that consciousness entails much more than just being "the tip of an iceberg", as it is expressed in well-known psychoanalytic metaphoric, and that analysis has room to meet a silence which cannot be filled by means of psychoanalytic theories, but which gives place for existential reflection about the finitude of life.[9]

Let us look at a couple of relevant psychoanalytic thoughts about death, contributions that concern the relationship of the existential death to the individual's early experiences before the individual in question was old enough for an existential awareness of death. Robert Jay Lifton (1996) points out that the fundamental question is not whether one can imagine the moment one was born or dies, but that one has a kind of attachment to the fact that

one has been born and that one will die. Focus is on our relationship towards death, which is more or less obviously present for us all the time. Even
if we do not have a developed idea of death from the beginning, it is present
in the form of so-called "death equivalents", which, to a large extent, are
"image-feelings" concerning *separation* (e.g., separations, weaning, empty
the bowels), *disintegration* (e.g., cuts, aches, bruises) and *stasis* (e.g., sleep,
immobility). These death equivalents have their counterparts in image-
feelings which are connected with the opposite of death, namely vitality and
affirmation: attachment instead of separation, integrity/wholeness instead
of disintegration and movement instead of stasis. Separation, disintegration
and stasis function as a kind of precursors to experiences which approxi-
mate death. When our idea about death begins to take shape at an early age,
it already has thus a historic source of experiences which in one way or another evoke associations to death. In particular, separation plays a central
role in the image/idea of death. And there is a mutual influence between the
so-called "death equivalents" and the images/ideas of death:

> Still extremely dependent upon those who nurture him, the child contin-
> ues for some time to equate death with separation. He thinks of the dead
> as having "gone away", an image that allows for the possibility of their
> return. He doesn't just model death on death equivalents, he also be-
> gins to model death equivalents on what he comes to understand about
> death. The three-year-old child who equates separation from his mother
> with her death now constructs frightening images of irreversibility – his
> mother permanently asleep, buried underground, forcibly carried off
> and murdered [...] We continue to construct our sense of death from
> our separations; to react to death with feelings of being annihilated or
> wiped out; to move back and forth in our minds between death and
> death equivalents.
>
> (Lifton, 1996, p. 68)

With reference to Sylvia Anthony, Lifton claims that the child around the
age of 8 years has an image/idea of death, which begins to look like the
adult's, and it is then that the child for the first time realizes cause–effect
relations between life and death.

Piven's (2004) ideas resemble Lifton's in that he maintains that death figures as a complex idea and has its origin in early emotional experiences,
when the child did not have any knowledge or apprehension of death. These
early emotional experiences are about separation, injuries and annihilation: an infantile helplessness that becomes the precursor and prototype to
a more and more developed death concept. Death is a conglomeration of
unbearable experiences that are kept together in the death concept with associating death derivates.[10]

It is, of course, important to consider that the existential death does not become reduced to the feelings and circumstances which function as precursors to the unique existential death. But these precursors are there as sources to all those associations and meanings as the person who is aware of their death associates with the possibility of their constantly present inevitable death.

Signposts towards death in this book

Although death has not played a central role in this book hitherto, there have been hints of its importance in order to understand masculinity. Here, I would like to develop some of these hinted significances. In my thesis that masculinity is a project, or more specifically an unattainable project, whose purpose is to elude existential conditions, such as vulnerability, helplessness and dependence, our mortality can be said to constitute the Condition of conditions. Death is the outermost horizon against which existence is understood, and then, of course, not least such experiences as vulnerability, helplessness and dependence. In line with this thesis, one can expect that men, generally speaking, have a more defensive attitude and are in a greater denial about their own death, which generally seems to be confirmed by research. The anthology *Death Anxiety Handbook. Research, Instrumentation and Application* (Neimeyer, 1994/2015) reports, among other things, studies that concern sex differences with respect to death anxiety. Even though the results are not unequivocal, women seem to display more death anxiety than men, which is not to be understood as if women would tend to be more open in describing their feelings. Research also shows that men, to a higher degree, tend to avoid thoughts about death.

Men's comparatively greater difficulty to affirm experiences of mourning is revealed in statistical studies, which show that mortality is bigger among grieving men who have lost their partner compared to women in the same situation (Skulason et al., 2012). When it comes to talking about one's terminal disease with specialized health-care personnel, only 30% of the men initiated the conversation compared to 80% of the women, a statistically significant difference. Even after an intervention in the form of an open question about future plans, the difference between the interests to talk about one's forthcoming death is significantly higher with women, although men's interest increased clearly compared to when no such intervention was made. In other words, the difference between men and women is obvious when it comes to confiding in others about one's forthcoming death (Skulason et al., 2014).

Within psychoanalytic literature, we find, among other things, that Freud (1927) makes a connection between the human being's helplessness in the face of death's indomitability and her infantile longing for a protecting father, which is his psychological explanation for religious belief. Piven takes

Freud's understanding a step further and postulates that the fear of death leads to motives for disgust and abhorrence for the body. The living body turns into a corpse and decays, and that which decays becomes despised – a destiny suffered female body fluids, menstrual blood and the placenta because they can remind the man of his decaying origins. There is a connection between misogyny and fear of death. In accordance with the philosopher Beauvoir as well as other psychoanalysts, Piven can establish that "menstrual taboo and the declaration that woman is unclean, corrupt, and sinful are not merely defenses against castration, incest, or bindings of procreative magic, but also emblems of man's fear and disgust toward mortality" (2003, p. 243).

Sexual potency can be a sensitive issue for a man: it does not only concern the possibility of sexual desire and conquering, but can precisely serve the function of escaping vulnerability, weakness, death anxiety and withering decay (Piven, 2004, p. 70).

If we also consider that feelings in connection with separation make up the primary precursor to an anxious attitude to death, it is not unreasonable to think that our mortality, generally speaking, has a specific character for the man. The separation process from the mother tends to be harder for the boy than for the girl. This separation process takes place simultaneously with the discovery of the sexual difference, which becomes a double challenge for the boy: to separate from the mother and to discover the sexual difference in relation to her. In Chapter 6, death came to our attention, in discussing Bion's and Winnicott's theories of the consequences of the child's experiences when it did not feel contained, even though this discussion did not take its point of departure from sex/gender.

The narcissistic masculine solution is represented by different manners of avoiding and defending oneself against the awareness of separation, loss and death. As stated earlier, there is a connection between our relation to death and to our capacity to mourn: "Our relation to mortality is nowhere more evident than in how we conceptualize and negotiate the task of mourning" (Frommer, 2005, p. 485). What is mourning? How does one mourn? are questions that men, not rarely, ask themselves. Our difficulty in coming to terms with our mortality can be displayed in many different ways. It is not just about using all available means to keep death away, invisible, but when one finally comes face-to-face with death, it is about dying in a dignified masculine way. In Chapter 4 (pp. 81–82), I quoted Robert C. Solomon's observation that there are masculine ways of dying. Here, a history full of wars has not least offered men the possibility of proving their masculinity to the last breath.

There are some interesting coincidences in certain age phases when both death and the sex/gender dimension receive a prominent place. Kenneth J. Doka (1995) points out that many circumstances contribute to an increased awareness about one's mortality in middle age, such as bodily processes, that the statistical mortality increases in that age as well as aging and death in one's parents' generation. Psychologically, the awareness of one's mortality in middle age may be the most significant phenomenon. In Chapter 4, I discussed how the entrance into middle age evokes feelings about the limitations of life and the forthcoming end. Diamond (2004) stresses that it is in middle age that men's phallic ideals may give way to identifications with the mother. Feelings that earlier on had been rejected, which are associated with femininity and motherly containing, allow themselves to be integrated with masculine traits. Diamond also maintains that in middle age the feeling of identity becomes less important in favor of the need for meaning. And in old age, when our mortality usually becomes more salient, grandiose masculine ideals give way for a striving to become a person (Diamond, 2013).

Finally, I would like to put forward that the analysis of masculinity in this book has implied that the idea of gender identity has undergone a deconstruction in several steps. To begin with, I emphasized that even though one, in a sense, is born as a man, woman or intersex, it is not possible to draw any conclusion concerning gender characteristics from this fact. Bisexuality is now a rather old-fashioned concept in the psychoanalytic thinking. Later generations of psychoanalysts have talked about surpassing the gender dichotomy, for example, concretized in the form of Benjamin's earlier quoted idea that a person can alternate between experience itself as "I, a woman; I, a genderless subject, I, like-a-man" (1988, p. 113). In my analysis of different forms of masculinities, I suggested one form, demasculinized masculinity, which entails a liberation from the masculine ideals and norms which ground phallic masculinity. In particular, in Chapter 6, I argued for going further in the deconstruction of gender than Benjamin, by claiming the possibility of going beyond the gender dimension, in favor of an ego-identity that is not gender constituted. The deconstruction of different identities, such as the striving for masculine identity, reaches its climax in the awareness of death: in the face of death, we can no longer shine with borrowed feathers. Identity and mortality are antithetical:

> Identity and mortality are inextricably and antithetically related. Our identities seem to tell us that we have essence, stability, and permanence. Our mortality tells us we are transient, ephemeral, and will cease to be. Identity, in this sense, opposes or negates mortality. But reifications of identity create their own prisons. They work to preclude who we allow ourselves to be and what we allow ourselves to be and what we allow ourselves to feel and express. When we make way for mortality, we loosen our grip on how we need to think of ourselves.
>
> (Frommer, 2005, p. 497)

I will be able to unfold the content of this quote when shortly discussing the meanings that an awareness of mortality can include. But, already now, I would like to pay attention to that which I emphasized in Chapter 6, namely that the ego-identity is a prerequisite in order to be able to affirm the value of authenticity. The ego-identity does not have the character of being a solidified limiting outlook at the world, on the contrary: it makes a subject's taking responsibility possible. And in a stunning manner, it is as if the awareness of our mortality strengthens and consolidates the self as well as loosens solidified views of oneself.

Important values that the awareness of death impart

Death is like a projection screen in the sense that it seems to be able to nourish the most various and opposite reactions. The spontaneous emotional reaction to death is probably that it exerts a destruction of meaning: it robs life of meaning. However, from a reflective stance, it can be argued that finitude is a prerequisite for experiencing meaning and meaningfulness. Death is profoundly paradoxical: at the same time as it is the most traumatizing and the most devastating imagination in a person's life and the most challenging for our wish of control, it is also a prerequisite for meaningfulness and authenticity. Besides, which I will develop shortly, it seems as if being in absolute nearness to death makes it possible to feel a joy of life which eludes us on other occasions.

De Masi compares death with psychosis and delusion, in that it is an "indigestible object" permeated with traumatic anxiety and something we never can overcome: "In reality, the perception of our own death remains dissociated from our awareness all throughout life" (De Masi, 2004, p. 114). Anxiety before our death is an anxiety which points not only towards the presence and towards the future but, in all time directions, towards our entire existence. The enigma of death reflects questions and arouses wonder about what life and existence are all about. Death points towards the past in the form of the prompting question: How have I managed my life? Furthermore, a flashback on my life gives an uncanny experience of how vanishingly fast a life goes. As we can read in Samuel Beckett's *Waiting for Godot*, women "give birth astride of a grave, the light gleams an instant, then it's night once more" (1953/2006, p. 82).

Death appears as the greatest challenge that we face in our lives. In front of it, we are completely bewildered, and our wish to control existence receives its final rebuke. The impact of death is not limited to the loss of one or several objects in the world. With death, the horizons disappear, out of which the objects can appear, and our connectedness with the world. How this challenge and human predicament can make up ground for realization of the most valuable possibilities that life can offer is truly enigmatic. The masculine project to deny our existential conditions goes against an attitude to affirm our mortality. I will next state some of the important values that an affirmation of our mortality can bring.

Let me reconnect to what was said above, that identity and mortality are antithetical. The awareness of our mortality helps us to liberate us from our petrified identities: it helps us to relate more flexibly and sensitively to the world and situations, as well to how and who we wish to be. Our worry whether we meet others' expectations can be soothed, and we can make decisions that are more anchored in ourselves. We can feel freer in relation to ideas about what life and existence are about. This flexibility and freedom in our way of being does not mean an impoverishment of the self, but a consolidation of the self: even if death implies the end of our individuality, the awareness of it can reinforce and consolidate our self. An impoverished self seeks narcissistic confirmation, whereas a consolidated self is an affirmation of existence. With reference to Hoffman, Frommer (2005) highlights the dialectic between a consolidation of the self and flexibility and elasticity. When we emotionally recognize our mortality, we can promote an existential consolidation of the self as well as flexibility, elasticity and freedom in our established self.

In connection with freedom and flexibility, we can get a grasp of how the awareness of our mortality corresponds to an improved possibility to authenticity and responsibility. We will be able to affirm more easily such things that are valuable for us and take responsibility for them. Taking responsibility for our choices and actions in the world should increase, but we also experience a deepened feeling of authenticity by affirming our feelings and our subjectivity. "Awareness of death, in fact, confronts us with the possibility of being ourselves, free from illusions" (De Masi, 2004, p. 68). Paradoxically, Hoffman suggests, we are most aware of the responsibility for our lives when we are most acutely and painfully aware of our helplessness in controlling our ultimate destiny (1998, p. 57).

In this connection, I would like to mention Marin Heidegger's (1927/1980) exposition about death and the possibility for *Dasein* (translated into English; "being there") to exist authentically. Mostly, *Dasein* exists as "the They" (*das Man*), that is to say, in a nonindependent and inauthentic way; *Dasein* loses itself in the world in a distraught way, where the possibility of death is something that does not concern the present, but is deferred to the future, nor does it have anything to do with my death but "one dies", "others die". However, in the anxiety in the face of death, the so-called "being-towards-death", when Dasein does not avoid its finitude then Dasein exists in an authentic way. However, being-towards-death does not imply any morbid broodings: it is when I open myself to my finitude that I can take responsibility and realize my possibilities.

In light of Heidegger's philosophy and Winnicott's concept "holding", Johan Eriksson (2015) highlights the importance of incorporating finitude in order to develop the capacity for psychological self-holding. By virtue of my finitude, I get a grasp of life as *my life*, and by the holding – the self-holding –

I am not lost in impressions and experiences. The self-holding implies that I structure, organize and canalize impressions and experiences, which also makes possible a reflecting and emancipatory attitude to life.

Another possible effect of the awareness of our mortality is an increased joy of life, about which many have witnessed, not rarely persons that suffer from serious diseases. Frommer reproduces a patient's reflection during a session: "My death feels real, at least right now, and it's odd [...] I'm almost embarrassed to say it, but in some way, it makes me feel joyful" (2005, p. 497). One may wonder what this joy of life contains. I will soon return to my idea about what its deepest meaning may be, which is particularly interesting owing to the thesis that I have argued for with respect to the project of masculinity.

When reading the literature about the weight of the awareness of our mortality, one is struck that the value, to such a high degree, is attached to doing, activity, actions and achieving, rather than to an experience of reception. De Masi writes that the prerequisite for experiencing our life as meaningful is that we "continuously invest our future projects, ambitions, aims and desires" (2004, pp. 73–74). And furthermore:

> There is no subjective self without the notion of development. The potentially infinite development, based upon the illusion of unlimited growth, is a constituent characteristic of the self. We can feel alive only if we can project ourselves into the future: this illusion is the background symphony that allows us to go on living.
>
> (Ibid., p. 74)

And another couple of quotes from De Masi: "The desire for immortality needs to be transformed into hope for what is still possible. Such hope, preserved until the end, is a gift to others, as well" (Ibid., p. 122). The value of life risks being constrained to what the person in question has succeeded in achieving: "As they age, people turn back to look at their past and wonder what they have achieved" (Ibid., p. 124). In Tor-Björn Hägglund, we can read the following:

> The last adaptive attempt at maturation in the mourning process of the dying person is the integration of the essential phases of his life and his relationships and the desire to share his concrete created product with others, as a gift, transferring one's narcissism so it will live on.
>
> (from Straker, 2013, p. 63)

What one does, performs, achieves or accomplishes is no doubt of significance from the horizon of the awareness of death, but the deepest joy that the awareness of death broods on should not be understood in instrumental terms or be filled with what one has achieved or with acquired ego-content. It is not about transcending – going beyond – the existent but about immanence and about an affirmation of that which is.

Existence as an unconditional gift[11]

If we talk about death in a figurative sense, it appears in enjoyable but very different contexts. We know from literature and in popular parlance how death and orgasm are likened to each other, and in many languages, orgasm is named "the little death".

In psychoanalytic theory, we have Laplanche's original interpretation of the sexual drive, where it becomes the most extreme expression of the discharge of the libido, it is the least civilized and least socialized part of sexuality and it functions in accordance with the principle of free energy and the primary process (Laplanche, 1979). Laplanche's death drive does not concern a biological, organic death, but has to be understood in a metaphorical, psychic sense. Thus, the death referred to in the death drive is not the death of the organism, but, as Laplanche stated, "the death of this 'organism' which, in human existence, represents the interest of the biological organism, that is to say, *the ego*" (italics in the original) (Laplanche, 1986, p. 14). From this enjoyable sexual pleasure, we can move on to that which is promised by spiritual guides, in religions and in wisdom teachings – to free oneself from one's self. In the Gospels, we read that "for whoever wants to save their life will lose it" – a sentence that catches a deep existential truth, by pinpointing the meaning of self-surrender and the letting go of the (controlling) ego. However, this existential truth is certainly a great challenge for the self, and not least the masculine ideal. Even if such a self-surrender corresponds with an experience of profound relief, liberation and enjoyment, it is, nonetheless, amazingly difficult to obtain and, if obtained, to sustain for more than a moment.

It is thought-provoking that such a liberating experience is so difficult to obtain and to sustain: it seems to be difficult also to contain that which is good. The deep bubbling joy is too powerful to fully harbor. My associations go to the sentence from 2 Genesis 33:20 that no one can see the face of God and live. Thus, it is not only aggression, hatred and pain that are difficult to contain but also their opposites, such as love, goodness and enjoyment. In psychoanalysis, one can discover many reasons for self-destruction and difficulties in receiving that which is good and would give peace and rest, such as guilt, envy and shame. However, here I want to draw attention to an existentially based reason for the difficulty in affirming the half-filled glass of water instead of the half-empty.

Such a kind of experience can occur when the ego is able to get a glimpse of a blissful existence free from narcissistic strivings, such as achievement anxiety, rivalry and comparison with others, and this blissful experience is even accompanied by the insight of how detrimental the narcissistic strivings are for oneself. Nevertheless, even under such circumstances, the narcissistic strivings and illusions are very difficult to give up. My point is that an effective obstacle for the ego to surrender, to letting go is the difficulty to accept death and finitude. There is a way of activating oneself which possesses the quality of turning one's back on death and finitude: one throws oneself into realizing projects and strivings to achieve that are narcissistically satisfying and give the illusion of an identity that would save one from the fate of being finite. Correspondingly, the letting go of the ego "risks" uncovering our finitude, vulnerability, lack of control and dependence. To turn this threatening feeling into something potentially positive requires quite a bit of psychical work in terms of containment of separation, loss, mourning and narcissistic humiliation.

Above, I quoted a patient who felt joy at the strong realization of being mortal (Frommer, 2005, p. 497). I will use a couple of more examples, when the person very concretely faces their death, and which offer the existence of a relief and deep joy that seems to be very difficult to experience unless one really is or has been very close to one's death.[12]

The first example is an experience that is not too uncommon among people who suffer from a terminal disease, here represented by a Swedish television news anchor, Ulla-Carin Lindquist (2007), who died of amyotrophic lateral sclerosis (ALS) some years ago. She has, in a very naked and moving way, described this disease process. It is a description of anger, despair, sorrow, but also a profound joy in the now that she never had been able to experience before. How is that to be understood?

The second example is from Horwitz's account of his death struggle after having gone into anaphylactic shock. First, an extract from his concrete death struggle:

> It is very difficult to describe time through this sequence. It ceased to be the medium through which I was moving. There was no forward, no backward, no future, no past – only a present that contained everything [...] There both was and was not an observer. There was no distinction between the me, the perceiver, and the it, the place [...] There was something basically wordless about the experience [...] It was some place, not 'no place', not an undifferentiated world of blackness, not a void, nothingness [...] Dying removed me from the clutches of time. There was no present for me – transient or otherwise – during this period.
>
> (1998, p. 9)

After this death struggle, which Horwitz calls his "mini-death", he felt an amazing lightness, and, a year and half later, when he recounts this experience, he can still feel touches of that embrace in his daily life. Let me resume parts of his description of this experience:

> These moments were what they were. They lacked nothing. They were complete in and of themselves. I could conceive of no happiness outside of these moments [...] There was nothing that I wanted to do or felt that I had to do. There was no vestige of self-importance left. It felt like death had obliterated my ego, the attachments that I had, my history, and who I had been [...] I had no identity in death (p. 10) [...] Personality was a vanity, an elaborate delusion, a ruse [...] I was lodged in the present. I had caught a glimpse of eternity, and I was content to dwell in its embrace (p. 11) [...] There was a lightness, which I have described, but there was also an indifference, a detachment from my world [...] indifference replaces other emotions, like anger and envy [...] Thoughts of death clarify and clear the blackboard of unimportant material (p. 13) [...] With less to cling to I felt surprisingly strong and considerably less vulnerable [...] I had witnessed how my life could end at any moment. It was this fact that gave pleasure to my daily life filled with its trivial actions [...] I was alive and living my life. I needed no more [...] Death adds a potency and concentration to life. It is a most reliable counselor (p. 15).
>
> (Ibid., pp. 10–13, 15)

It seems as if sustaining the proximity of death can facilitate an opportunity to open oneself to existence in an entirely exceptional way. I will end this chapter by some reflections on the kind of self that is involved in this experience of lightness and profound joy. One may ask: what characterizes the self that is disclosed in the liberating experience of surrender or letting go? I would like to maintain that it shows itself as an unmotivated surge of joy and well-being; it is an experience which highlights my existence – that I AM. Let me try to sketch some traits constituting this type of self-experience.

First, the paradoxical nature of self-surrender means that it involves a relinquishing of control and a dismantling of the defensive barrier, simultaneously with an expansion of and a release for the self, as well as increased trust and confidence.[13] Self-surrender implies a living in the present. It is the spontaneous pre-reflective character that gives it a focus on the present and a strong affirmation of existence. There is a transforming power in the affirmation itself that can be seen in the psychoanalytic process, when affirming painful feelings and experiences. The affirmation of, for example, one's vulnerability or the feeling of being very small in a situation can make up the difference between feeling lost, disintegrated and full of anxiety and being in touch with oneself, and feeling collected and present. My point is that there is a psychic growing in the affirmation itself. The affirmation of difficult and painful feelings is then not, first of all, a means of ridding oneself of something (that would be to reduce the affirmation to an instrumental value), but the "affirmation-in-itself" entails psychical growth. I think that it is this quality in the affirmation that can explain patients' common paradoxical description in the course of the psychoanalytic process that they feel worse than ever and at the same time stronger than they have ever felt before.

Second, what stands out in this experience is that one feels joy, lightness and security. This reminds us of Levinas' ideas about the self and enjoyment. According to him, the original dimension of life is enjoyment. To despair of life can only be understood on the condition that life is originally enjoyment. Levinas claims that "(l)ife is *love of life*" (italics in the original) (1969, p. 112). Everything that we are *living from* – food, drinks, ideas, sleep, spectacles, light and so on – is not to be conceived of as something instrumental (they are not tools) that satisfies needs; his point is that the act in itself, the doing, contains enjoyment. The basis of the self is enjoyment. "Enjoyment is... the very pulsation of the I" (Ibid., p. 113). One becomes a self, something separate, egoistic (although not in an ethical sense) in the enjoyment of life. In other words, existence itself is inherently good.

Third, I think that in this experience of oneself, one can discern an experience of being contained by something transcendent and good. It entails an affirmation of existence in its pure form, existence when it is purged of aspirations and coincidences: affirmingly received as an unconditional gift.

It is this kind of experience of oneself, sketchily presented in the above three points, which the masculine project not only misses but constitutes its antithesis.

Notes

1 Martha Nussbaum writes:

> Our finitude, and in particular our mortality, which is a particularly central case of our finitude, and which conditions all our awareness of other limits, is a constitutive factor in all valuable things, having for us the value that in fact they have [...] [T]he removal of all finitude in general, mortality in particular, would not so much enable these values to survive eternally as bring about the death of value as we know it.
>
> (from Hoffman, 1998, 18)

2 De Masi writes:

> To my mind, psychoanalysis has investigated the issue of death from three main points of view. The first concerns the presence or absence of the representation of death in the unconscious; the second links with the wider theme of separation, loss of objects and loved ones; the third concerns the part played by annihilation anxiety in causing mental suffering. Whilst all three are present in psychoanalytic literature, it is the second, separation anxiety that appears most frequently.
>
> (2004, p. 24)

3 Hoffman writes: "Instead of an unconscious belief in immortality, the defensive formulation suggests an idea of mortality that is fended off in favor of a conscious belief in immortality, one that is compatible with the 'narcissistic system'" (1998, p. 36).

4 In my view, it is unfortunate that psychoanalysis has paid so little interest in consciousness, when it, in many respects, is significant for psychoanalysis. To begin with, we can roughly count on two levels of suffering in psychoanalysis that I would maintain require different etiological explanations as well as therapeutic approaches. The earliest suffering has to do with deficits in the intentionality of consciousness/self-consciousness due to an insufficient containment and yields difficulties in affirming existence, in contrast to a neurotic suffering due to repressed unconscious intrapsychic conflicts. When it comes to problems in the sphere of consciousness/self-consciousness, our interventions do not concern interpreting unconscious conflicts "behind" that which is said or expressed as with Freud; here we are dealing with something more basic: what it is the patient experiences or attempts to experience (cf. Alvarez, 1992; Karlsson, 2004, 2010; Monti, 2005). The question concerning "what something is" is the first question, and it does not require the same developed psychic capacity as, for example, the question about "why something is". Since there is suffering that has to be understood on the basis of the structure of consciousness, phenomenology and its systematic and thorough excavation of consciousness becomes highly relevant for understanding the psychoanalytic field of investigation.

It is beyond the scope of this chapter to discuss the question of the meaning of the unconscious in psychoanalysis. A few remarks have to suffice. Despite the fact of Freud's claim that the unconscious is the distinguishing mark for psychoanalysis, its meaning is utterly unclear. It signifies differently between psychoanalysts as well as within one and the same authorship. When it comes to the relationship between consciousness and the unconscious, I would claim that consciousness is prior to the unconscious, both in time and from a (phenomeno) logical point of view, which I believe is implied even in some of Freud's writings (e.g., 1905, 1920). One way to describe the difference between consciousness and the unconscious is that the intentionality of consciousness entails a synthesizing, harmonizing and structuring character, whereas the unconscious has a dissolving character; the unconscious is thus to be understood as being the opposite of meaning/intentionality/consciousness. It can be argued that the unconscious in its most radical version is a theoretical construction that thus never has been experienced or can be experienced, but is nevertheless needed for psychoanalysis in order to explain such suffering that is not comprehensible on account of consciousness.

Above I pointed out the relevance of phenomenology for psychoanalysis due to suffering that has to be understood on the basis of consciousness. In addition, phenomenology has a role in epistemologically clarifying the conditions upon which the psychoanalytic unconscious can be constructed (see Karlsson, 2007, 2010, chs. 4–6, 2020).

5 In Merleau-Ponty, we can read the following:

> Neither my birth nor my death can appear to me as my personal experiences […] and thus I could not genuinely conceive of my birth or my death. Thus, I can only grasp myself as "already born" and as "still living" – I can only grasp my birth and my death as pre-personal horizons: I know that one is born and that one dies, but I cannot know my birth or my death.
>
> (1945/2012, p. 223)

6 Eriksson writes:

> It is easy to get the impression that Freud in these discussions [the tendency to reduce death anxiety to castration anxiety] somehow invokes psychoanalytic concepts with the purpose to, all the time, obstruct a deeper existential recognition of the constitutive role of death in human life.
>
> (2015, p. 116)

7 Anna O, whose real name was Bertha Pappenheim, underwent a kind of suggestive and hypnotic treatment with Breuer in the beginning of 1880s and is included as a case study in Breuer's and Freud's *Studies on Hysteria* (Breuer & Freud, 1895).

8 Searles writes:

> We tend to forget, for example, when a phobia about death is being discussed, that even after the *symbolic* meanings to the patient of 'death' have been brought to light, and there has been a resolution of the neurotic anxiety concerning heretofore-unconscious affects (concerning sex, aggression, passivity, or whatever) which have presented themselves in the guise of anticipated death, there will still remain the *reality* of death itself, and the anxiety realistically associated with it.
>
> (italics in the original) (1961, p. 656)

9 See Razinsky (2013, ch. 9) for a discussion about the different ways in which death has been reduced and neglected in psychoanalysis.

10 Freud also thinks that the development consists of a series of threats, where the original anxiety arose in the birth when the child was separated from the mother (the "primal anxiety" of birth). This separation from the mother is followed by a separation from the genitals in the form of castration anxiety, which in its turn is followed by superego anxiety. The last transformation concerns death anxiety: "The final transformation which the fear of the super-ego undergoes is, it seems to me, the fear of death (or fear for life) which is a fear of the super-ego projected on to the powers of destiny" (1926, p. 140).

11 The rest of this chapter is almost identical with a part of my article "Psychoanalysis and the question of self: A dialogue with spiritual traditions", published in *Journal of Consciousness Studies*, vol. 23, no. 1–2 (2016), pp. 179–195. I thank the journal and the publisher for the permission to publish this part of the article here.

12 Frommer writes: "Finding the liberating potentiality of mortality is, at best, an unstable achievement that is not won easily. But how is it won at all? Strangely, psychoanalysis has little to say on the matter" (2005, p. 482).

13 Winnicott's article, "The use of an object and relating through identifications" (1971/1991, ch. 6), has given rise to interesting reflections around the problematic that I am dealing with here. In particular, I am thinking of an article by Eigen (1981) and one by Ghent (1990), who understand Winnicott's idea of the use of the object in the same manner but express it differently; Ghent talks, first of all, about "surrender" and Eigen about "faith". I mean that these terms – surrender and faith – capture two sides or aspects of one and the same thing. It probably wouldn't take too far to also see the connection between Winnicott's idea of "the use of an object" and the meaning that death can have. I am, first of all, thinking about the immutable nature of death: death does not allow itself to be manipulated or controlled, and precisely because of this, it can have a containing function which makes experiences of meaning, meaningfulness and health possible.

References

Alvarez, A. (1992). *Live company*. Routledge.

Beckett, S. (1953/2006). *Waiting for Godot*. Faber and Faber.

Benjamin, J. (1988). *The bonds of love. Psychoanalysis, feminism, and the problem of domination*. Pantheon Books.

Breuer, J. & Freud, S. (1895). *Studies on hysteria. The standard edition of the complete psychological works of Sigmund Freud, 2*.

De Masi, F. (2004). *Making death thinkable. A psychoanalytic contribution to the problem of the transience of life*. Free Association Books.

Diamond, M.J. (2004). Accessing multitude within: A psychoanalytic perspective on the transformation of masculinity at mid-life. *International Journal of Psychoanalysis, 85*(1), 45–64. Doi:10.1516/3PFY-NQMU-C95F-HH0W

Diamond, M.J. (2013). Evolving perspectives on masculinities and its discontents: reworking the internal phallic and genital positions. In E. Ester Palerm Mari & F- Thomson-Salo (Eds.) *Masculinity and femininity today*. Karnac.

Doka, K.J. (1995). The awareness of mortality in midlife: Implications for later life. In J. Kauffman (Ed.) *Awareness of mortality*. Baywood Publishing Company, Inc.

Eigen, M. (1981). The area of faith in Winnicott, Lacan and Bion. *International Journal of Psychoanalysis, 62*(4), 413–433.

Eriksson, J. (2015). Döden och psyket – om ändlighet, dödsdrift och psykologiskt självhållande. [Death and the psyche – on finitude, death drive and psychological self-holding]. *Divan*, (3–4), 114–125.

Freud, S. (1900) *The interpretation of dreams. The standard edition of the complete psychological works of Sigmund Freud, 5*.

Freud, S. (1905). *Three essays on the theory of sexuality. The standard edition of the complete psychological works of Sigmund Freud, 7*.

Freud, S. (1913). *The theme of the three caskets. The standard edition of the complete psychological works of Sigmund Freud, 12*.

Freud, S. (1915). Thoughts for the times on war and death. *The standard edition of the complete psychological works of Sigmund Freud, 14*.

Freud, S. (1916). On transience. *The standard edition of the complete psychological works of Sigmund Freud, 14*.

Freud, S. (1919). The "uncanny". *The standard edition of the complete psychological works of Sigmund Freud, 17*.

Freud, S. (1920). *Beyond the pleasure principle. The standard edition of the complete psychological works of Sigmund Freud, 18*.

Freud, S. (1923). *The ego and the id. The standard edition of the complete psychological works of Sigmund Freud, 19*.

Freud, S. (1926). *Inhibitions, symptoms and anxiety. The standard edition of the complete psychological works of Sigmund Freud, 20*.

Freud, S. (1927). The future of an illusion. *The standard edition of the complete psychological works of Sigmund Freud, 21*.

Freud, S. (1928). A religious experience. *The standard edition of the complete psychological works of Sigmund Freud, 21*.

Frommer, M.S. (2005). Living in the liminal spaces of mortality. *Psychoanalytic Dialogues, 15*(4), 479–498. Doi:10.1080/10481881509348845

Ghent, E. (1990). Masochism, submission, surrender – Masochism as a perversion of surrender. *Contemporary Psychoanalysis, 26*(1), 108–136. Doi:10.1080/00107530.1990.10746643

Heidegger, M. (1927/1980). *Being and time.* Basil Blackwell.

Hoffman, I.Z. (1998). *Ritual and spontaneity in the psychoanalytic process. A dialectical-constructivist view.* Routledge.

Horwitz, T. (1998). My death. In J. Malpas & R.C. Solomon (Eds.) *Death and philosophy.* Routledge.

Jonte-Pace, D. (2001). *Speaking the unspeakable. Religion, misogyny, and the uncanny mother in Freud's cultural texts.* University of California Press.

Karlsson, G. (1998). Beyond the pleasure principle: The affirmation of existence. *Scandinavian Psychoanalytic Review, 21*(1), 37–52. Doi:10.1080/01062301.1998.10592662

Karlsson, G. (2004). The conceptualization of the psychical in psychoanalysis. *International Journal of Psychoanalysis, 85*(2), 381–400. Doi:10.1516/002075704773889805

Karlsson, G. (2007). The construction of the libido in psychoanalytic theory on the basis of conscious sexual experiences. In J.T. Locks (Ed.) *New research on consciousness.* Nova Science Publishers.

Karlsson, G. (2010). *Psychoanalysis in a new light.* Cambridge University Press.

Karlsson, G. (2016). Psychoanalysis and the question of self. A dialogue with spiritual traditions. *Journal of Consciousness Studies, 23*(1–2), 179–195.

Karlsson, G. (2020). The function of phenomenology for psychoanalysis. In C. Bodea & D. Popa, (Eds.) *Describing the unconscious. Phenomenological perspectives on the subject of psychoanalysis.* Zeta Books.

Kotkavirta, J. (2015). Hur ska vi tänka på döden? [How should we think about death?]. *Divan,* (3–4), 73–81.

Laplanche, J. (1979). Une métapsychologie à l'épreuve de l'angoisse. *Psychoanalyse à l'Université, 4,* 709–736.

Laplanche, J. (1986). La pulsion de mort dans la théorie de la pulsion sexuelle. In A. Green, P. Ikonen, J. Laplanche, E. Rechardt, H. Segal & D. Widlöcher (Eds.) *La pulsion de mort.* Presses Universitaires de France.

Levinas, E. (1947/1987). *Time and the other.* Duquesne University Press.

Levinas, E. (1969). *Totality and infinity.* Duquesne University Press.

Lifton, R.J. (1996). *The broken connection. On death and the continuity of life.* American Psychiatric Press, Inc.

Lindquist, U.-C. (2007). *Rowing without oars. A memoir of living and dying.* Penguin.

Merleau-Ponty, M. (1945/2012). *Phenomenology of perception.* Routledge.

Minerbo, V. (1998). The patient without a couch: An analysis of a patient with terminal cancer. *International Journal of Psycho-Analysis, 79*(1), 83–93.

Monti, M.R. (2005). New interpretative styles: Progress or contamination? Psychoanalysis and phenomenological psychopathology. *International Journal of Psychoanalysis, 86*(4), pp. 1011–1032. Doi:10.1516/5MKF-NDD8-QFBM-8XJK

Neimeyer, R.A. (Ed.) (1994/2015). *Death anxiety handbook. Research, instrumentation and application.* Routledge.

Piven, J.S. (2003). Death, repression, narcissism, misogyny. *Psychoanalytic Review, 90*(2), 225–260. Doi:10.1521/prev.90.2.225.23551

Piven, J.S. (2004). *Death and delusion. A Freudian analysis of mortal terror.* Information Age Publishing.

Pontalis, J.-B. (1978). On death-work in Freud, in the self, in culture. In A. Roland (Ed.) *Psychoanalysis, creativity, and literature.* Columbia University Press.

Razinsky, L. (2013). *Freud, psychoanalysis and death.* Cambridge University Press.

Searles, H.F. (1961). Schizophrenia and the inevitability of death. *Psychiatric Quarterly, 35,* 631–665. Doi:10.1007/BF01563716

Skulason, B., Jonsdottir, L.S., Sigurdardottir, V. & Helgason, A.R. (2012). Assessing survival in widowers, and controls-A nationwide, six- to nine-year follow up. *BMC Public Health, 12*(96). Doi:10.1186/1471-2458-12-96

Skulason, B., Hauksdottir, A., Ahcic, K. & Helgason, A.R. (2014). Death talk: Gender differences in talking about one's own impending death. *BMC Palliativ Care, 13*(1), 8. Doi:10.1186/1472–684X-13–8

Straker, N. (2013). Psychoanalytic literature on the treatment of dying patients. In N. Straker (Ed.) *Facing cancer and the fear of death. A psychoanalytic perspective on treatment.* Rowman & Littlefield.

Winnicott, D.W. (1971/1991). *Playing and reality.* Routledge.

Author Index

Subject Index

Note: Page numbers followed by "n" denote endnotes.

For Product Safety Concerns and Information please contact our EU
representative GPSR@taylorandfrancis.com
Taylor & Francis Verlag GmbH, Kaufingerstraße 24, 80331 München, Germany

www.ingramcontent.com/pod-product-compliance
Lightning Source LLC
Chambersburg PA
CBHW050610280326
41932CB00016B/2988

9 781032 402772